ESCAPE

In Search of the Natural Soul of Canada

ROY MacGREGOR

M&S

National Library of Canada Cataloguing in Publication

MacGregor, Roy, 1948-
    Escape : in search of the natural soul of Canada / Roy MacGregor.

ISBN 0-7710-5601-X

1. National characteristics, Canadian.   2. Wilderness areas – Canada –
Psychological aspects.   3. Vacation homes – Canada – Psychological
aspects.   I. Title.

FC97.M316 2002   155.8'971   C2002-903543-0
F1021.2.M32 2002

We acknowledge the financial support of the Government of Canada
through the Book Publishing Industry Development Program for
our publishing activities. We further acknowledge the support of the
Canada Council for the Arts and the Ontario Arts Council for our
publishing program.

Typeset in Minion by M&S, Toronto
Printed and bound in Canada

This book is printed on acid-free paper that is 100% ancient forest friendly
(100% post-consumer recycled).

McClelland & Stewart Ltd.
The Canadian Publishers
481 University Ave.
Toronto, Ontario
M5G 2E9
www.mcclelland.com

1 2 3 4 5   06 05 04 03 02

Contents

PROLOGUE

One winter morning, with the snow falling so fat and thick and soft it muffled our coming, I chanced upon four deer here in the clearing. They stared at me and the dog with eyes dark as death, raised their white tails and simply vanished, so soundlessly the poor old dog, her snout buried in the light snow in search of Lord knows what, never even noticed they had been there. Bandit, understand, is not a particularly alert dog – think of her as a Border*line* collie. She has also missed a half dozen wild turkeys moving through the underbrush, a fox that slipped silently across the path and disappeared into a dark skirt of spruce, a pure white rabbit caught in a snowless Christmas, a wolf that left its tracks for us to puzzle over, and a black bear that so alarmed the nearby high school that the police had to call in the rangers and tranquilizer guns. She is, however, good company, the type of dog who would happily lick the face off a child, and the two of us rarely miss an afternoon walk here; nor, for some reason, does she ever seem to miss the slightest sound or movement made by the resident squirrel population.

This place is called Alice Wilson Woods, named after a nature-loving pioneer, and is in the small suburban community we live in just to the northwest of Ottawa. It is a simple park; someone driving by on the nearby residential streets would not even notice it, a five-acre tract of mixed hardwood and stubborn granite and, once in a while, a noisy pileated woodpecker. But for Bandit and me, it is our daily escape.

We come here in spring looking for that certain day when, with the trilliums in full bloom, it seems as if the snow has magically returned under a hot May sun. We come in summer, when the leaves are so thick it is like entering through the flap of a large, cool tent as we turn in off the official walking trail and set out on the astonishing series of spider-webbed paths we and a few others have stitched through this small wood. We come in fall, when the maples are red and the sumac is just beginning to bleed. We come in winter, bushwhacking our trails through snow that, at times, will reach to my thigh and cause the old dog to bound ahead and turn with a look on her face that asks if this is truly a sensible thing to be doing.

"I do not understand," Marjorie Kinnan Rawlings, author of *The Yearling*, wrote, "how anyone can live without some small place of enchantment to turn to." That is what Alice Wilson Woods is to me, some small place of enchantment I can turn to when in need – or even when not in need. I use it the way others might turn to drink or afternoon naps. For me, it is one of those treasured places where, as Colorado naturalist John Murray once put it, "we go to turn our backs on the world, the places where we go to try and get back into the world." I walk and drift off; the dog could walk forever. I lose myself in my thoughts, though admittedly not to the degree of Charles Darwin, who also had his own little nearby woods and paths, and who had to come up with an ingenious method of turning over a cache of small stones with his boot as he passed a certain point – otherwise he would never know when to quit and return home for his evening meal.

I am not the only one fascinated by Alice Wilson Woods. There is a local teacher who photographs here every lunch hour. He now has approximately a thousand photographs through the yearly cycles, and shrugs his shoulders as to why he does this or why anyone else would care. There are a couple of women who walk their dogs along the same paths and who know the names of such fleeting treasures as wild leeks and dutchman's breeches and wild columbine. There is an older man who thought he should clean it up after a vicious ice storm struck one January and who, eventually, came to the conclusion that the woods are their own best keeper.

They call this a "woods," and I think of it as such because it has a simplicity and an easy familiarity to it. But I know that this is more an American than a Canadian term, that "woods" are what Thoreau preferred, with a sort of order, convenience, and limit to them, very different from what we in Canada refer to as the "bush." The bush has no order, no limits, and usually no convenience. The Canadian bush is, to Alice Wilson Woods, what the English countryside is to the English garden, plus. It is what the American woods are to the American backyard, plus. "Bush" means Australia to most Americans. But not all. A great many have already discovered, and more discover each year, that there is something about the Canadian *bush* that is unlike any other place on earth. Something awe-inspiring, something magical. My great hero in Canadian journalism, Bruce Hutchison, who was almost as old as the century when he died in 1992, knew what it meant to him when he left his work and travelled up the interior of Vancouver Island to his Shawnigan Lake retreat, where he could feel all the cares of work vanishing in the dust clouds that trailed his car. "For myself," he once said, "the return to my swamp and the whispered welcome of the forest seems like release from a luxurious prison." He is not alone.

I have always been an escape artist. My mother, a sweet and giving woman, who was herself most comfortable and happiest heading off into the bush, used to strap me in a harness and tie me to a tree so she could get her work done in a house with three, then four, active and growing children and a husband who worked six days a week, sometimes months at a time in winter, deep in the bush of Algonquin Park. With great laughter she told the story of tying me to various trees and even kept the little harness for years after to prove it. (There is a photograph somewhere of me tied to a spruce by the clothesline.) I hold no grudge about this. Had she not harnessed me to a tree I might be at the bottom of the Muskoka River or nothing but picked-over bones in the deep bush back of our Huntsville home or, more likely still, lost off the high rocks at Lake of Two Rivers, where we spent our summers in the log home of her father, the Algonquin Park ranger.

I daydreamed through school and survived, as daydreamers do, to move on to matters infinitely more pleasurable than algebra or Latin. My notebooks were filled with intricate drawings of pond life, the drawings from mid-winter showing where the beaver and snapping turtles and leopard frogs were sleeping and waiting, just like me, for the coming release of summer. Away from my beloved point at Two Rivers, I would draw it endlessly, if poorly, through the long Canadian winter: the old ranger's hand-built log home sitting below the high pines, the three little clapboard cabins where our family slept and cooked from joyous school-out to dreaded school-in, the Union Jack snapping on the flag pole (and God be with the child that let it touch the ground when we lowered it each evening), the huge floating dock, usually with a large snapping turtle staring menacingly from under the log booms, the red cedar-strip canoe out on the water, the little wooden fishing boat heading off in the evenings when our father was home from the lumber mill, a small cloud of blue smoke rising from his old three-horsepower Evinrude, a small cloud of white smoke rising from the Players fine-cut roll-your-own smoke that hung from his mouth as if it had been nailed to the side of his upper lip, the glistening steel line from the trolling rod stretching far out behind in search of the lake trout that lay off the point.

All my cells have been replaced a dozen times over or more, but I am little different today. I no longer draw – I never could – but the miracle of modern technology and the computer chip have given my imagination a summer retreat with year-round access from anywhere in the world. It is my answer to those who say, "You only get to use a summer place for two or three weeks of the year – what's the point?" I use this escape every single day of the year, no matter where my work as a journalist might take me. A digital photograph of a small, rustic cottage – nothing, really, compared to the old ranger's magnificent log house – sitting on a deep cold lake on the western edge of Algonquin serves as the screen saver on the laptop computer that represents my office far more than any downtown building. And I can change the image to fit the mood – flying off to the Stanley Cup playoffs with the view from the dock to escape into, flying off to the Olympics with the view from the deck where the hummingbirds come to feed, flying off to cover an election campaign with a lovely, sweeping twilight shot of the bay to turn to when the speeches begin to drag.

We don't always need to be at the lake to enjoy it. I visit when I'm shovelling the driveway in February. I lie on the deck with a cold beer and a good mystery novel when I'm stuck in traffic. That's not me napping on the living-room couch, that's me at work, planning and organizing complicated summer projects, whacking down the undergrowth back of the outhouse, helping put in a new dock, finally locating that secret speckled-trout lake that supposedly lies somewhere just back of the dam. We're talking year-round retreat, instant access. C. S. Lewis's wardrobe. Alice's mirror. Track 9¾ for the Hogwarts Express. All I need to get me there is to think of what Henry James once called the two loveliest words in the English language: "summer afternoon."

It was while walking Bandit in Alice Wilson Woods that I first thought of the possibilities of a book on escape. It began as a simple enough notion. The great Canadian literary critic Northrop Frye, after all, had lectured and written for decades that fear of the bush was at the core of who Canadians were. Novelist Hugh MacLennan had argued that the essence of Canada lay in its rivers, while popular historian Pierre Berton had published two bestsellers claiming that our national lifeline came from the railway. Why, then, could I not look for the soul of the country in the desire to escape? After all, it was escape from famine and war and persecution and economic repression that brought most of us here, escape that still brings most visitors to Canada today, and, I would contend, it is the promise of escape, however temporary, that makes everything from black ice to conference calls bearable for the rest of us in our everyday lives.

But it was only when I took out a small advertisement in *Cottage Life* magazine requesting thoughts on this percolating theory that I came to realize the Canadian census-takers have a problem. They think, after they have knocked on enough doors and analyzed enough forms, they have a pretty good idea of where Canadians live. In fact, they have very little. There are millions of us who fill out a street address and a postal code, but this tells only where we do what is necessary to get to where we truly live: the lake, and the bush around it.

It was no bigger than a thumbprint, and yet that little classified ad pushed more buttons than I could possibly have imagined. Dozens and dozens of letters and e-mails came flowing in, all with charming variations on the same theme.

A man from Hamilton told me he "escapes" every day of his life, even when he might be stuck in rush-hour traffic. "I think in thoughts that wouldn't make sense as sentences," he wrote. "I am content to drift from the city to the north, from age seven to yesterday."

A woman who has a demanding city job in the mental health field wrote to tell about her own therapy, a cabin in the deep bush that has no running water, no electricity, no telephone, not even a cooking stove. "My husband says I do nothing at the cabin," she told me. "It is my respite . . . my escape from all the routines and obligations of urban life. I escape from protecting my kids from cars and strangers, walking my dog who can run free, noise, pollution, cars, neighbours, phone calls, faxes, shopping, laundry . . . the list is endless."

Other letters told stories of returning the ashes of loved ones to the lakes they had escaped to only temporarily during their working years but where they always dreamed of being permanently; of windswept islands where luxury was a door on the makeshift outhouse; of places by certain lakes that became the "roots" of families posted overseas. They spoke of places down difficult lanes or over unpredictable bodies of water that had kept their sanity, preserved their marriage, and, in several cases, even returned them to sobriety.

"I'm only nine hours, door to door," wrote Mark McMurray, a geologist who has a home in Calgary, Alberta, but claims he *lives* on Raven Lake near Dorset, Ontario. "Leave the house, park-and-fly at the airport, check-in (sometimes with dog), boarding, four hours in air, deplane in Toronto, baggage, car rental, traffic, two- to three-hour drive up the 400 and 11, across 117, and down 35 with a co-ordinated pickup at the landing, followed by two miles across the lake." This past year McMurray made the trip five times, completing the last leg sometimes by boat, sometimes by snowmobile. In summer the whole family, Abby the golden retriever included, drives from Calgary, 3,500 kilometres, in three nights and four days, breaking into "O Canada" when the Dorset fire tower comes into view. "The dog hates to travel," wrote McMurray. "She won't lay down! Needless to say, she is exhausted by the trip."

Personally, I think McMurray has misread his dog. She doesn't hate to travel at all. She just hates how long it takes to get there.

The late Canadian historian W. L. Morton observed nearly half a century ago that the "alternative penetration of the wilderness and return to civilization is the basic rhythm of Canadian life." Nothing has changed. "Summer cottage, canoe trips and the northern lights," famed environmentalist David Suzuki wrote much more recently, "are quintessential Canadian experiences. We boast of nature on our license plates, lure millions of tourists here to experience it, and lionize the artists who capture it. Our flag is graced with a maple leaf, and the beaver and goose are stamped on numerous Canadian products. What would Canada be without bears, loons, salmon, cedar trees, or fall colours?"

This sense of nature and escape goes far, far beyond the cottager, however. It belongs to the camper, the tripper, the hiker, the climber, the walker, the Sunday driver, even the noon dog-walker who heads, as always, to the shelter of Alice Wilson Woods no matter the season, no matter the weather, because there is something waiting there that defies articulation, not something that rises in the mind and can be illustrated by the tongue, but something that is of the heart and in the bones and needs no explaining whatsoever to those who feel the same.

American writer Annie Dillard once talked of a special place she would stroll to in her little neighbourhood as often as possible, a small park where the whine of tires on the freeway could still be heard and where houses were visible through the bare branches of winter, but where there was always a quick fix of contentment to be found which was never so handy elsewhere, nor always guaranteed.

"I come to Hollins Pond," she wrote, "not so much to learn how to live as, frankly, to forget about it."

In other words, to escape.

Chapter One

THE SEARCH FOR ERMINE LAKE

"It is not down on any map; true places never are."

HERMAN MELVILLE, *MOBY DICK*

By the third summer, the search for Ermine Lake was verging on obsession.

There were nights – lovely, thick-starred summer nights, with the children singing around a campfire and the grown-ups laughing over wine on the porch – when John and I would find ourselves inside and staring, stone-faced, at the topographical maps that he had framed and put up on a back wall of the old log cabin that sat, all alone, below the highest hill along the south shore. If we appeared hypnotized, it was because we were: the pale green official government survey of the western edge of Algonquin Park our swinging pocket watch; the soothing voice of suggestion nothing more than our own muttered oaths that this year, finally, we would make it in to Ermine Lake.

Maps have always held a certain fascination for me. I can stare at an atlas for hours, delighted by memories that suddenly get dusted off by a glimpse of Copenhagen or Nagano, surprised by the discovery of countries like British New Guinea that keep showing up in places they surely shouldn't be. When I fold out a road map, it is often less for direction than for distraction. Instead of wondering how to get there, I am one who imagines being there. I am, in my newspaper work, never so happy as when I turn my rental car out the airport exit and onto a highway I have never before driven, my entire knowledge of where I am headed limited to the next turn in the road. If the highway is away from centres of population, so much the better, for – apologies to Orwell – two lanes are better than four. And better still is one lane, with grass growing up like an arching back in the middle. There

3

are a great many of us with this affliction; we are the ones who require no explanation when we hear of Wilderness Society founder Bob Marshall's abiding passion for "blank spaces on maps."

In this case, John and I would stare endlessly first at sheet 31 E/7 West of the National Topographical System representation of our immediate area, every twist in the gravel road familiar, even our respective little cottages acknowledged by tiny little dots about the relatively unencumbered shoreline of Camp Lake. John's map offered no resolution to the various debates of the locals – was it Blueberry Island, as the south shore knows the lake's smallest island, or Mouse Island, as the people on the nearby larger island call it? – and no answer at all as to whether little Blue Lake, just to the south of us, was its own body of water or, as the locals claim, nothing more than a culvert extension of Tasso Lake, which itself isn't really a lake but an ancient river the Ontario government dammed at the north end to get better control of the waters flowing out of Algonquin Park and, ultimately, into the Muskoka River system. There were the area landmarks – Toad Lake, Martencamp Lake, Flossie Lake, Sly Lake, Samlet Lake, the Oxtongue River, the Big East River, Distress Dam, Ragged Falls, Doughnut Creek, and the Split Rock rapids – exquisite, imagination-firing names that conjured up a hundred fond memories of one-day canoe trips and weekend bike treks and fall hikes and spring fishing trips, perhaps even one or two of them successful.

But there was also the entrancingly named Ermine Lake, a small, tadpole-shaped body of water that lay just inside the Algonquin Park boundary and offered, according to John's other framed map – Ontario Ministry of Natural Resources Map No. 1017665050300 – an unsullied shoreline and as many as three small, unexplored islands. As enticing as the "blank spaces" that surrounded Ermine on the map was the confirmation, from Natural Resources, that at some point in the previous decade the lake had been stocked with trout. If it was as truly inaccessible as the map suggested – no roads going in, no creeks leading in – then it stood to reason that the lake would be not only pristine to view, but never before fished.

"This year," I said, raising a beer glass holding nothing but the foam that hadn't found its way onto my moustache, "is the year we find out."

"Guaranteed," John agreed, turning to click one empty glass against the other.

It is a wonder the beer glasses did not shatter, for our luck in finding Ermine Lake had, up until this point, been as elusive as the creature after which the lake had been named.

Twice before, we had gone in search of Ermine. The first attempt, two summers earlier, had involved just the two of us, the topographical map, and an unhealthy amount of male arrogance. We knew, from an aerial photograph of the area, that there were a number of logging roads that spread out into the park from a main depot not far from the road that led in to Camp Lake. The aerial photograph was a tree-generation or two old, however, and the actual logging had been done years, perhaps decades, before the picture had been taken.

No matter, we knew the bush like the back of our hands – *where did that liver spot come from?* – and so we had set out, the two of us, in my old tin fishing boat with the forty-year-old six-horse Johnson fouling the air of an August day so warm and still the lake seemed filled with dark syrup rather than water. With the bow gargling through the water and the wake slapping the shoreline behind, we pushed through the shallow narrows, past the rickety, tilting hunt camp, up across the centre of Flossie Lake, past the campsite, and down the long, ever-narrowing bay-creek that leads from the little trickling falls that carry the runoff from the Algonquin highlands.

It was a quiet run, the only sound the cough of a regularly missing outboard, the cut and boil of the bow, and the burring vibration of the oarlocks on aluminium seats. We passed by the water lily stand where, on an early morning and in a much quieter canoe, you can sometimes come across a bull moose feeding. We passed by the beaver lodge with no sign of its tenant, passed the small point where spruce and pine have lain scattered like pick-up-sticks since a small twister touched down ten years earlier, passed the log where the huge snapping turtle prefers to take his sun, and turned into the shallow, weedy bay where we planned to leave the boat.

I killed the engine, the air at once silent but for the chuckle of the little falls as they dropped the last few feet down the slanting rock face on the other side of the bay. I stood to yank the propeller up free of the rocks just as a large great blue heron took off from its one-legged stance in the shallows. It swept toward the falls, and then back and over our heads, a modern pterodactyl, heading south over the trees. It was so close at one point, we could hear the sighs of its vast wingspan, and we sat in silence, staring straight up as the bow of the boat grounded into the muck and stones and waterlogged beaver chews of the shore.

"Beautiful," I said.

"Ever notice," John said, "you never see a small one?"

I stabbed out with an oar, dislodging us from the suction of the black muck. "That's true," I said. "I don't think I have."

But then, I'd also never seen two great blue herons together, which makes you wonder not only what they reproduce, but when and how they ever mate. Nor do you ever see a nest, suggesting that perhaps the great blue heron is indeed the pterodactyl it so resembles, a sixty-million-year-old creature who just happened to be so far back in the Ontario bush when that meteorite slammed into the prairies that it somehow managed to carry on, blissfully unaware that history had passed it by.

We pulled the boat up onto the shore by a mucky, moss-covered opening where, according to the potholes in the mud, moose came down to drink. I tied the bow line to some alder branches while John set out the pack, opened up the map, and folded it strategically for convenient reference. We were ready to go.

I felt slightly like another John, John Muir, the nineteenth-century Scot who became the driving force behind the Sierra Club and who never felt more invigorated than when he could "throw a loaf of bread and a pound of tea in an old sack and jump over the back fence." The difference in this case was we had no bread and no tea, nothing in the pack but a plastic map holder, a bottle of bug spray, a hatchet, and a couple of plastic bottles containing lukewarm drinking water. Still, it wasn't far removed from our "back fence," given the short distance from John's log cabin, and it wasn't as if we were heading out into the unknown: after all, we had a map.

We also had limited knowledge. We just didn't know how limited. We knew, from earlier explorations, that a passable old logging trail ran the circumference of Camp Lake and Flossie Lake and even this slow tributary by the little falls. Winter snowmobilers and, to a much lesser degree, summer all-terrain vehicle drivers had kept it fairly open despite the overgrowth. The previous summer my teenaged son, Gordon, and his best friend, David Rider, had circumnavigated the two lakes, Camp and Flossie – an eight-hour bike trek that left them drained of energy and, thanks to raspberry bushes, hawthorns, spruce and balsam branches, and bramble, drained as well of an impressive portion of their personal supplies of blood – and earlier this same summer we had made our own exhausting loop of the lakes by sometimes riding, sometimes walking, sometimes carrying our bicycles. We knew, at the very least, where the first trail ran, and we knew it was open.

We followed a creek up to the trail, hopping along the rocks and stepping carefully up the roots of yellow birch that grew along the route. It took us to higher ground, mixed forest giving way to hard-wood bush, the undergrowth all but vanishing and the forest floor dark and dank beneath the maple and beech canopy. The going was easy, almost too easy.

We walked until the first fork in the trail. The fairly open path of the bicycle expeditions headed north and east to where it would swing back over the creek that flowed just above the little falls. We turned the other way, the way less taken, and it most assuredly made all the difference.

Now, instead of easy going, we were pushing through small spruce and balsam as if through a subway crowd at rush hour. The old logging road was easily discernible to the naked eye; all we had to do was stare straight ahead and slightly up and we could see where the hemlock and maple, the birch and red pine and even cedar, grew high on each side of what appeared to be a green "ditch" running through the deep forest. The ditch, however, had no bottom, its floor covered by the stabbing green tops of the tens of thousands of white and black spruce, balsam and alders that had grown to roughly the height of an average man along the trail.

"This is not going to be easy," I said back to John.

He was studying the map. He was turning it in his hand, almost as if he could not determine whether it was upside down. I realized he was also holding the aerial photograph, now unfolded, and trying to align it with the topographical map so both corresponded to the flow of the rough trail ahead.

"This is the right trail," he said. "If we follow it for about half a mile, there should be a second branch heading off to the right and then what looks like a huge bog or swamp – then there's another fork, and if we keep to the right then, we should be dead on the mark for Ermine."

I leaned over his shoulder, studying the various shades of what looked like a poor black-and-white photograph of nothing. He ran a finger along what appeared to be a crease.

"I'd say we were right here," he announced.

I agreed; I had no idea where on earth we were.

John struck out, confident in his map, his aerial photograph, and his own gall.

Why not? I figured. You could always read the line of the old logging roads, even if at times it seemed they were nothing but an impenetrable blockade of scratching green branches. We weren't going far. We had a map. We knew enough about the bush to know when one was getting into trouble – even if, in a literal way, we were already in over our heads.

We walked for an hour or more, each taking turns pushing through the scratching, sweeping spruce and balsam branches with our shoulders, our walking sticks, and, at times, our shins. The worst part of it was being unable to see anything below one's waist and being forced to step forcefully ahead on faith alone – a faith that was from time to time sorely tested by a fallen branch or small log across the path that could not be seen until a swinging leg slammed into it.

It was hard going. The old logging road, perhaps more accurately the *hint* of an old logging road, twisted and turned – deliberately so, for the convenience of hauling as many logs out of the area as possible – and climbed over hills and skirted swamps and bogs and kept jutting off into quick dead ends where old log depots had once been. The high ground was easier, the sightlines better in hardwood bush than along the swampy tangle of the bogs and swamps and creek crossings. The lower ground also held the bugs, the late-summer mosquitoes stirred up by our kicking through the timothy and sedge and despised thistle.

The presence of the timothy, at least, was proof that we were still on old logging grounds, the type of grass unknown to the park before the logging companies got horses to do the winter hauling and had to have hay brought in over the ice roads from distant farms. The horses ate and hauled and pooped, and the timothy spread easily throughout the logging routes, the first, but most assuredly not the last, new species introduced to the park. Once, we found a rusted cache of oil cans and filters from the last time the bush had been worked by men and machine, but the height of the spruce and balsam and the girth of the maple and beech suggested it had been many years since any logging of any sort had taken place on the road to Ermine Lake.

We came to a split in the trail, neither route dominant, both quickly being erased by new growth.

"We turn right here," John said.

We checked the topographical map, then the aerial photograph. John pointed to the photograph as if, somehow, he could make out my sweaty ball cap through the branches and shadows.

"We're here," he said, tapping a dark splotch with his finger.

I didn't argue. He seemed so certain. Besides, it was his map and his photograph.

Right we went, up over more hills and past more bogs until we came to another split.

"Right again," he said.

More hills, an almost impassable swamp, a bog, a creek that we hobbled down over slippery, unstable rocks while flailing our ball caps at the horse- and deer flies that suddenly came out to greet the heat of the day and the foolish, unprepared explorers.

At times like this I have understood perfectly what that Récollet brother meant in the early 1600s when he wrote back to France that the worst "martyrdom" to be suffered in New France was not the marauding Iroquois and the torturing and the burning stakes. It was the bugs, the blackflies and no-see-ums of spring and the mosquitoes of early summer.

Still, I sometimes think I find blackflies and mosquitoes preferable to the dreaded horsefly or the slightly smaller deer fly. Both have an uncanny knack of getting footholds on human hair while they chomp out slabs of flesh. No needle noses or stingers for these guys – like winged piranhas, they prefer to chew their food.

Scientists say a moose can lose a cup of blood a day to the horseflies when the insects are at their worst. In the park, horseflies have been known to drive moose out onto the highway in search of relief in the breeze of an open space. It works better in theory than practice for the moose, as it also leads to a summer-long series of road accidents at dusk. Only a few miles from where we tramped toward Ermine Lake, one unlucky fellow rammed into a bull moose so hard it all but ripped off the roof of his car. Then, the ambulance rushing him to hospital in Huntsville was demolished by another bull moose frantically scrambling up out of the fly-infested bush. A second ambulance had to be dispatched to bring in both drivers.

My mind was clearly wandering.

"Left," John said. We turned left.

"Right."

"Right again."

I was beginning to feel a bit like Professor Summerlee in Arthur Conan Doyle's *The Lost World*: "'We have spent two long days in exploration,' said he, 'and we are no wiser to the actual geography of the place than when we started. It is clear that it is thickly wooded, and it would take months to penetrate it and to learn the relation of one part to another.'"

I was, by now, silently cursing Ermine Lake and the folly of our great adventure. John, however, suddenly became possessed with new energy and moved ahead to the cusp of the next hill, his topographical map and his aerial photograph in hand and his head flicking from side to side in search of landmarks.

He hurried down the path. I stumbled after him, sweat pouring off my face and trickling down the small of my back. It was even coating my legs, stinging now into the scratches and scrapes along my shins.

"I CAN SEE WATER!" John shouted back.

I hurried toward him. He was standing triumphant and pointing. Up ahead, through the trees, I could see a flash of blue lake.

"Thank God!" I said.

"This way," John said, cutting away from the old logging road and heading down what appeared to be a dried-up creek bed. I followed, both of us heading down, down, down.

"It's beautiful!" he called back.

I had to agree. There is little in the bush more beautiful after a long day of slogging than to feel a sudden coolness tickle along the hairs of your arms, the almost imperceptible coolness that comes from nearing water, and to see light ahead through the branches, to stare high over the treetops and to sense, for once, that there is an opening ahead rather than more bush and more bush and more. I could see the water rippling blue through periodic breaks in the tree cover. I could smell the lake, fresh and airy compared to the rot and must of the forest undergrowth.

I hurried to catch up, coming shoulder to shoulder with John as he pushed through some alders and came out along the shore, the lake spreading blue and beautiful before us.

I'd tried to imagine what the shoreline of Ermine would look like. It seemed, as I should have known, little different from the lakes we had just left – lily pads in the shallows, a few deadheads sticking up, the water dark blue and rippling in a slight wind.

We stared across the little bay before us, both stopping abruptly with the same realization.

Someone else was here!

Someone with a small boat and motor. The boat was hauled up on the mucky shoreline while the invaders were off having a lunch of fresh trout or napping.

John was first to comprehend. He started giggling.

I pushed farther out through the alders to see what was so funny – and then, a beat behind John, I knew too.

"It's my boat," I said, voice cracking.

"We went in a complete circle," John added unnecessarily.

I leaned out more, as if there were any need to confirm the obvious. The tin boat and the old oars were as undeniable as the old Johnson six-horse tilted up out of the water.

I could hear the falls now, the water tumbling down in what sounded like a whispered, hissing laugh.

We failed again the following summer. It was a hot, sticky, end-of-July day, and we should have known better. We only had a few hours, and we kept telling ourselves that it was just an "exploratory" run to establish the correct logging trail into Ermine, but after three hours of mosquitoes and horseflies and deer flies buzzing about our heads and cicadas buzzing in our ears, we were no closer, really, than our first foolish attempt.

They were beginning to laugh at us. They were also beginning to wonder about us, John and I endlessly hauling out different maps, even laying them over each other to see if one cartographer's notion of Ermine's exact location coincided with another's. When we found two maps that disagreed – one a road map of Ontario, the other a canoe route guide to Algonquin Park – we began to wonder ourselves if perhaps Ermine, like Brigadoon, might have mythical properties.

And why not? Is our world not filled with places that can no longer be located? Do people not believe in Atlantis, though it cannot be found by any modern explorer, treasure hunter, or television specialty channel? Our imaginations overflow with places that have been lost, misplaced, have disappeared, or never been found in the first place: The Neverland in *Peter Pan*; the Duchy of Grand Fenwick in that wonderful Peter Sellers movie *The Mouse That Roared*; the legendary French town of Lubec, which is perhaps left well enough alone, since the men of Lubec must store their genitals in the town hall and only remove them when absolutely necessary; the floating islands of

Ojibway oral history, which the gods supposedly keep for their own pleasure in Lake Superior and move about so no human can ever land; Brigadoon, the little Scottish village in the Highlands, which appears on no known map, is supposedly surrounded by a high, impassable forest, and comes awake only once every one hundred years; Mark Twain's Curious Republic of Gondour, which no one can ever find and is a little hard to believe in, because everything is supposed to work perfectly there, unlike in the real world.

Perhaps Ermine Lake was merely a Canadian version of the infamous false-front villages Russian Prince Grigory Aleksandrovich Potemkin erected back in the late 1700s to convince Catherine the Great that he was doing a crackerjack job in the provinces. When Catherine came to check on her young lover's progress, Potemkin flew her horse-drawn coach so quickly past the villages that the poor lovestruck empress never even noticed that the paint was still tacky. In many cases, there was nothing behind the shining new facades but peasants cringing under the threat of instant death. The illusion gave birth to one of politics' most lasting credos: perception is reality.

Certainly, we began to see Ermine Lake differently from then on. The more they laughed at our inability to find the obvious, the more we covered up with elaborate explanations. The lake, I put forward, existed only in winter, which is, of course, why it's called Ermine Lake. What we needed to look for in summer, I argued, was Weasel Lake, an off-season version of the glorious ermine, one that was brown and dirty instead of white and clean, and renowned for its sneakiness. Weasel Lake, like its namesake, was just giving us the slip.

I even read up on the little winter beast to see if perhaps a clue might be found in its particular traits. "The ermine, or Stote," recorded Samuel Hearne in *A Journey to the Northern Ocean*, which he published in 1792, more than two hundred years before our brave venture into the unknown, "is common in those parts, but generally more plentiful on the barren ground, and open plains or marshes, than in the woods; probably owing to the mice being more numerous in the former situation than in the latter. In Summer they are of a tawny brown, but in Winter of a delicate white all over, except for the tip of the tail, which is of a glossy black. They are, for their size, the strongest and most courageous animal I know: as they not only kill partridges, but even attack rabbits with great success. . . . I have taken much pain to tame and domesticate this beautiful animal, but never could succeed; for the longer I kept it the more restless and impatient it became."

No clues there. And the only ones growing restless and impatient were the two of us. We had to find Ermine. We had to put an end to the laughing and ridicule and the rising concern that two grown men were becoming obsessive about something they could not find and had never seen, something that no one else on the face of the earth seemed concerned with, even in the slightest. To justify ourselves, we began to work on the youngsters of the lake, telling them over and over again that there was something so special about Ermine that it required a full-blown expedition – the Algonquin equivalent of Stanley to the Congo, surely – to prove once and for all that this was a lake like no other.

There was, I told them, evidence of another dimension just beyond the bog, some wormhole through space, perhaps, that would let us pass from the edge of Algonquin Park to the outer edges of the Milky Way. Or maybe, on the shores of Ermine Lake, there was an alternative society to ours – what else could explain their having a boat identical to mine? – with magnificent cottages that no one could see until they arrived there.

Ermine Lake, I told the kids, had a marina and a ski jump. It had a small store that sold ice cream cones that never dripped and candy that was good for you. It had endless sunny days and perfect calm – unless you wished to sail, and then a breeze would rise at the snap of a finger. It held fat trout that had never so much as glimpsed a hook and would be certain to leap at anything, even those dreadful nitrogen worms with the green dye that ran all over our hands and clothes and boat. At Ermine Lake, the people were always happy, the refrigerators full and inviting, the drinks on ice, the campfire a perfect deep-red glow for marshmallows, and no one in Ermine Lake had ever heard of let alone seen a mosquito, a blackfly, a horsefly, a deer fly, a leech, or a snapping turtle.

I would even walk around at times singing or humming an old bluegrass tune:

> In the Big Rock Candy Mountain
> You never change your socks
> And little streams of alkyhol
> Come trickling down the rocks . . .
> There's a lake of stew
> And gingerale too
> And you can paddle
> All around it in a big canoe
> In the Big Rock Candy Mountain

"When can we go?" they wanted to know.

"Soon," we told them.

But it would be another year before we would launch our third assault on the treacherous climb to Ermine Lake. We would spend Thanksgiving blowing steam off our coffee as we stood, once again, in front of the framed topographical map and tried to figure out where we had gone wrong. We would buy more maps and compare them to each other as if the true location of Ermine were some great carto-graphical in-joke. We would exchange e-mails throughout the winter talking about when we'd go and how we'd go and how this year, finally, we would reach our destination. Or else.

The choice was simple: find it or spend the rest of our summers the butt of endless jokes.

A man on the north shore, a hunter with a wonderful sense of the bush, told us that he knew exactly where Ermine Lake was, because that was "where I got my moose." I pointed out to him that Ermine was – according to the several maps we now owned – located inside the Algonquin Park boundary and therefore protected from hunters. If he'd shot his moose there, he was, in effect, a poacher.

"No," he said, "that's where I saw the moose. I trailed him until he stepped outside the park boundary, then I shot him."

It was a suggestion too preposterous even to entertain, as if the park were surrounded by one of those knee-high light beams like they have in classy art galleries, a small alarm going off just as the foolish moose took a single step in the wrong direction, followed by the echoing discharge of a .308. But he said he had been there. He pointed it out on the map and ran a thick finger along what he claimed was the "trail." "Easy to find," he said. "You can't miss it."

Later that spring, we ran into another man from a neighbouring lake at a cottagers' association function. He went on at some length about the wonders of travelling by all-terrain vehicle and how he and his son had roared and blue-smoked and ground their knobby tires along hundreds of miles of old logging trails in the area. Caught up in the moment, we happened to mention that we, too, had travelled over the old logging trails in search of a particular lake.

"Yeah, which one?"

"Ermine."

"Been there."

I sincerely doubted it. The logging roads we had travelled would not allow passage of a Sherman tank, let alone a Yamaha ATV. We had seen no tire marks, no broken spruce. We had heard nothing but the red-eyed vireo and cicadas on our trek in to Ermine – or at least as close to Ermine Lake as we had yet reached.

"You should get yourself an ATV," the burly man said as he popped the top off another beer. "Or rent a couple – you can rent 'em in town, you know."

We did not know. But we also did not care. For one thing, ATVs are banned in the park, meaning we'd be breaking the law even if one could make it up those trails, which seemed unlikely. We'd also be destroying trees and churning up mud and scaring animals and birds. And besides, we'd be cheating. The idea, after all, had always been to hike in, to walk the pitiful little distance between the landing by the falls and the little park lake that, on some maps, was beginning to look less like a tadpole and more like a sneering, lopsided grin.

The man burped loudly and rubbed his chest and stomach with enormous self-satisfaction. "I got my ATV and my GPS," he said, pausing for a second smaller burp. "I can go anywhere you want to see."

Thanks but no thanks, we said. But almost immediately we began talking quietly about the possibilities of a GPS. These little hand-held gizmos – full name "global positioning system" – were becoming increasingly popular that summer, and not only among hikers and canoe trippers. Car rental companies had been offering them as an option on higher-end models for some time, and while covering the Stanley Cup playoffs in Denver, I had been astonished to see what they could do. A Canadian sportswriter friend had rented a Chrysler with a GPS tracker sticking up off the floor like the shift in an old half-ton. Another journalist had booked a tee-off time at a suburban public golf course, and four of us Canadian hockey writers were headed there with only a half hour to spare and not the slightest notion of how to get to the course. All the driver had to do was enter the name of the golf facility and the GPS immediately took over. As we hurtled down freeways and over turnpikes and looped around cloverleafs, every now and then a mechanized voice would say things like "Move into ... the right-hand lane. ... You ... will ... be ... taking ... the next exit," and "Be prepared ... to ... turn ... right ... at the next ... traffic light." Without a single missed turn, we arrived in excellent time, teed off, and by the fourth hole were all in agreement that the next huge scientific leap for mankind would be GPS coordinates fixed to golf balls.

Entranced, I began reading up on GPS. The idea came out of defence research. By using more than one satellite, the theory went, it was possible to fix the position of anything that the satellites could pick up. By the mid-sixties, the Americans were using it to track submarines, and by the early seventies the U.S. Department of Defense was using its NAVSTAR system to track everything from troop movements to shipping. They spent some $10-billion to produce an intricate twenty-seven-satellite system that one day, thanks to miniaturized computer chips, digital programming, and backlit screens, would put the tracking capability in the hands of anyone with a few hundred dollars to pass to the cashier at the local Canadian Tire. Farmers were even hooking their tractors up and using special computer programs to control their seeding so that, by early summer, airplane passengers flying overhead could look down and see the Mona Lisa mysteriously smiling up from a wheat field in Alberta.

Their capabilities – increasing by the month, it seemed – were astonishing. By using three different satellites at once, and a fourth to remove the margin of error, the little hand-held cheaters could tell a hiker precisely where he or she was on the map. Not only that, but a more sophisticated one would also supply the direction you had been travelling in, the average speed of your hike, the distance to the pro-grammed destination, and even the estimated time of arrival, taking into account the terrain and your average walking speed.

An article in *Discover* magazine compared GPS to the Marauder's Map in the Harry Potter books, which charts the movement of every creature within the grounds of the Hogwarts school of wizardry. I would go a step further, saying it comes close to Big Brother in George Orwell's *1984*, the all-seeing eye that keeps track of every single person and their movements. One California company was said to be devel-oping chips so small and flexible that they could be sewn into cloth-ing. "Our vision," the founder of the company was quoted as saying, "is to bring location awareness to virtually everything that moves."

Vision to him, perhaps; nightmare to others. Was this not "yet another death for the powers of human observation?" wondered the article's author. We wanted to go in to Ermine Lake to see it, not merely find it and then get out by the shortest route possible. If all that sailors now had to do to navigate was hold out their GPS, did it not matter what they saw in the stars and wind and the changing hues of the water? Surely sailing was all of these sensations and observations rolled up into one hugely satisfying intelligence for the successful sailor. And what of the farmers, who, as we so love to say, "know their fields like the back of their hands," if they now can seed and plough and harvest with their eyes closed?

There was, however, one huge attraction to the relatively inexpen-sive GPS John and I checked out at the local Canadian Tire. For a few dollars extra, we could get one with a "map" page, an ingenious little option that meant if you aimlessly walked into the wilderness with your GPS on, it could create a map you could follow back out. Given our previous experience with Ermine Lake, that might just be a handy little tool to carry in the pack.

"I don't know," John said, turning from the display case.

I could sense him weakening. I cleared my throat. "It wouldn't be the same thing as finding it on our own."

He was too polite to say, "Of *course* it wouldn't be the same thing! For a start, we wouldn't have to spend another day travelling around in a complete circle! We wouldn't bust our shins and scrape our arms and twist our knees hobbling down creek beds to find an impassable bog. For Christ's sake, MacGregor, we wouldn't become the laughing stock of an entire lake because we can't walk in a straight line over a couple of hills!"

"I guess you're right," he said instead.

"What if we just took a compass?" I suggested.

"A compass?"

"Yeah, a compass. Then we could check it against your map just to make sure we were on line. Just a back-up. In case . . ."

"Good idea," he said. "You've got one?"

I nodded. In fact, I had several. One, which I treasure, is in a wooden case polished so smooth by one man's hand that the wood feels more like ivory than cherry. It dates from around the First World War and belonged to my grandfather, Tom McCormick. He used it for all the decades he was a fire ranger and then chief ranger of Algonquin Park. I keep it on my work desk to remind me of him, a tall, imposing man whose idea of a fine Saturday off was to take a grandchild or two with him and simply strike out into the heart of Algonquin. Together, we would trace old logging trails and forgotten portages and all-but-grown-over tree blazes back to abandoned camboose logging camps where, with luck, he might be able to step out the lines where the old foundation logs had been laid or, once in a while, find a rusted square blacksmith nail by kicking up the earth or turning over a few stones. He could walk for hours, hard and straight ahead with nothing but his axe in his left hand for occasional fresh blaze marks, and never once did he ever seem even the slightest uncertain as to where he was going. He would hike for miles back into the bush, the underarms and back of his old worn green khaki ranger shirt turning dark with sweat. Those grandchildren he took along with him, of course, were constantly petrified that a second heart attack would fell him dead in the middle of the Algonquin tangle, and we'd be so far lost we'd never get out. I inherited his wonderful old compass, but none, apparently, of his natural sense of direction.

I wouldn't risk losing that family heirloom in the bush, but there was an easy second choice. My wife, Ellen, had purchased a cheap combination compass/whistle that she had attached to the boat key, it now being law to carry a source of emergency sound in the boat as well as a bailer, a life jacket for each person, and a rope in case one of them tumbled overboard. The whistle was cheaper than a horn. The compass was a bonus, as the lake was small enough to see all of the surrounding shores at once – the perfect lake, someone might have suggested, for the likes of John and me.

We determined that this summer we would do it. We would make one significant change – the compass – but there would be no other cheating. We would go prepared this time, with packsacks holding the maps, the now-badly-torn-and-worn aerial photograph, some light food and drink, and, for once, the essentials no one is ever supposed to head into the deep bush without: rope, matches, water container, bug spray, sun block, dry clothes, a hatchet, a good knife, a couple of fishing poles, some tackle, and a whistle. The whistle, of course, was attached to the compass, which I would carry in my pocket.

Our plans made, word soon spread around the lake. Those who weren't ducking behind their hands to hide a snort of derision seemed genuinely interested in our finally reaching Ermine, as if our now-legendary failures somehow reflected badly on them – or worse, on their fickle and fragile property values. Who, after all, would ever want to pay good money for the opportunity to summer on a lake where people like us might paddle, uninvited, up to their dock? Presuming, of course, we could find it.

Denis, from the north shore, even offered to come along. This was an unexpected development. Denis was a newcomer to the lake, the result of a second marriage, to Merryl-Jeanne, whose family had been lake "originals." A charming, outgoing francophone from the Eastern Townships of Quebec, Denis had, in a few short summers, become known and widely welcomed around the lake. Perhaps it was because, as one woman so succinctly put it, "All the men want to hang around with him and all the women want to sleep with him," but perhaps, too, it was because, in such short time, he had himself become part of the recent mythology of the lake.

Camp Lakers were still talking about Merryl-Jeanne and Denis's wedding, and will likely still be talking about it for generations to come. A ceremony on the shoreline and dock, conducted by a minister and overseen by a local caterer who somehow managed to cart a prepared banquet over twenty miles of bad road and serve it up in grand fashion. They made their own wedding wine, wrote their own words, and even built their own latrine, digging a great hole off one end of the dirt "dance floor" and erecting a plank outhouse over it so no one would have far to go . . . to go. One day they may sell a poster of Merryl-Jeanne, resplendent in her white wedding gown, sitting in the outhouse, the upper half of the dutch doors open, with a great contented smile on her face and a bouquet of fresh flowers in her hand. The world's most natural air freshener.

But there was more to the growing legend than the wedding. Denis had such a knack for dressing for the occasion, we eventually came to the conclusion that the rough shed he kept back of the cottage was not, as he claimed, a place to store the fishing boat for the winter, but the wardrobe department of a Hollywood studio. If he came to dinner, it seemed he had just stepped out of the pages of *GQ*. He was so perfectly dressed and suavely casual, it's a mystery that we kept asking him back. If he went fishing, it seemed he had just stepped from the pages of *In-Fisherman*. We once got our signals mixed up on a plan to go fishing, as Denis preferred, or golfing, as John would rather, and at 6:15 A.M., just as the sun was beginning to burn off the mist, Denis slipped out of the fog in his fishing boat, landed at our dock, and hailed me from a sound sleep. He was wearing a golf cap, a fishing vest over a golf shirt, a pair of bush pants over golf shorts, and a pair of work boots with grey socks. His golf shoes were in his golf bag, which lay by the live well beside his rod, already set out with a sharpened lure and tipped with a minnow. He was, I like to think, the first golfer in history happy to be headed for the water.

That is not, however, to suggest that Denis was an expert at fishing – any more than he was a golf professional. He had the equipment – one of those carpeted bass boats with an electronic fish finder, an electric motor, and seeming suitcases of tackle, all of which he had inherited from his father – and he had such passion for fishing that he could be found setting out most summer days at dawn, the steam of his ritual coffee and cognac mingling with the swirling mist as he delicately, methodically let out his line and steered into the channel that runs between the two islands, heading for deeper waters.

He insisted on trolling where still fishing was best, still fishing where others would troll. He cast with lures so large they could pass for depth charges. They crashed into the water near other fishermen who were trying to cast not so much as a shadow, let alone a fat heavy lure that looked like a Christmas tree. We tried to explain to him that this was a small freshwater lake, not the Atlantic Ocean, and that this was freshwater fishing, not *The Hunt for Red October*, but to no avail. He had his methods and he would stick by them. He also had no luck. None.

Denis did, however, have a great curiosity, and a sparkling delight in adventure. Once he heard that Phase III of The Search for Ermine Lake was about to be launched – complete with compass – he was interested in joining. In fact, out of Denis's enthusiasm grew a virtual crusade to find the lost lake, with Alannah, John's wife, and their three children – twelve-year-old Shauna, ten-year-old Logan, and eight-year-old Hope – deciding to come along if the weather turned fine.

This, of course, had the effect of downplaying the gruelling dangers we had previously faced in seeking Ermine – two healthy males against the elements, determined to return one more time at whatever imaginable risk – but there was also a strong sense, by now, of what-the-hell?

Less "share the adventure" and more "share the ridicule."

Certainly, if we failed a third time, there would be more than enough to go around.

I rose around dawn and began packing for the trip. I packed water and fruit drinks and granola bars and apples. I packed a hatchet to help clear the trail, a Swiss army knife and a hundred-foot coil of nylon rope in case we got entirely lost and had to build a cabin to spend the winter, a warmer shirt, a pair of shorts – we'd be wearing long pants for the hike in – sun block, insect repellent, a camera, flashlight, an extra roll of film, toilet paper, matches, telescoping rod, reel, and a small plastic container of essential fishing tackle.

Since there were kids going, I added two other essentials. A long, hot summer had brought out the wasps, and so many people on the lake had been stung – some of them multiple times – that it made sense to carry some sort of antihistamine in case of allergic reaction, so I tossed in a box of hayfever pills. I also knew that most kids had one fear far greater than getting lost, so I put in the Bear Guard as well. The year before, prior to heading into the park on our own family canoe trip, I'd ordered it from British Columbia to ease the highly imaginative mind of our youngest daughter, Jocelyn. It was, essentially, a spray can of cayenne pepper, and while I had serious doubts that it would have any effect on bears, except perhaps to make the meat palatable, it had had the welcome effect of calming Jocelyn's fears. Neither she nor any of our other three children were around for the trek to Ermine, but John and Alannah's children were not without their own wild imaginations.

Denis showed up as if Wardrobe had dressed him for the part of Tom Thomson. Turn-of-the-century collarless cotton shirt, faded fishing vest, floppy hat, bush pants with what looked like an artistic smear of blue-grey paint down one leg placed there by the continuity people – the effect being one of Tom having just painted his beloved canoe before heading out on a sketching trip – and a pair of work boots with leather laces laddered up halfway and then hitched around the back and tied again in front. The toes were perfectly scuffed to the point where the steel toe shone through on the right foot, almost as if someone had sat with it pressed against a stone grinder until the scuffed and burnished toe had taken on the look of a logger's boot that had been used repeatedly to turn over fresh-cut timber for grading.

Denis, too, carried a pack. No one asked what was in it and he did not offer to show us.

In two boats, we set out for the narrows, and the long shallow run that ended at the little falls. Denis, Hope, and I rode in my tin fishing boat, and we were first through, our arrival in the quiet channel sending a blue kingfisher looping along the shoreline as if it were hanging bunting in the trees closest to the water. Perhaps in anticipation of our triumphant homecoming later in the day.

John and the rest of his family came in their bigger, faster boat, and the sound of a larger outboard coming up fast sent the great blue heron angrily squawking from his shallow hunting grounds high over the treetops and away. With both engines killed and tilted up, we drifted and poled our way into the shore, the only sound now the distant wash of the wake on the shoreline behind us and the murmur of the falls.

"It's so quiet," one of the kids said.

The heron, now almost out of sight, was still disputing the point.

We hauled up and tied the boats. We put on our packs, warned the kids about how tough it was going to be, and set out, the sun now rising full for the morning and leaking down through the roof of the hardwood forest in bright, sparkling shafts of light. The bush smelled both very alive and very dead at the same time, the heavy wet odour of plant and muck and rot and fungus lying somewhere between a lung's desire to fill all six hundred million alveoli with the rich air and the throat's natural reaction to gag.

We set out up the rock-cluttered dried creek to the first of the old logging trails, the one most passable and the one most certain to give hikers a false sense of confidence. Everyone was content, happy to be together, happy to be in the cool shade of the forest, happy to be on the easy road to Ermine.

Soon, of course, the easy trail fell away and the bush began tightening around it. Raspberry and blackberry bushes began taking over those sections of the trail that opened into sunlight, the ripe red berries so inviting to the free hand and mouth, the sharp-spined cane so alarming to the legs, even if covered, trying to wade through the bramble scratch.

"What's that?" Hope called out behind us.

Denis and I went back. She was pointing to what appeared to be a Plasticine replica of an elaborate Ben & Jerry's ice cream concoction, a dark, almost black base, sprinkled freely with blue and red berries.

It seemed fresh. And not only fresh, but large.

A bear.

"Raccoon," I said.

"Fox," said Denis.

"Which one?" Hope asked, a note of challenge in her voice.

I looked again, pretending to re-evaluate. I poked it with a stick. Soft. Very fresh. At least it wasn't steaming.

"Wolf," I decided. "A few days old, too. Don't worry."

But of course she did. And so, too, did we. I discreetly moved ahead, unzipped the pack, and worked out the Bear Guard. It came in a black holster with a Velcro flap to keep the can from bouncing out. I quickly looped it into my belt and then, again discreetly, faded back to the rest of the hikers.

"You put the bear spray on," said Shauna. "Why?"

"I just have it on," I said. "That's all."

"For raccoons?"

"Wolf," I said. "I said it was a wolf."

"Yeah, sure."

We walked on, the trail turning to young spruce and balsam and alders and more and more bramble. The sun was higher now, the day picking up in heat, and we were all sweating under long sleeves and pants. There were, however, few flies about, and, thankfully, no wasps.

It was even tougher going than the last time. The spruce seemed a little wider, the branches a trifle thicker, the drag of raspberry bramble just a little more irritating. The kids were tiring quickly and we stopped regularly for water breaks, at times spraying our faces and necks to bring a little relief from the heat, which seemed to rise the farther we moved away from any body of water.

The lake we had left was soon far behind us. The lake we sought, Ermine, was somewhere over the coming hills. We checked the map regularly and always used the compass. We double-checked with the aerial photograph, now almost in pieces, and agreed that we were where the compass and the topographical map suggested. Three different logging trails, three or four steep hills, two dried creek beds, and a long, surprising meadow and we figured we were halfway.

Every time we turned, I took out the hatchet and struck a new blaze on the side of a handy poplar or beech, the slight wounds shining white or pale yellow, like airport landing lights in the shadows of the surrounding higher trees.

"Why are you doing that?" Hope wanted to know.

"So we can find the trail back," I said.

"You think we're going to get lost?"

"No."

"Then why are you doing it?"

I had no answer. I moved on ahead, taking the lead over from John and pushing through the increasingly resistant growth to a small, baking clearing, a former log depot now home to yellow wood sorrel and forget-me-nots.

We found another dropping, large and fresh.

"Moose," I confidently declared.

"It's the same as what you said was wolf," Logan said.

"Whatever. Wolf or moose. They're much the same."

"Bear," said Hope. She'd already decided. She knew. She didn't seem in the slightest concerned. I tapped my holster for comfort.

John again took the lead. It was becoming hard slogging now. Alannah quietly wondered if the kids could make it. They were wet with sweat and the insects were out. We sprayed everyone down with bug repellent and continued, the trail becoming so close to impassable that, at one point, Denis struck off into the bush and found the going easier among the large maples and beech and hemlock. We followed suit for a while, but then turned back to the dreaded overgrown logging road, because at least it provided some guidance for direction.

The other guidance came from the compass and maps. We had passed over high hardwood hills, low bog-ridden swamps, over creeks and old logging depots and branches in the trail that seemed, from one angle, like the only possible way to go, from the next angle impenetrable.

John held the aerial photograph in one hand, the topographical map in the other. He kept switching his gaze from one to the other.

"Let me see that compass," he said.

I pulled the little compass out and placed it over the map. We adjusted until north lined up, checked the sightlines against the next split in the trail, and checked again.

"If we go cross-country from here," John said, "it should be only one good-sized hill and then another and we'll be there. Straight south from where we're standing."

I checked his calculations. On the map it looked simple. When I looked ahead into the trees, it seemed impossible. Instead of "one good-sized hill," when I looked up I saw hills rising in layers. If Brigadoon were surrounded by a high, impenetrable forest, it had nothing on Ermine Lake. The kids were almost exhausted. We were stopping more often now. The heat of the midday sun had brought out the horseflies and deer flies. Cicadas were starting up and winding down like miniature chainsaws every few twists along the trail.

On John's recommendation, we once again took to the bush, where the going would be easier, and headed cross-country. This would be the last chance. We were leaving the trail, and every subtle turn we took – an opening here, a fallen tree there, a rock outcropping ahead – meant the trail was not only soon lost from view but gone, as well, from memory.

I checked the compass. We were headed east.

"You said south, didn't you?" I called over to John.

"Straight south," he called back.

"Then we need to turn right."

We did, and stumbled on for a while. Kids fell, adults slipped, everyone grew quieter and quieter as John's one hill became a second, then a third. At one point we were headed straight toward a rock face and had to skirt around it to the east before turning south once more. We were well on our way to creating our own maze.

I crossed a small creek that had turned mostly to mud and came across a clump of pink-and-white lady's slippers. They were late bloomers, like we all hope to be, and I seemed to recall once reading that native medicine men used to collect the delicate little slipper-like flowers and grind them down to treat "delirium."

Even more appropriately, the showy lady's slipper is the fool's gold of wildflowers, a gorgeous, tall orchid that sends out the scent of nectar but has no nectar at all. Insects think there's something there, squeeze in past the pouting lower lip of the flower, find they've been tricked, and are forced to squeeze out again through the rear, where their backs are coated with pollen before they fly on to the next flower, get fooled again, and end up unwittingly pollinating each slipper they enter for no reward.

Perhaps Minnesota has already claimed the lady's slipper as its state flower, and Prince Edward Island has claimed it as its provincial emblem, but, at this point, this elegant trickster was a far, far better symbol for Ermine Lake, the scent of which had now been fooling us for better than three years.

We were about to give up. The children were exhausted. Alannah was clearly concerned. John was twisting his topographical map in his hands as he walked – always a bad sign – and Denis was so far off to the right that he had vanished from sight.

"A loon!" Logan suddenly shouted.

"What?" I called back.

"A loon! I can hear a loon!"

We all came to a stop. The quiet was so sudden that we were instantly struck by the hideous, destructive racket we must have been making as we had spread out and begun bushwhacking in a southerly direction. Branches snapping, undergrowth brushing against clothes, stones tumbling underfoot, grown men swearing – we had become so caught up in the push south that we had been unaware of the noise.

Now there was not a sound to be heard anywhere, not even our own breathing. I have never seen a "wildlife census" done for Algonquin Park, but University of Illinois scientists once calculated that in ten square miles of the eastern American forest there were approximately 300,000 mammals, of which 220,000 would be mice and other small rodents, 63,500 squirrels and chipmunks, 470 deer, 30 fox, and 5 black bears – and yet we had not seen or heard anything but songbirds and insects for hours.

"There!" Logan announced.

And we all heard it, the quick territorial call of the common loon.

"Where's it coming from?" I asked.

Logan pointed through the trees.

"It's gotta be Ermine!" John shouted, and began moving ahead fast through the forest. Everyone else followed.

There was still another small hill to go; nothing in the wild carries quite like a loon call. We pushed through the undergrowth and over felled rotting trees and stumps from the last logging days, past more tangle and yet another outcropping of rock, crested the hill, and stopped.

It was as if the forest had cracked and broken open. Ahead of us there was still the near black-green of immediate bush, hardwoods now mixing with thick cedar and spruce and pine, but there was also a break here and there, and through each break flooded light and blue and, it seemed, even a different smell.

Ermine Lake!

We pushed down through a glorious stand of white birch and came to the pine and cedar that fringes all lakes of the Canadian Shield. The forest floor here was riddled with tiny maple saplings that would eventually eliminate one another. There were squirrels and chipmunks now, all complaining and nattering about us as if we'd somehow missed them from the census. The loons were calling again, the sound as welcome to the ear as the breeze off the water was to our sweat-soaked and dirt-caked faces.

We came out onto an old beaver lodge, hundreds of chews of various length and thickness laid up against the shore, and used it to step out for a clearer view of the lake.

I felt like Sigurd Olson, the American naturalist and writer who was once president of the Wilderness Society. Olson, who, had he lived past his eighties, would have passed the century mark this summer, had, like John and me, become entranced with the notion that, somewhere out there, lay the "perfect lake," and he spent most of his long life trying to find it.

"Always before me was the ideal," he wrote in *The Singing Wilderness*, "a place not only remote, not only of great beauty, but possessed of an intangible quality and spirit that typified to me all of the unbroken north beyond all roads."

The Chicago native became convinced of one thing, that this perfect lake lay somewhere in Canada, and he eventually found it, he believed, at Saganaga Lake, which lies along the Ontario–Minnesota border between Ontario's Quetico Provincial Park and Minnesota's Superior National Forest.

"My first glimpse from the western narrows was enough," he wrote when he reached Saganaga, "and as I stood there and looked out across the broad blue reaches to the east with their fleets of rocky islands, the hazy blue hills toward the hinterlands of the Northern Light Country, I knew I had reached my goal. How I knew without having explored the lake, I cannot say, but the instant I saw the lake, I realized it was the end of my search, and that there was nothing more beyond the hills. I shall never forget the sense of peace and joy which was mine at the discovery. Perhaps I was ready for Saganaga; perhaps all the searching that had gone before had prepared me. Whatever it was, I was content at last, knowing that I would find in this lonely solitude the realization of all my dreams."

That's about half of what I felt having finally reached Ermine. Truth be told, my feeling was rather more like the last sentence Olson ever wrote, fifteen simple words his wife, Elizabeth, found on a sheet of paper still rolled in his old Royal typewriter after he'd suddenly passed away at the age of eighty-two after an afternoon of snowshoeing.

"A new adventure is coming up," he'd written, "and I know it will be a good one."

It was even more beautiful than I had imagined. The sky was clear, which made the water the darkest blue. Small gusts of wind tickled along the surface and a loon bobbed up from below and turned sideways to stare at us. I could see islands, one fairly large one in the centre, a smaller one beyond it, and tiny little archipelagos of stone and blueberry bush stretching off the east end of a third, larger, island toward the far shore.

No cottages. No motorboats. No marina. No store. No ski jump. No plastic greenhouse bubble over top to create an eternal summer. No alternative society living their perfect lives hidden away from interlopers carrying topographical maps and aerial photographs – not to forget that little pocket compass.

"Thank God for the compass," I said.

No one answered. They were all too busy checking out the lake of a thousand fantasies to be bothered about what magic had brought them here. For a brief moment I wondered whether, in fact, I would have preferred not to have found Ermine Lake. In some ways the outrageous fantasies had been as much fun as the planning and kidding about our constant failure to track this place down.

It was, admittedly, a pretty little lake. But so, too, were dozens of others within a day's hike or less. As long as Ermine had remained an imaginary lake it stood out from all the other lakes in all of Algonquin Park. Once it was found, it took on the appearance of every other small body of water in the region: clear, clean water, rough shoreline that was mostly a tangle of dense brush and a jumble of dead and fallen trees surrounded by large broken stone haphazardly arranged by the last retreating glacier, a couple of loons, a herring gull, beaver chews along the shore, horseflies, dragonflies, damselflies, and God only knows what beneath the blue rippling surface of the water.

No one else, however, seemed in the slightest disappointed. Ermine was likely precisely as they had imagined it. A lake. Different in shape, perhaps, but essentially the same in every other respect as the lake we had left, the lake we had travelled across and the lakes we had hiked in to on other summer days just to see what they looked like and whether there were any fish in them.

Denis already had his rod and line hooked up and was delicately balancing out on the end of the largest log caught in the pick-up-sticks jumble of the abandoned beaver lodge.

He made a cast. The lure – once again far too large – slapped hard on the water, sank like an anchor, and instantly his line went taut and the rod bent hard, bouncing.

"Got one!" Denis cried, perhaps for the first time in his life.

John and I stared incredulously. One cast and already Denis had a fish. One cast with one too-large lure and no bait, and a fish had gone for it. Denis reeled in hard, the fish putting up little fight, and he leaned out with his arm and gently lifted the catch free of the water.

A little perch. Not a trout, which we had hoped were here, but a fish all the same. And caught by Denis, first cast.

We had no idea then, but within twenty-four hours we would all accept that Denis's bad luck had turned forever with this one cast. Early the next morning, at a secret location a short drive from Camp Lake, Denis would snag a five-pound giant that would take him fifteen minutes to land and win him, on Labour Day weekend, a fabulous wood carving of a fish, the trophy for the best catch of the entire summer.

Proof, we believed, that the world had changed irrevocably with the discovery of Ermine Lake.

We found a small moss-covered clearing by the beaver lodge and settled down, kicking off our boots and struggling out of the sweat-dampened long-sleeved shirts we were wearing. The kids were exhausted, and hungry, and thirsty.

This, I knew, was my cue. I unzipped the pack and began pulling out rope coils and knives and matches and extra clothes and sun block and fly dope and . . . apples. Apples and fruit drinks and granola bars and fresh water. I began to hand the food about like a relief worker.

But then Denis opened his pack. He carefully removed, and unwrapped, a perfect little bottle of Heineken beer, still cold, the sweat forming instantly around the neck as he set it down on a neatly laid-out orange plastic tarpaulin. He then reached deep in the pack and began to remove pieces of barbecued chicken, each one individually wrapped in Saran Wrap. He passed the chicken to eager small hands that only moments before had held my apples.

We ate and the kids stretched out, moaning and groaning from the effects of the difficult walk in. The sun was high and hot now, and the shade of the cedars welcome. A nap before the long hike back seemed the sensible thing to do, but the younger ones couldn't settle down.

Denis reached once again into his magic sack. He came out with a mittful of *Archie* comics.

"Like something to read?" he asked.

The kids scrambled for the comics, rolled back onto the tarpaulin and settled down to read. Soon they were asleep in the warm shade. My apples lay beside the granola bars, ignored in favour of chicken and *Archie* comics. Denis – not John, not Roy, not the expedition leaders who had just brought them to this promised land – was the hero of the day; we were merely the Jugheads tagging along.

The adults got up and stood on the abandoned beaver lodge, staring out at the islands, green and gleaming like emeralds in the sharp light of the midday sun.

"When I was twelve years old," Denis said to no one in particular, "my dad left me on an island for a week."

The three of us turned at once.

"What?"

He was staring off at the main island, seemingly lost in memory. "He took me and a friend of mine out and dropped us off with a tent and sleeping bags and a frying pan, and a week later he came back and picked us up."

"He just left you?" I asked.

Denis nodded.

I shook my head. Shauna, John and Alannah's oldest, was twelve years old. She spent weeks every summer canoeing through Algonquin Park and Quetico Park and Temagami, yet to imagine her and another twelve-year-old being dropped off on an isolated island to fend for themselves for a week – with no cell phone, no radio, no guns or Bear Guard, not even a hand-held GPS to tell them how to walk out if they could get to shore – was incomprehensible. If Denis' father were to try such a thing today, he would be charged with everything from failure to provide the necessities of life to child abuse and abandonment.

"It was the best thing that ever happened to me," said Denis.

His friend Noel, he explained, had just moved to the Sherbrooke area from the francophone region of northern Maine with his six siblings and a mother who had just lost her husband in a tragic accident. Not knowing what else to do, she had come back to her Quebec family.

Noel turned to sports to handle his grief, and it was sport that brought the two youngsters together. Denis and he made the school basketball team together and spent weekends fishing and hunting in the lakes and rolling hills around Sherbrooke. In the summer of 1964, Denis' father took the two twelve-year-olds fishing on Lake Boissonneault, a twisting five-mile-long body of water in the Eastern Townships of Quebec. The lake had cottages in one restricted area, but the southern three-quarters of the lake was all crown land. There were no cottages, two medium-sized islands, and wonderful fishing for northern pike and smallmouth bass.

The boys got it into their heads that they would like to camp and do nothing but fish and explore for a week, and when they mentioned their dream to Denis' father, he not only agreed but took it upon himself to convince the boys' mothers that they would be safe spending a week alone on a wilderness island. Somehow, he got the mothers to agree. He took the boys down the lake towing a smaller boat behind and dropped them off with the supplies they would need to set up camp and enough food to get them through the first few days. Then he left.

"It was the greatest adventure of my life."

For five days they fished and explored the empty lake. They swam from island to shore and back again. They caught fish, cleaned them, and ruined their first meals trying to cook the flesh too quickly over too high a flame. But by the third day they had learned the little tricks of cooking over an open fire. They found a spring on the far shore where cold, clean water bubbled up. They found a place in the nearest bay where the bottom was littered with sunken logs, and they dived after lost lures they could see sparkling below when the sun was high overhead.

They spent their evenings around the campfire, two boys living the life of Tom Sawyer, and at night they tried to fall asleep to the eerie calls of the loons and the hoot of a barred owl in the trees back of their campsite. They cringed at the sound of movement around the tent and campfire as the nightly parade of mice, shrew, raccoon, rabbit, fox – perhaps even bear – began shortly after dark. They awoke each morning delighted to have survived the night.

"Why would your father do something like that?" I asked.

Denis shrugged. "I can only guess. My dad had this good friend, we called him Ti-Noir, whom he had grown up with, and the two of them had probably done much the same thing when they were young. I guess he felt that this was the right thing to do."

"What did you learn from it?" I asked, a little too seriously.

Denis grinned. He placed his two index fingers under his tongue and blew a shrieking whistle that bounced off the far shore and rattled around the lake.

"Noel taught me how to do that. I can do it without fingers, too."

"We believe you!" said Alannah.

The loons were calling back. Perhaps they thought one of their own had been wounded by the aliens who had just set up camp by the old beaver lodge.

We all stood around for a while longer, gazing out over the water, watching wind gusts tickle portions of the lake to goosebumps, then corduroy, before dying down to leave a surface so smooth it might have been spread by butter knife.

"I think I'll swim out to the island," Denis announced.

"What?"

He was nodding, staring far off toward the island. I stared out, the distance between shore and island suddenly growing as if someone had pulled in a telescopic lens.

"I'll go," said John.

"Sounds good," I said, less than convinced.

We hurried off to the side of the beaver lodge, past a convenient stand of cedar and into a second clearing where, in a moment, the three of us had stripped down to our underwear.

John and I in Anglo, middle-class, purely functional white Fruit-of-the-Loom and Stanfield's.

Denis in multicoloured pinstriped Versace jockey shorts.

He looked like one of those nonsensical advertisements in *GQ* or *Vanity Fair*, where the celebrity athlete or movie star stands around casually in a million-dollar setting as if his jockeys were merely a hot-weather tuxedo. John and I looked like we'd just run out into the street to escape a fire at a rundown rooming house.

Denis stepped down, using the sun-bleached beaver chews for footing, and slipped off the end of the abandoned lodge into knee-deep water, and from there entered the deeper water without so much as a splash. John and I scrambled down among the sharp, tilting rocks, screaming as insteps turned and toes stubbed.

We waded out over our knees, dropped down quickly with a splash, then rose again in slightly deeper water, standing on a ragged bottom of dead pine needles, black muck, unexpected stones, and the sharp shells of freshwater clams.

We stood there, bracing to take the plunge, and we knew, the moment we looked at each other, that there could now be no turning back.

Of all the known colours on this earth, the ugliest, by far, has to be the sickly pink of the male bottom through soaking wet white underwear briefs.

Denis was already swimming well out into deeper water and headed in a straight line for the island. We dove after him, as much to remove our hideous pink bottoms from sight as to give chase to our middle-aged Tom Sawyer.

The water was cool, refreshing, and stinging. I could feel every swipe of raspberry cane. I could feel the large, oozing bump on one shin from an unseen log on the way in. I dove down, hands back along my sides, and dolphined across the bottom, turning onto my back as I rose.

Alannah was also coming. She'd changed into her bathing suit and was leaping off the deepest edge of the beaver lodge. I was glad to see her. She is a former competitive swimmer; I, on the other hand, am a swimming fraud. I have a number of strokes down, at least fairly well, but I swim with a secret fear that I am often one stroke away from flailing and sinking and drowning. I turn on my back not to show off, but to collect my breath. I suspected the same was true of Denis, who was also on his back, laughing at the sight of Alannah diving in to join us, but seemingly relieved that at least one person on this spur-of-the-moment folly might know what to do if cramp, fatigue, panic, or rogue snapping turtle happened to attack.

At least I was wearing clean underwear – and getting cleaner every stroke – for the air-ambulance ride.

John noticed as well that Alannah was coming. A good swimmer himself, he is also conscientious. "I'll stay with the kids," he said, turning back and kicking toward the shore.

Denis and I swam ahead, keeping time with each other, aware that neither of us was quite the swimmer the high crawl strokes, the buried head, the snorting and spitting suggested.

We turned again onto our backs, pretending to check whether anyone needed our help, when we both noticed we were no longer the only swimmers in the middle of Ermine Lake. The two loons had paddled over and were skirting us like gunboats trying to determine our intentions. Had Alannah been Katharine Hepburn, had Denis been Henry Fonda and had Ermine Lake been Golden Pond, Alannah might have called out, "Norman! The loons! The loons! They're welcoming us back!" But there was nothing welcoming with these two: even without expression they gave off an unmistakable message of deep suspicion.

Loons surprise up close. They seem to have had their colouring determined on a drafting table rather than by any natural arrangement of feathers. While wood carvings of other birds rarely look like their subject, loons tend to look like, well, wood carvings. At least they do until they suddenly rise up in the water, white chest flashing, and flail away with both wings and lungs at whatever might be bothering them. Which one of them was doing at this moment.

Then there is the red eye. Perhaps it is what gives the loon its unnatural air, for the eye looks like a designer's costly afterthought, the job finished off with a sparkling ruby. The eye cannot be read the way we can read the stare of most other beasts. Eye contact is unintelligible, if not impossible, and all the more disconcerting as they breach alongside and suddenly turn so that the other impenetrable red eye can take you in.

I do, however, love loons, even though I have several times witnessed them to be the vicious, territorial creatures they are. As a child, I stood on the rocks at our grandparents' place on Lake of Two Rivers and watched three loons gang up on an intruder and pound him with their wings until they had broken his neck. Our father rowed out and lifted the heavy, dead bird out of the water, brought it in, and buried it back of the outhouse. As an adult, I have watched a large loon pound and harass a smaller one until our daughter Jocelyn paddled over to attempt a rescue. She managed to frighten off the bully and hauled the beaten loon out of the reeds, where it seemed he had gone to die. He looked like he'd lost a bar fight to a chair leg and a broken beer bottle, not a brief skirmish over a calm bay at the far end of Canoe Lake.

But I love the way they glide about a lake as if they are of the water, not merely on it. I love the way they carry their very young on their backs, and how when the young begin attempts to dive, they can't, no matter how hard they try. Someone once said it was like watching diving ping-pong balls. I love the way the adult loons dive, the way they arch their bodies and slip instantly under, the water closing over them without so much as a ripple. I love those very rare moments when I have seen them under the water, in full flight as they pass under the canoe or past the deep end of our dock.

I love the way they are so helpless on land – early Canadian settlers called them "arsefoot" – their tiny legs and clumsy big feet seemingly attached to the wrong part of their sleek bodies. I love the way they take off for flight, literally running over the water as though the lake were some huge mud puddle that threatened their dress shoes – one biologist on a slow day once calculated their foot size to be, in human terms, 45 RRR – and how they always seem, at takeoff, like a float plane that has sadly overestimated the length of runway.

It is often said that, according to the laws of physics, the bumble-bee cannot possibly fly, but in Canada, we should speak of the loon as the engineering enigma of nature.

But mostly I love their voices. I like the Cree notion that the calls are slain warriors signalling back to the land of the living. Thoreau thought the loon's call "perhaps the wildest sound that is ever heard." Scott Young, long one of my favourite sportswriters, once said he thought his famous son, Neil, sounded rather "loon-like" when he sang, and sure enough, when the naturalists who run A Wing and a Prayer, a small bird rehabilitation centre near here, ended up with a lonesome loon chick who wouldn't stop wailing, they quietened him down by playing Young's "Long May You Run." I find that song very soothing myself.

Their curiosity sated, the two loons slipped away, heading back toward the far side of the island.

I turned again, looking for Alannah. She seemed farther behind now. I knew this couldn't be due to excessive speed on our part, so I flipped over, treaded water, and looked again. She was going back to land, nearing the shallow ledge leading out from shore, and in another moment she was standing on it, wading toward the abandoned beaver lodge.

What if we started drowning?

Later, I would ask why she would come halfway across the lake and then turn back, particularly since she was such a strong swimmer.

"Do you really want to know?" she asked.

"Yes."

"Well," she said, giggling, "I couldn't quite imagine myself prancing around a little island with two men in their underwear, neither of whom was my husband."

But suddenly it no longer mattered that there was no one around to dive down and yank me – probably by the elastic band of my white Fruit-of-the-Looms – off the bottom. The bottom had risen to meet us, and both Denis and I were now touching down and wading the rest of the way to the island.

We drew, dripping, to the shore, the sand giving way to rock. The bush seemed to guard the island. We could see into it, and pick out clearings and even patches where the sun broke through in bright, dusty columns, but along the fringe it seemed unwilling to open up and let us onto the island.

"Over this way," Denis said.

The two of us made our way over slippery rock and soft, oozing dark sand.

We came to a cave-like opening between a jagged rock and a spruce tree, and Denis ducked down and scooted through.

I followed, the spruce branches like harsh wool on my back.

It was as if we had entered a building. It was cooler and darker, the air more pungent and alive. There were small animal paths – raccoon probably, perhaps rabbit – heading all through the undergrowth, but for grown men in bare feet and underwear, it was almost impassable. Dead pines lay everywhere over the spongy carpet of the island floor.

We had to pick our way through, snapping off limbs and ducking under branches and stepping over fallen trees and small bushes and hundreds of massive stones. The light was so bad and the going so ragged it seemed almost primeval, and my instinct was to head straight back for the welcome water and the swim back to the abandoned beaver lodge.

"What's this?" Denis said. He bent down to pick up a long bone.

He handed it over. It was light. Almost as if it was not bone at all but a plastic reproduction.

"Here's more!" he called. He began picking up more bones. Bird bones, like turkey bones, only longer, thinner, lighter. They seemed everywhere.

Where had we come? Some Algonquin Park graveyard where beasts never before seen came to die?

I began looking around. There were broken eggshells at the foot of a cedar. I picked one up and examined it. It was larger than a chicken egg, and light blue, with a rubbery white lining.

"Look at this!" I called.

Denis came over and took the shell, examining it carefully. He clearly had no idea what it was.

"Loon?" he said.

I didn't think so.

"There's more over there," Denis said, pointing to at least four broken shells at the side of a moss-covered stone.

"And more here!" he shouted.

We began moving about the island, sometimes finding bones, sometimes more of the strange shells.

Denis looked up, as if for inspiration – and found it.

"Look at that!"

I stared up. He was pointing to a tall white pine that seemed almost dead. Most of the needles had fallen, the bark had shredded, branches had broken off, some of them hanging precariously, and yet high up in the tree it seemed as if someone had built a substantial tree fort.

I was amazed that something so large could be sitting up there. How had it got there? Who had built it?

"There's two of them!" Denis said. He had circled around to the other side of the sickly tree.

I circled from the other direction. "Three," I corrected, pointing up.

We stared for a while and then moved away, looking up now instead of down.

"There's one!" Denis said, pointing into a high hemlock that also seemed to be dying.

"Two there!" I shouted.

We counted eight in total. Eight huge fort-nests on one small island.

"Here's another one!" Denis called from near the shore on the far side.

But he wasn't pointing up. He was pointing down toward a large clump of sticks and brush and hair and moss and leaves and branches.

"It must have fallen," I said.

"There's another," he said, pointing off in the other direction.

We found four more on the ground, each one with the fractured blue-and-white eggshells, as if it had been dropped from a great distance.

"Great blue heron," I said, remembering an occasion when I had been deep in the bush – this time in the dead of winter with a couple of beaver trappers – and came across a sight like this, minus the nests on the ground and the broken shells. "It's a colony. It's extremely rare to find one, you know."

We would later learn just how rare. Finding out where the lonely blue heron nests is not that far removed from discovering the mythical elephants' graveyard. Herons like to keep their private lives private. They hunt alone, but each night return to curious little condominiums like this, where they have their nests and raise their young. They are the forest's commuters, their daily work a substantial flight away, returning to a bedroom community each night.

We had come at the end of the nesting season, which partially explained the broken eggshells. But only partially. The blue heron, it turns out, so fastidious in its own demeanour, so elegant and deliberate in its movements, is not particularly adept at building nests or landing on them. They so dread raccoons stealing their eggs that the herons construct enormous platform-like nests that feature sharp branches sticking out like guard stakes, and not only are the huge structures liable to topple in gusts of wind, they often collapse under a bad landing. Perhaps this explained the bones.

This was just a small colony, tiny by comparison to some that have been discovered. Once, a heron rookery was found in Ontario with 389 nests, which on a windy day would make it dangerous to prance about beneath the trees in wet underwear. The danger extends to the trees themselves, as the droppings of the birds are so acidic they kill the trees they nest in, and it sometimes happens that a tree will simply keel over in a high wind and take several active nests with it.

The mortality rate among chicks is astonishingly high. If the raccoons don't get them, then the ravens might, or the hawks, gulls, owls, and jays that feed on the light blue eggs and even the hatchlings. Then there is always the danger of a poor parental landing before the chicks are old enough to fly, the chance that the wind will pick up the nest, the slightly lesser chance that the tree will fall down, and the chance, even, that the heron chick, perhaps anxious to escape such danger, will attempt to fly before it is ready and go crashing down through the branches.

No wonder they hide out. No wonder they choose, when they can, an island so isolated that no intruders will ever discover them, a place so off the beaten path that these fastidious, elegant shoreline hunters can conduct their sloppy off-hour lives in private.

We stayed on the island for a good hour, walking about in silence, in awe, two men in their underwear absolutely aware they were now intruders.

"We should get back," Denis said.

I agreed. The others would be rested and anxious to get going.

We also had an incredible story to carry back to shore, one that would let the magic and mystery of Ermine Lake continue for as long as campfires glow and the red wine lasts on Camp Lake.

After all, I had found precisely what I had said would be here.

An alternative society.

Chapter Two

A SHORT HISTORY OF ESCAPE

"*I would like to learn, or remember, how to live. I come to Hollins Pond not so much to learn how to live as, frankly, to forget about it.*"

ANNIE DILLARD, *TEACHING A STONE TO TALK*

On a cold afternoon late in the fall of 2001, there was a fresh blanket of white snow on the ground as I drove into Whitney. Early snow meant easy tracking, and in the backyard of the first house at the bottom of the hill, a freshly killed bull moose was being butchered on an orange plastic tarpaulin as more than a dozen hunters and villagers looked on, all waiting patiently for the amateur butchers to complete their work and divide the bounty.

A grisly scene, of course, but oddly comforting. I had just spent two months travelling about the country for the *National Post*, talking to Canadians in every region about the effect on their everyday lives of the September terrorist attacks in New York and Washington. And one of the places I most wanted to go back to was Whitney, a lumbering village on the eastern edge of Ontario's Algonquin Park, where, in 1948, I was born in the little Red Cross outpost.

A moose being chopped and sawed to bits over a blood-spattered tarp might not seem like a confirmation of life, but this time it certainly was. It was the solid reality of bush life that gave comfort. The hunters had been successful, the butchers were being efficient, even if some work required a chainsaw. The women, wearing rubber boots, were putting huge chunks of moose meat into doubled-up green garbage bags, which they then threw over their shoulders before hiking off home to fine-cut the roasts and steaks and stewing meat and freeze most of it for later in what is always, in this part of the country, a long winter.

I drove around Whitney on my own before dropping in on various relatives. I checked out the dam where the Madawaska begins its long, twisting run east to the mightier Ottawa River. I drove out to the even more isolated community of Airy, where we had once lived on the shore of Galeairy Lake and where our mother once had to deal with three children in diapers, no running water or electricity, and a husband gone all week in the bush. It seemed a million miles from anywhere. It no longer is in the age of cable and modems, of course, but still, after visiting with relatives and old friends who were deeply rattled by the events of September, it was clear that they were greatly comforted by where they lived.

I had found the same was true in little villages on the north coast of Prince Edward Island, in the mountains of British Columbia, and in the little prairie towns of Saskatchewan. It was hardly a surprising discovery. The first inclination of many frightened Americans had been to head for the countryside. Some were even convinced that the time had come to arm themselves and take to the woods, much as they had in the Revolutionary Wars. As the fears increased – first, with deadly anthrax in the mails, then the possibility of massive war – Canada had seemed increasingly to take on a new glow for Americans as the nearest safe refuge. Real-estate offices in Toronto began reporting an influx of inquiries from the United States. And marinas in the New York City area claimed there was an unexpected rush on used boats that could serve, if necessary, for escape north to the Canadian Atlantic provinces.

There were even, in the weeks of the aftermath, reports of a new "survivalist" trend emerging in the United States. Small-centre Americans were making sure that one of the family cars was fully fuelled, with food stashed in the trunk and cash hidden in the upholstery, ready to flee for the Canadian border at the first sign of further trouble.

"I feel very safe there," Rhode Island banker Georgina Cormier told the *Ottawa Citizen*, "There is a sense of safety and security when I go to Canada. If I had to go somewhere, that's where I would want to be."

For anyone wishing to get away from it all, I could not recommend any place more highly than this lovely little village at the northwestern end of the Madawaska Valley. Certainly, few places in this already isolated country are farther removed from the world than Whitney. It owes its existence to a railroad, the Ottawa, Arnprior, and Parry Sound Railway Co., which was pounded through the bog and the Canadian Shield in the nineteenth century in an effort to take critical transportation as far away as possible from the United States' border and its recent civil war. It was populated with Poles fleeing repression, Irish fleeing famine, Scots fleeing the highland "clearances." And as recently as the late sixties and early seventies, Americans fleeing their own country.

Founded on escape, Whitney today thrives on escape, only those who come here now do so for the park and its canoe routes, the campsites and wilderness lodges. It is what I would call a *splendid* isolation, the sort of sanctuary American West Coast writer Annie Dillard was surely thinking of when she wrote of the need for places where one can go "not so much to learn how to live as, frankly, to forget about it." That is what Whitney provides its visitors. To those who live here, it gives a sense of place. And, when necessary, a sense of comfort.

I remember my father's tale of going down to Toronto back in the 1950s with a group of Whitney bush workers. They had been called to a labour board hearing concerning an effort, unsuccessful, to establish a union at the local mill, and they left reluctantly under subpoena. He talked about how alarmed they had been by the big city, how the men jumped when they saw sparks flying from the streetcar lines, and how one of them, Eddie Kuiack, was completely astonished at the sight of a woman talking on a pay phone.

It reminds me of my own first memories of Toronto. A lumber buyer had given our father tickets to a hockey game at Maple Leaf Gardens, and off we went, both parents and four children, in the old '54 Chevrolet to see the Leafs play the Detroit Red Wings on a Saturday night and to stay over with family friends living in Port Credit.

I have two strong memories of that trip that have nothing to do with the game played. First was going to the washroom between periods with my older brother, Jim, and being too intimidated to go when we saw the mile-long stainless-steel urinal and the lineups waiting for position at it. It was a strange reaction, as we had never had trouble going among company in the two-seater outhouse, but this was like a four-hundred seater to us. The second is of our parents' first experience with traffic lights and highway clover leafs, and how petrified they were that if they missed their turn they would be forced to drive off the end of the world.

It was in the back seat of that old green Chevy that I learned there is another side to the widely held belief that Canada is the story of a people terrified of the bush.

There are, I swear, at least as many, if not more, petrified of cities.

Northrop Frye was a great scholar of both Blake and the Bible, a brilliant literary critic – but what if he got it wrong?

It was Frye, the bespectacled, roly-poly University of Toronto English professor, who established the ground rules that still hold for Canadian literature, and, by extension, for so many observations that are made on the Canadian personality and psyche. It was Frye who wrote in *The Bush Garden: Essays on the Canadian Imagination* that there is, in this fragile northern imagination, "a tone of deep terror in regard to nature. . . . It is not a terror of the dangers or discomforts or even the mysteries of nature, but a terror of the soul at something that these things manifest."

I have long been troubled by this interpretation of the Canadian soul. For my parents, one could have substituted the word "city" for "nature" and it would have held equally true. For them, "terror of the soul" had to do with too many people, too much noise, too much traffic, too much confusion. In nature they found their peace; in nature they found comfort; in nature they found themselves. And not only were they not alone, they were in the vast majority of all the Canadians I have ever known – though, admittedly, I come from a rural and small town background.

Northrop Frye – known as "Norrie" to his friends and, by all accounts, a most lovable little man – was born in a city (Sherbrooke, Quebec, in 1912) and raised in a city (Moncton, New Brunswick) before heading off to first Toronto and then Oxford, England, eventually graduating as a United Church minister before switching to academia at the University of Toronto's Victoria College, where he would make his mark. A most impressive resumé, but devoid, it would seem, of any real experience of Canadian nature.

Foolish as it would be for someone without such credentials to call Professor Frye a fraud – and no one is suggesting for a moment he was – it is surely fair game to point out that one of his best-known comments on the Canadian psyche came not from personal experience but from sitting in a comfortable office and imagining that experience.

The abiding presence of terror in regard to nature, Frye once wrote, was something that the earliest explorers and immigrants to this country felt the moment they sighted land. It was one thing to immigrate to America, he said, to enter friendly waters beneath the welcoming gaze of the Statue of Liberty, but quite another to enter North America at a higher latitude.

Canada, the eminent critic wrote, in an essay for the *Literary History of Canada*, "has, for all practical purposes, no Atlantic seaboard. The traveller from Europe edges into it like a tiny Jonah entering an inconceivably large whale, slipping past the Strait of Belle Isle into the Gulf of St. Lawrence, where five Canadian provinces surround him, for the most part invisible. . . . To enter the United States is a matter of crossing an ocean; to enter Canada is a matter of being silently swallowed by an alien continent."

This is a brilliant metaphor – the mouth of the St. Lawrence opening up like the mouth of the biblical whale that swallowed Jonah – and has stuck fast to all subsequent study of the Canadian imagination and literature.

It is also pure hogwash.

Those who survived the treacherous two-month sail across the Atlantic, who had seen their children or parents die along the way, who had lived in filth and vomit and human waste for weeks, who had suffered in stinking, cramped quarters, who counted themselves fortunate if scurvy was the only disease they suffered – each and every one of them thanked his or her god and cheered, if able, when the verdant banks of the St. Lawrence came into view.

This was no monster about to swallow them whole; this was land, about to make them whole again.

Susanna Moodie was aboard the *Anne* in the last week of August 1832 when the morning mist cleared to reveal the rocky shore that Frye believed struck such terror in the minds of those entering the St. Lawrence. "Never had I beheld so many striking objects blended into one mighty whole!" she recorded in her journal. "Nature had lavished all her noblest features in producing that enchanting scene."

Frye's brilliant metaphor could only have been arrived at in one possible manner: by sitting in his office and staring at a map. Those who came to this country – the first explorers, the later immigrants, most of them illiterate – had not the slightest sense of the gullet-like structure of the St. Lawrence as it appears in an atlas. Nor would even the educated have gained such a sense moving toward it from the North Atlantic. It is simply the inspired imaginings of a man staring at a wall map.

It was this sense of being swallowed up by the dark unknown that helped Frye come up with his "garrison mentality" theory of Canadian literature. According to Frye's theory, as expressed in *The Bush Garden*, the Canadian experience was one of Europeans who came and founded "small and isolated communities surrounded with a physical or psychological 'frontier.'" Frye's own views of the malevolence of nature come through dramatically in his praise for E. J. Pratt, whose "Brebeuf and His Brethren" Frye considered the "greatest" of Canadian poetry. Brebeuf, the Jesuit martyr who died at the hands of the Iroquois in 1649, is portrayed as the heroic visionary, burned at the stake by "savages who are in the state of nature, and who represent its mindless barbarity." Frye's idea was that the fierce landscape reinforced the fear of nature already held by nearby arriving Europeans. Seeing it as threatening, they concluded it must be tamed. Thinking it untrustworthy, they concluded it must be curtailed. Because of this, he decided, the Canadian imagination developed a distinct fear-response to nature.

Sounds good, and undoubtedly true of Northrop Frye himself, just as it was true of so many writers and artists who came and peered at the Canadian wilderness and then hurried back to their comfortable lives to describe it – often in deliberately embellished terms. They embellished to impress, and often to sell, for there was money to be found in the Canadian wilds that had nothing to do with clearing the land for farms, felling timber, or hunting, trapping, and fishing. It had to do with the lecture circuit and its late nineteenth- and early twentieth-century brother, publishing.

It is in his diaries, not published until very recently, that the true nature of Northrop Frye himself is revealed. He was, like a great many other city dwellers, ill at ease in the country. He suffered from debilitating hay fever that kept him away from the countryside in its most embraceable time. He rarely ventured away from the comforts of his Victoria College office and his home in the very heart of the city, where the greatest threat was the black squirrels that raided the bird feeder.

Frye was not much for the outdoors. In his diaries from the year he spent on sabbatical at Harvard, 1950–51, he notes how dearly he enjoyed simple rides into the ordered New England countryside and the small seaside towns where he could happily amble along the beach amid all the bathers. Not for Northrop Frye the unknown at the end of the portage. Not for him the shifting winds of a summer storm, a darkening trail in winter, the night sounds of spring.

For some, the imagination can be a curse when applied to the unknown, and never did Frye reveal his own mental tendencies as clearly as when he scribbled in his diary on January 30, 1949, his reaction to his wife's reaction to minor surgery she was about to undergo. "It's vividness of imagination that produces cowardice . . . ," Frye wrote. "The operation is pure routine, the merest trifle, yet a little imp inside one keeps nagging constantly yes, but just supposing. Such cowardice is a perversion of imagination, from its true function of establishing patterns of possibilities into a false one of probabilities."

Give that imagination a branch snapping in the dark underbrush, a pair of yellow eyes blinking at the edge of the campfire, and it is easy to see how the "garrison mentality" theory came to fruition.

"The Lord's work for me," Frye wrote in his diary, "is sitting still in a comfortable chair and thinking beautiful thoughts, and occasionally writing them down."

Such as the thought that the St. Lawrence River opened up like the mouth of a whale rather than the arms of a sheltering motherland, and writing it down so that it was not the whale doing the wholesale swallowing, but Can Lit students from the Gulf of St. Lawrence to the Straits of Juan de Fuca.

There is a dramatic contrast between the written record of the explorers who travelled by canoe and those who began exploring the land and its creatures through books. The earliest explorers were far too businesslike to bother waxing poetic about anything they saw. John Cabot, who was looking for China when he bumped into Canada, left behind little on his two trips apart from the notes of his son, Sebastian, who remarked on the white bears and stags like horses (moose? caribou?), but deemed it "a very sterile land."

"That sense of wonder is the essence of all good nature writing," writes Canadian author Wayne Grady in his introduction to *Treasures of the Place*, "and is missing in the early accounts of 'encounters' with the New World. Columbus and the other Europeans who came to North America at the end of the fifteenth century were not all that interested in nature, except as something to be subdued and exploited."

There is, however, quite a different reading experience to be found in the accounts left behind by those who took the time to explore the vast interior, the rivers and lakes of the northern half of the continent. "There is very little in the way of terror in the journals of David Thompson or Samuel Hearne," writes Grady. "What there is is a continuous sense of wonder at the vastness and the splendour of the Canadian wilderness."

The explorers marvelled at the beauty and longed to get back into the isolation and the wilderness; the writers feared it, often despised it, and longed far more to get back to their lecture circuit with their inflated and often quite deceptive words. In reading these lecture-circuit writers, with their penchant for drama, exaggeration, and self-aggrandization, and not knowing for himself, it is perhaps no wonder a nervous Norrie Frye would come to the conclusions he reached and so effectively passed on.

The phoney is as much a part of Canadian literature as the braggart is of American. Grey Owl, by far the most truthful and best of the lot and the author of the hugely successful *Tales of An Empty Cabin*, was, of course, never the "full-blooded Red Indian" the posters promoted on his European speaking tours. He was a full-blooded Englishman named Archibald Stansfield Furmage, later changed to Belaney. He dyed his hair black, used henna to redden his skin, flattened his nose, it is said, by rolling a spoon back and forth across it, performed "Apache" war dances while singing gibberish, and wore an Indian headdress he'd picked up in a London souvenir shop. I give Belaney full credit, though. He had no fear of the wild, loved it passionately, and knew it in all seasons, under all conditions. His work stands up; his conceit is excused.

The poet Pauline Johnson, daughter of a Mohawk chief and an Englishwoman, certainly had a strong sense of the Canadian outdoors – "The Song My Paddle Sings" is a work of wonder – but she soon discovered she "sold" much better as Princess Tekahionwake. She filled the English theatres as she travelled about in buckskin, telling her gullible audiences that her beaded belt was, to her, the equivalent of the British soldier's Victoria Cross. Much of what some of these performers wrote was hopelessly inaccurate as well as exaggerated. Sir Charles G. D. Roberts, who is still held up as the father of Canadian nature writers, left us such wilderness inanities as "The Solitary Woodsman," in which he claimed the wily woodsman could find in "the partridge drumming,/The belated hornet humming,/All the faint, prophetic sounds/that foretell the winter's coming." It would be a short summer, for even the foolish partridge has enough sense to drum during the spring mating season.

Frederick Philip Grove was another fake, a renowned Canadian nature writer who managed to keep secret his entire life that he was actually Felix Paul Greve, the rich son of a Hamburg merchant. Grove died in 1948 and wasn't found out until 1972, years after he had published an autobiography called *In Search of Myself,* in which he ignored such details as his real name, his true background, his running off with another man's wife to Italy, and his spending a year in prison after being found guilty of fraud. He also believed, much ahead of his time for a Canadian writer, that "Canada owes me a living."

Ernest Thompson Seton was, like Belaney, an Englishman who changed his name, only Seton did it so many times he eventually reached the point where he was asking perfect strangers to address him as "Black Wolf." His strange personal history leaves no doubt why he would once ask his siblings to place but one word, "misunderstood," on his gravestone. Another Nervous Nellie, Seton was so affected by stress that his eyes would cross when he felt tense. He was not only afraid of the deep bush but terrified of nocturnal emissions and, to prevent them, deliberately slept on boards and frequently splashed his tortured private parts with cold water.

Unlike Belaney, Seton preferred to keep to the ordered rural lands on the city outskirts and liked to have a guide around to take care of him as he sought out his animal tales. He found enormous success with these, applying human characteristics such as intuition and emotion to Canadian wildlife and convincing a generation of readers back in England that the hedgehog was not the only charming animal on God's earth. Had Frye only read certain works by Seton, he might have considered the Canadian wilderness little more threatening than Winnie-the-Pooh's Hundred Acre Wood. His stories so enraged U.S. President Teddy Roosevelt, who fancied himself a bit of a bush man, that Roosevelt launched an angry campaign against such "Nature Fakers" and "yellow journalists of the woods."

Roosevelt's attack, however, was mild compared to that which would come from respected American naturalist John Burroughs. Those who dared to write as Seton did, Burroughs said, in a devastating review of the Canadian's work in *Atlantic Monthly*, ran the risk of "the danger that is always lurking near the essay naturalist, the danger of making too much of what we see and describe." As Burroughs put it, "Such dogs, wolves, foxes, rabbits, mustangs, crows, as he has known, it is safe to say, no other person in the world has ever known. Fact and fiction are so deftly blended in his work that only a real woodsman can separate them . . . those who know the animals are just the ones Mr. Thompson Seton cannot fool."

The fact that the reading audience that mattered tended to be elsewhere – usually Britain – had a profound effect on early Canadian literature and, one presumes, on Northrop Frye's early reading. It seems, for the most part, to be the estate of those who came from elsewhere, who pretended to be something they were not, who visited rather than stayed, in good weather more than bad, who had the luxury of education and time to write, and who delivered back exaggerated stories they believed, correctly, that their distant readers and theatre audiences would want to read.

For accuracy, it is better to turn to the Strickland sisters, Susanna Moodie and Catharine Parr Traill. The two sisters, born to privilege in England, had two decidedly different points of view. Susanna wished to see British culture transplanted to the colony and fought throughout her life to force a semblance of the gentry upon the colony to which she and her somewhat bumbling husband, John, immigrated in 1832. Yet even after the Moodies had left the land for town life in Belleville, she could never find it in herself to love this harsh land. Frye would have had his own tremblings confirmed by Susanna Moodie, who also fancied herself a poet, albeit hardly one of light verse. "Oh! Land of waters," she once wrote, "how my spirit tires,/In the dark prison of thy boundless woods . . ./Though vast the features that compose thy frame,/Turn where we will, the landscape's still the same." Susanna's early enthusiasm for what she saw from the deck of *Anne* certainly waned over time. "If," she wrote in *Roughing It in the Bush*, "these sketches should prove the means of deterring one family from sinking their property and shipwrecking all their hopes, by going to reside in the backwoods of Canada, I shall consider myself amply repaid for revealing the secrets of the prison-house and feel that I have not toiled and suffered in the wilderness in vain."

Her sister, bless her soul, was of quite a different mind, accepting a far harsher reality and the bush as so many others have, and coming to love it for what it was rather than what it could be. Catharine Parr Traill, despite a helpless husband and poverty, took matters far more at face value, and some of her works, such as *Studies of Plant Life in Canada*, are so wonderfully accurate and filled with discovery that they are as fascinating for readers today as they were for readers more than a century ago. In 1894, Catharine published her memoirs, subtitled *Notes of an Old Naturalist*, in which at the advanced age of ninety-two she argued that nature was no dark threat to the soul, but rather an open invitation to wonder.

If only Northrop Frye had stuck with her.

One wonders if there might not be a profound difference between those who read, or, for that matter, don't read, but are familiar, and even quite comfortable, with the outdoors, and those who write about the woods, the bush, the deep unknown. When Frye spoke about the way the imagination could roll when considering minor routine surgery, he could just as easily have been speaking of dozens of brave wordsmiths who have sought to tie outdoor experience to indoor reading and found the task a challenge. It is far from merely a Canadian affliction.

"So woods are spooky," the American writer Bill Bryson writes in *A Walk in the Woods*. "Quite apart from the thought that they may harbor wild beasts and armed, genetically challenged fellows named Zeke and Festus, there is something innately sinister about them, some ineffable thing that makes you sense an atmosphere of pregnant doom with every step and leaves you profoundly aware that you are out of your element and ought to keep your ears pricked. Though you tell yourself that it's preposterous, you can't quite shake the feeling that you are being watched."

There is an assumption here, a literary conceit, that those who write these words and read them share an urban identity: "You are out of your element," says Bryson. He is, after all, writing (charmingly) about the well-travelled, well-mapped, sign-posted, and shelter-equipped Appalachian Trail, not Alaskan grizzly country. My own counter-experience may itself be limited, but my mother, born and raised deep in Algonquin Park, and my father, who worked his entire life in the bush, both read voraciously, everything from Plutarch to

Andy Capp in the case of my father. For them, a profound awareness of being "out of your element" was the opposite of what Bryson suggests. The cities were where danger lurked, where the unknown played its tricks with the imagination. And I do not consider them unusual, but, rather, typical of those who have lived in a rural, even bush, setting. They may be fewer in number than those who dwell in cities, but this does not render their perspective less valid.

Margaret Atwood, who spent a portion of her early childhood in the bush of northern Quebec, examined this sense of being out of one's element in *Survival*, her slim but significant 1972 study of the literature of Canada. She even named her second chapter "Nature the Monster," and later on makes reference to her beloved Frye's notion that Canadian *lettres* are overflowing with "the conquest of nature by an intelligence that does not love it."

"There is a sense in Canadian literature," Atwood writes, "that the true and only season here is winter: the others are either preludes to it or mirages concealing it. There is a three-line poem by Alden Nowlan called 'April in New Brunswick,' which puts this case perfectly: 'Spring is distrusted here, for it deceives –/snow melts upon lawns, uncovering/last fall's dead leaves.'

"The key word is 'distrusted'; Canadian writers as a whole do not trust Nature, they are always suspecting some dirty trick. An oft-encountered sentiment is that Nature has betrayed expectations, it was supposed to be different."

Much of the problem had to do with transferred sensibilities. Poets went out in search of landscapes similar to the gentle Lake District, which had so inspired the Romantic poets of English literature; others thought the Canadian landscape should be a northern version of what had moved Thoreau and Emerson. Too often the long winters, the stinking bogs, the mosquitoes, and the impenetrable tangle overwhelmed them and, in many instances, changed them. Rarely was the shift so profound as in Susanna Moodie, who arrived in Quebec City noting that "Nature had lavished all her noblest features in producing that enchanting scene," and not too many years later was bitterly noting that "my love for Canada was a feeling very nearly allied to that which the condemned criminal entertains for his cell – his only hope of escape being through the portals of the grave."

Thoreau himself found the real bush to be terrifying, even though he remains the rural icon for America. He much preferred the ordered farmlands and the "woods" to the "bush," and lived not so much in the wild as on the edge of town, where he could stroll in to pick up his mail and even some fresh baking. In 1846 he was talked into taking a trip to the Maine interior for a brief hike, an experience that so unnerved him it left him "near hysterical."

That the imagination can run away with even the best minds is hardly new. Pliny the Elder, in his *Historia naturalis*, even included a map of the true world as he knew it in the first century: dog-headed humans, men with heads in their chests, mermaids, islands with demons, and springs that could grant eternal life.

There are a great many mysteries to life, but one of the greatest, surely, is how long it took humankind to "discover" nature. Part of the problem may be that for centuries thinkers showed far more interest in looking up rather than down. Plato argued for his two-sphere world, a dome of stars above the world, nothing beyond, and the sun circling round the stationary earth within a sphere formed between earth and the stars. It was not until Copernicus came along in the early sixteenth century that anyone considered the possibility it was the earth that was in motion, and that so many natural mysteries, from seasonal changes to the difference between night and day, flowed from that simple precept.

Copernicus, of course, was dismissed. Thinkers of the day preferred to agree with the Danish astronomer Tycho Brahe, who was granted a magnificent island off the coast of Denmark by his king and spent a lifetime staring up instead of down. Brahe counted exactly 1,000 stars and declared the heavens fully calculated. He "proved" Copernicus wrong by firing two cannonballs in opposite directions, arguing (with great success) that if the earth truly moved then one cannonball would fly farther than the other, which it did not. He also built his own false nose out of silver, having lost his fleshy one in a duel, but that is getting off topic.

It was the glass lens that changed everything. Oddly enough, no one has a clue who actually invented it, only that the ability to magnify captured the imagination of Galileo Galilei, and he was able to change the whole notion of "perception," which eventually caused men to look around themselves in a different manner, as well as upward to the heavens. The changed perception brought no reward for Galileo; he was dismissed by the "natural philosophers," who believed one could believe only what the naked eye could see, and he was branded a heretic by the Church for challenging the accepted order of the universe. Galileo would be much happier with his life as it is seen by history than he could possibly have been as he was actually living it. In a cruel irony, he went blind in his later years, and, beaten by critics, he even recanted his beliefs and apologized to the Church in the hope of escaping his prison cell. It did not work, for he died in prison after eight miserable years.

But think what Galileo left behind. The use of lenses to see clearer, better, deeper. The development of telescopes that showed the Milky Way was a cluster of stars, and, unbelievably, that the stars, far from being fixed in Plato's dome, were scattered through a universe that might, in fact, go on and on and on forever. The production of magnifying glasses that allowed for closer examination of the previously accepted. And the invention of microscopes, for the exploration of a new world never before considered.

The microscope was to nature what the ship was to geography. It took us to new worlds. It meant exploration without the expense or the Crown's blessing. And it soon meant new discovery of creatures "lesser than any of those seen hitherto." The planets had been figured out, the continents had been found; it was time now to begin the exploration of nature.

Daniel J. Boorstin, in *The Discoverers: A History of Man's Search to Know His World and Himself,* says that for 1500 years European scholars had turned their backs on nature because they relied, instead, on what they could read from texts, usually ancient, such as Pliny's *Historia naturalis,* on herbs and animals and the like. Scholars did not think to look for themselves, presuming that if it was already written down it must be true. The greatest shortcoming was in botany, where the world of plants continued to be ruled by the works of Dioscorides, a Greek surgeon who had travelled with the armies of Emperor Nero and had carefully recorded the plants he came across, including whatever medicinal and food values he could determine. The fact that no similar plants occurred in Western Europe did not seem to inspire anyone to do their own studies. They simply ignored the issue.

Zoology texts were not much better. What information there was tended to be contained in medieval "bestiaries," which were both hugely popular and hugely inaccurate – though accuracy was not considered as significant as, say, illustration of a Christian moral value. The lion, claimed one of the best-known works, uses its tail to rub out prints so it cannot be followed. Its kits, the same book stated, are born dead and come to life only when the father comes along and blows life into them. They sleep with their eyes open. They have been known to mate with many different creatures, including the ant . . .

In some ways, the Age of Discovery – the glory years of sea exploration – only served to hinder the accurate assessment of the closer world. Sailors would return with wild tales of serpents and sea monsters, of mermaids and giant land creatures, and those who heard such tales had little desire to satisfy their curiosity by going to see for themselves.

Slowly, however, the Age of Discovery spread to include the backyard. Intricate wood cuttings changed the state of botany, biology, and, later, zoology. Aristotle had argued that there were only five hundred creatures on the entire earth – he also believed that leeches sprang to life instantly if hair from a horse's mane fell into water – but soon the count was well into the tens of thousands, and growing rapidly. Konrad Gesner published his *History of Four-Footed Beasts* in 1658 and, increasingly, people began to look at the world around them as if it might contain hitherto unknown surprise. Species began to be catalogued and classified, and even those without training began to take to the world of plant gathering and close examination.

Some scientists were particularly adept at arousing the curiosity of a new audience for their work. Sweden's Carolus Linnaeus found that nothing fired the eighteenth-century public imagination quite like sex and shock, even when applied to the supposedly dry world of botany. The calyx of a plant, he might say, was much like a man's foreskin. The poppy, he would lecture, was so promiscuous in its regeneration that it resembled "twenty males or more in the same bed with the female."

The backyard, the world beyond the cleared field, was taking on dramatic new perspective.

It was Linnaeus, Boorstin suggests, who sparked the worldwide quest for new plants to study and understand. Linnaeus sent his most prized student, Peter Kalm, off to North America where, in the summer of 1749, he travelled through Canada gathering plants and making what was, for the times, remarkably prescient observations. Struck by the frenzy of land clearing that he witnessed, Kalm noted that "the forests are pretty much cleared, and it is to be feared there will be a time when wood will become very scarce."

Another Linnaeus protégé, Daniel Solander, became librarian to Sir Joseph Banks, England's great patron of natural history, and Banks's influence caused Solander to be sent to collect plants and small creatures on Captain James Cook's long voyage of the *Endeavour*, from 1768 to 1771. So successful was Solander's research that it became customary for all exploration ships to carry along a naturalist, and usually a documenting artist as well.

Sixty years later, HMS *Beagle* set sail with a twenty-two-year-old naturalist by the name of Charles Darwin aboard. And a quarter century on, in 1859, Darwin published his *Origin of Species*. The world, apparently, had not been created in six days so that everyone could rest from the seventh on. It was constantly evolving, forever changing, and required the closest examination at all times. Sunday, in fact, was the perfect day for further exploration.

The public might not have cared for such thinking at first, but it did have one profound effect that would alter forever the way people looked at their world. The eyes had come down from the heavens to focus on matters close enough they could be touched rather than imagined. Nature, it would turn out, was every bit as great a mystery as God Himself. And, many would eventually come to believe, perhaps not all that different.

Nature quickly took on new meaning. It was seen – now – as having its own history, as being directly connected to science. It was also a subject for talk, new talk, exploratory talk. Not only could the professionals debate, but amateurs could go up against professionals, and even the family dinner table could become a forum for natural history and theory and shared learning.

"The investigation of nature," wrote Thomas Henry Huxley in 1871, "is an infinite pasture-ground, where all may graze, and where the more bite, the longer the grass grows, the sweeter is its flavour, and the more it nourishes."

The natural world would never be the same.

It would, however, take considerable time for such an open attitude toward nature to filter down, in any form, to the vast hordes who were now immigrating to North America. They were largely uneducated, had no time for "the investigation of nature," had pasture ground yet to carve out of an unyielding wilderness, if indeed they could, and had but one priority in their lives: survival.

It was a time of massive immigration to Canada, and often those who came were in desperate straits. "It would be impossible to describe the state of the poor among us," a Sligo journalist wrote during the worst of the Irish famine. "To know all, you should put your head into a cabin containing perhaps ten or fifteen squalid inhabitants who had fasted forty-eight hours; hear the cries of the children, behold the tears of the mother, and the worn, heavy countenance of the father, who has neither work to do nor strength to do it. The prospects of another year are gloomy in consequence of the ground remaining unplanted for want of seed potatoes."

Parish priests were at first reluctant to give their blessings to any departures, fearing that the lure of better land in Canada would bleed the parishes of the faithful. But eventually even the priests' sense of self-preservation gave way to their sense of humanity. As the Bishop of Limerick put it, "At present they are in a state of hopeless, despairing recklessness. Give them hope, and they will endure."

Hope. A chance of escape. The poor Irish raced to take their chances, especially after the first group of emigrants sent back encouraging messages that created "a perfect mania for going to Canada." By 1825, Canada was viewed throughout Ireland as The Promised Land.

That promise was not easily brought to fruition. The emigrants died on the way over the Atlantic and died of cholera once they reached Canadian shores. They were quarantined on ships and perished in such numbers at Grosse Île that the ships were said to be waiting in "Cholera Bay."

It was here that Susanna Moodie first arrived, and her description gives some sense of the desperation: "A crowd of many hundred Irish emigrants had been landed, and all the motley crew – men, women and children – who were not confined by sickness to the sheds (which greatly resembled cattle pens) were employed in washing clothes or spreading them out on rocks and bushes to dry." Moodie also gave an early hint of the sense of social structure she intended to import to this new land, complaining how the Irish immigrants were "all shouting and yelling in his or her uncouth dialect, and all accompanied their vociferations with violent and extraordinary gestures.

"They have no shame – and under no restraint."

If they had no shame, they would also have had no chance had they stayed in Ireland. Here, in Canada, they would at least have that, and a chance is all they sought. Canada represented escape from hopelessness. Nothing could be as bad as what they were fleeing.

They came by the thousands and tens of thousands. In 1818, 20,000 Irish crossed the Atlantic, most of them Protestant, and they soon assumed prominent positions in Upper Canada. By 1823 the British government was subsidizing the exodus of Irish Catholics, and they poured into the Ottawa Valley. Between 1825 and 1845, nearly a half million Irish landed in Canada, outnumbering even the vast numbers of Irish emigrating to the United States. In the 1840s, when the potato crop failed completely, it is estimated a million died in Ireland while a million attempted to escape to a new life in the New World.

In 1847, known in Ireland as Black '47, 20,000 of them left their homeland only to die on the voyage or in quarantine camps on Quebec's Grosse Île and on New Brunswick's Partridge Island. But still they came, until by 1870 it was estimated 900,000 Irish were now located in the new Dominion, making the Irish the largest ethnic group in Canada after the French.

It was not the first time Canada had seemed a sanctuary to people discouraged with their lot. The Acadians had come and found freedom as early as 1605, only to have their dreams shatter when, in 1755, the British decided the French-speaking settlers could not be trusted to live so close to Quebec. The British controllers subsequently expelled the Acadians to the more southerly North American British colonies. Many, however, later came back, still sensing in this northern country opportunities they could not find elsewhere.

Canada hardly has a perfect record – the Acadian expulsion, the reluctance to accept Hutterites, the refusal to accept more Jewish immigrants and refugees prior to the Second World War – but it is still possible to argue that the general history of Canada has been the story of others finding escape here. The Irish and the Scots, Mennonites, Ukrainians, Poles, Germans, Asians, and Africans. It is a common thread through Canadian history. Irish found escape from the potato famine. Blacks used the Underground Railroad to flee slavery. East Europeans found respite from revolution and war. The "boat people" found the peace and prosperity that had been denied them in Southeast Asia. The effect has been profound. Toronto alone has people from 169 nations, and they speak more than one hundred languages. Even today, more than one out of every five Canadians was born elsewhere.

The vast majority of Canadian immigration – the flood from the British Isles in the mid-1800s, the opening of the West in the early years of the twentieth century – happened as attitudes toward nature were changing throughout Western Europe. In pre-Thoreau North America, there had been no particular love for any concept of "nature"; it had, instead, been regarded as a general impediment to homesteading. The land was stubborn, difficult to clear. The cold could be unbearable. Storms and fire destroyed crops. The woods held dangerous animals, even dangerous people in the years of the American Indian wars. The overriding Puritan ethic was that God's kingdom would be expanded by the taming of the wild, for had not Genesis instructed believers to "be fruitful and multiply, and fill the earth and subdue it"?

Even the very word "wilderness" was a highly suspect term in English. "For decades," naturalist David James Duncan writes in his introduction to a book on Thoreau, "'wild' in America meant the same as it meant to the British: 'uncivilized, treacherous, pagan, dirty, bloodthirsty, and sexually nasty.' And 'wilderness' was deemed guilty by association."

But a change, however slow, was underway. "It is only within the last hundred years," writes American author Joseph Brochac in his essay *Understanding the Great Mystery*, "that the idea of wilderness as a positive thing has crept into European consciousness with the creation of a conservation ethic. The influence of Thoreau is important. But few seem to know that the New England transcendentalist's ideas were shaped not only by Asian thought but also by the American Indian vision of spirit in nature."

This growing notion of "wilderness as a positive thing" did not catch on as quickly or as firmly in Canada as it did in the United States. Perhaps it was partially because the wild in Canada could feel so utterly overwhelming, as certain writers, including Frye, have found it, whereas in the more populated U.S.A. there was a much earlier recognition that it was a finite resource. Perhaps it was merely a story of latitude, with the American "woods" and "forest" so much more accessible and, for that matter, survivable, than the more rugged terrain of Canada. Perhaps it had to do with the audience receiving the messages coming from the deep woods, American wilderness lovers able to speak to their own and more easily survive on their writings with a home-bred readership, whereas so many of the Canadian writers of the Great Outdoors were tailoring their impressions for speaking tours and publishers back in Britain.

Whatever, Canada had no John Muir to spearhead an early movement. The Scot who would go on to found the Sierra Club was, in many ways, the patron saint of escape. He had spent his childhood in Dunbar, Scotland, where he had fallen under the spell of his maternal grandfather, meat seller David Gilrye, who had a stirring passion for long, instructive nature walks with the grandchildren in tow. The grandfather imparted such a sense of adventure into the youngsters that John and his brother, David, used to crawl in under the covers on dark winter afternoons and play a game called "voyages around the world," where they would imagine they were in far off places seeing strange and unusual beasts and plants.

Muir's father, Daniel, a strict, humourless Presbyterian, wanted to immigrate to Canada and even went so far as to have his growing family board a ship sailing for the colony in 1849, only to have passengers with other ideas talk him into trying the western United States instead. One can only wonder what would have become of John Muir had he ended up Canadian, but he was then only twelve years of age and did not much care where the family ended up so long as it offered the opportunity to explore.

The Muirs moved onto an eighty-acre farm near the Fox River in Wisconsin, and delighted in it from the first moment. "This sudden plash into wilderness," Muir later wrote of Fox River, "baptism in Nature's warm heart – how utterly happy it made us! Nature streaming into us, wooingly teaching her wonderful glowing lessons, so unlike the dismal grammar ashes and cinders so long thrashed into us."

It is remarkable that such a joyous spirit could come out of such a background. Daniel Muir was a cruel, bitter man who took out his frustrations on his family, beating the children at the slightest provocation and treating the entire family in a manner that can only be described as sadistic. A combination of Presbyterian spartanism and his own obsession with money meant that he allowed his own family to suffer needlessly, for the farm was relatively prosperous. He would not allow them enough food. He was so stingy with heat that the children would wake in the morning and find their boots frozen to the floor.

John Muir found two means of escape from this nasty reality. In the daytime he had the woods, where he became infatuated with simple streams and wildflowers and songbirds. At night he had books, and would hide in a story each evening, much to the outrage of his father, who considered any reading apart from the Bible a sinful waste of time. They fought bitterly, and, finally, Daniel Muir agreed that the strong-willed boy could read what he wished in the early mornings before the rest were up; that way, the father would not have to see the son wasting God's time.

The youngster took to heading for bed the moment darkness began to fall, and rose earlier and earlier in the morning until, eventually, he was up and about at 1:00 A.M., racing downstairs in the freezing cold "to see how much time I had won. . . . I had gained five hours, almost half a day! 'Five hours to myself!' . . . I can hardly think of any other event in my life, any discovery I ever made that gave birth to joy so transportingly glorious as the possession of those five frosty hours."

He read voraciously, borrowing books from whatever neighbours had them, and read through Milton, Shakespeare, Plutarch, and the Romantic poets in those early hours when his father preferred not to know what his son was doing or where, in his imagination, he was headed.

In 1864, when Muir was in his mid-twenties and the United States deep in Civil War, the young man declared war "so unsightly a monster" and headed north into Canada.

He may have been the first of many thousands of draft dodgers to come to Canada.

Biographers such as Gretel Ehrlich refer to this time as John Muir's "lost years." A compulsive journal writer, he left nothing of his time in Canada, and all we know is that he worked a while in a mill in Meaford, on Georgian Bay, and that he suffered an accident in which he lost much of the sight in his right eye.

I like to think it was these years that made John Muir realize his ambition. Until he came to Georgian Bay, he had thought of himself as an inventor, and his ability with machinery was truly remarkable. He was, it would appear, a genius, as capable of coming up with a new processing system as he was of quoting at length from Milton. The accident in Meaford that so severely injured his eye set in motion his reassessment of what to do with his life. Certainly, he took long walks around the glorious Georgian Bay shoreline as he slowly recovered his vision. And surely it is safe to presume that, from then on, he placed more value on natural beauty and how fragile its connection to man can be, whether the threat was to the eyesight or nature itself.

"I only went for a walk," Muir declared many years later, "and finally concluded to stay out till sundown, for going out, I found, was really going in."

Muir would return to the States, would become a passionate mountaineer and an effective critic of the voracious timber industry, but his legacy would be that he was able to do, on a far larger scale, precisely what Grandfather Gilrye had done as they walked down by the cowslips and riverbanks in Dunbar, Scotland: point out the obvious, and wonder about it.

"Wilderness," he eventually came to believe, "is a necessity." What the mountains and streams and woods and rolling hills had to offer "tired, nerve-shaken, over-civilized people" was that in going out they would really be going in, in through a magical door that was, to Muir, the real "home" for humanity.

"I care to live only to entice people to look at Nature's loveliness," Muir once said. "Everybody needs beauty as well as bread, places to play in and pray in, where Nature may heal and cheer and give strength to body and soul."

Muir died on Christmas Eve, 1914. He was seventy-six years old and still had faith that nature would prevail, once humankind came to realize there was far more value to be found in preservation than in exploitation.

"This grand show is eternal," he had written before his death. "It is always sunrise somewhere; the dew is never all dried at once; a shower is forever falling; vapour is ever rising. Eternal sunrise, eternal sunset, eternal dawn and gloaming, on sea and continents and islands, each in its turn, as the round earth rolls."

It was a passion that he would pass on to generations of American nature writers, including John Burroughs, Aldo Leopold, Calvin Rutstrum, and Sigurd Olson. It was Olson, the Chicago native, who like Muir also fell in love with the Ontario landscape, spending so much time exploring northwestern Ontario that he was eventually issued an Ontario guide's licence. And it was Olson, on his return from Canada, who brought to his American audience the charming notion of the "singing wilderness."

In Olson's singing wilderness, peace was not to be mistaken for silence. It was Olson's belief that anyone – even the busy stockbroker who races off to the bush for a short canoe trip – can develop an easy oneness with nature that is energizing and sustaining.

Olson even said, early in his life, that there were only two known states that could make a person feel so alive: wilderness and war. War, because it posed a constant threat against that which is held most precious. And wilderness, because it "is a spiritual necessity, an antidote to the high pressure of modern life, a means of regaining serenity and equilibrium."

That "serenity and equilibrium" is something so many have found in the Ontario bush. Not far from Camp Lake, where I take my sustenance, is the small village of Dorset, where E. B. White, the author of *Charlotte's Web*, became a part owner of a children's summer camp, Camp Otter, in 1929, the year of the stock market crash that presaged the Great Depression. White's final children's book, *The Trumpet of the Swan*, which was written in 1969, is all about that camp, called Kookooskoos in the book.

The year after White bought in to Camp Otter, he brought his great friend James Thurber up to Dorset on the instructions of Harold Ross, the famous editor of *The New Yorker*, who feared for Thurber's state of mind as he was going through a difficult marriage breakup. Thurber and White had just published a bestselling humour book, *Is Sex Necessary?* with White producing the text and Thurber the illustrations, and the two were the toast of New York City.

Thurber drew the small woodland creatures about the camp, smoked his pipe and relaxed, but he never found in this retreat what White had hoped he would. But then, as one of White's biographers once wrote, White was forever fleeing the city: "Always craving the country, White spent his life trying to leave disaffection, bad nerves, and overwork."

The famous children's author bought a canvas canoe from Hughie McEachern in Dorset – the family is still there – and used to talk about how he was going to paddle from Dorset through Lake of Bays and on through to the Trent Canal and into Lake Ontario, then into the Erie Canal, the Hudson River, and, eventually, Manhattan, where he would show up for work as if he had just stepped off the subway.

White found something at Camp Otter that strikes a chord with all who dream of escaping in the other direction, from office to dirt road to the lake. He himself took on the persona of "Sam Beaver," the wise old bushman in *The Trumpet of the Swan* – forget that there are no swans in this part of the world, it's unimportant – and he noted that the time spent here "were the pleasantest days of Sam's life, these days in the woods far, far from everywhere."

The words of a practised escape artist.

I left Whitney the following day in search of another American philosopher, Al Capone, who is as far removed from the likes of John Muir and Sigurd Olson and E. B. White as is possible to imagine. With one critical exception. Like those writers, and other Americans who have been casting their eyes northward since September 11, the Chicago mobster may have seen in Canada a natural refuge.

With the snow fast melting and the last maple leaves headed for the ground, I headed back along Highway 60, past numerous hunting parties, turned south on Highway 62 at Barry's Bay, then along the Madawaska River toward Latchford Bridge and, eventually, Quadeville. At the little village of Quadeville, I turned north, heading up a gravel road past a swampy stretch, until I reached a long curving hill.

Here, according to an old man I visited at Latchford Bridge, I would find Al Capone's hideout.

"Keep your eyes peeled to the right – you can't miss it."

You cannot. It sits up a twisting path, a curiously long structure of rough-hewn and squared logs, heavily chinked, with windows that seem out of all proportion to the bulk of the building. It looks more like a fort than a cottage, which it once claimed to be, or a hunt camp, which it recently was, or even an abandoned cabin, which it is today.

There is a small red-and-black PRIVATE PROPERTY sign on the twisting path up to the cabin, but no indication as to who the owners might be or when they were last here. It seems ludicrous to think it could once have been a "cottage," for there is no body of water nearby and no vista apart from a rather strategic view of the gravel road as it loops up, largely unused, from the sleepy little village to the south.

Even the bush seems impenetrable here, the deep Ontario tangle so dense that a weasel would have trouble twisting through the scrub and suckers and deep-skirted spruce.

Just the way The Boss wanted it, some of the older locals will tell you.

This, they claim, is where Al Capone came when he just had to get away.

The basement – its windows now kicked in and littered with evidence that the only bandits hanging about in the twenty-first century are raccoons – is said to have once contained the entrance to a secret tunnel that led through the hill and out into the deep woods, just in case American G-men or Canadian Mounties happened to stage a raid. Given the tangle, however, and the rough, impenetrable terrain beyond, Al Capone's chances of survival might have been better in a shootout.

There are, of course, no photographs of The Boss in a wading pool or blowing bubbles on the back deck. But there are endless stories to be gathered about dark men in even darker cars, fancy-looking women wearing too much makeup, and intimidating stares from the tiny windows should any locals chance up isolated Letterkenny Road. There are even older men about the village today who will claim there was one particular man who sometimes visited whom they were told to call "Uncle Al."

The cabin was built, to specifications, out of squared pine timber in 1942. The man who built it, according to local legend, travelled to the States to collect on an outstanding construction bill for $1500, only to be threatened by a gun-carrying henchman wearing a blood-splattered butcher's apron who informed the visitor that "Da Boss" would deal directly with him later in the day. The builder turned tail, ran back to Quadeville, and the outstanding account was never again mentioned.

Madawaska Valley historian Harry Walker first wrote about the cabin and the Capone connection decades ago but could produce no sources, as area oldtimers refused to speak on the record about what they'd seen and heard. "Even today," Walker wrote in the early 1970s, "the memory of the event instils fear in those who came in contact with the gangsters."

There are also many who doubt "Da Boss" was ever in the area, who believe Capone wasn't so far from the truth when he said, "I don't even know what street Canada's on." The Chicago mobster was released from jail – where he'd been serving time for income tax evasion – at the time of construction, but he was unwell, often hospitalized, and died of syphilis just five years later, in 1947. It is hard to imagine him roughing it in the Canadian bush during those years, far from the comforts of electricity and running water and with medical care hours away over bad, often impassable, dirt roads.

Others argue that if Capone came to Canada at all, he did it in the 1920s when he was just establishing his bootlegging operations. And indeed, Capone did go missing for three months in the summer of 1926, despite the best efforts of a three-hundred-man special detective unit set up to track him down. Some said he was in Wisconsin. Others thought Michigan. A few even claimed he'd fled to Italy. But a lot of the older residents of Moose Jaw, Saskatchewan, will say he was right there on River Street, hiding out in an underground maze of secret tunnels. The tunnels had been built before the First World War by immigrants hiding out to avoid paying Canada's notorious "head tax" on Chinese immigrants, and, the story goes, Capone's men had come to Moose Jaw to establish a Canadian beachhead in the rum-running business. Prohibition ended on the prairies a full nine years before it would in the United States, and Moose Jaw's proximity to the border and the secret underground maze for hiding out and liquor storage made the little city perfect for Capone's needs.

Those tunnels, now excavated, spruced up and well lit, have become a tourist attraction known as "Little Chicago," and the claim that Capone used them is widespread though, once again, there is no concrete evidence. Laurence "Moon" Mullin, an elderly resident of Moose Jaw, claimed several years ago that he used to earn twenty-cent tips running errands for the gangsters, and another local said her barber father used to be called down into the tunnels to cut Capone's hair. But nothing a respectable historian would dare stake a reputation on.

Back in Quadeville, the men who gather over morning coffee at Kauffeldt's little rural post office are more interested in talking about the fall moose hunt than they are in going on the record about any possibility that Al Capone ever actually hid out up Letterkenny Road.

"We used to go up there when we were younglads," one says, "but we never saw nothin'."

"Once the rumours started about it being Al Capone's place," says another of the morning coffee drinkers, "people started breaking in. "I don't know what they thought they might find – there's nothing there."

But it's not what *they* thought they might find that attracts me to such places.

It's what Al Capone, if he ever did come, found there that I'm chasing.

Chapter Three

UP THE CROW RIVER

"Every so often a disappearance is in order. A vanishing. A checking out. An indeterminate period of unavailability."

Joʜɴ A. Mᴜʀʀᴀʏ, Cᴏʟᴏʀᴀᴅᴏ ɴᴀᴛᴜʀᴀʟɪꜱᴛ

Never would I suggest that wild animals have a sense of occasion, but on this brilliant midsummer day, as we drove up Highway 60 into the heart of Algonquin Park, I could not help myself. We were headed into the interior with friends from rural Saskatchewan, a young family that had canoed all over the Prairies and the Far North but had never seen the high white pines of Algonquin that tell the history of this region as much as the railroad tells the history of theirs. It was just past dawn, the August sun an explosion every time our two vehicles, each wearing a red canoe like a jaunty cap, crested one of the hardwood hills heading east toward Lake Opeongo and our chosen launching spot.

Our visitors – Don and Marcia Harris, both teachers, and their sons Brandon, sixteen, and Vaughn, thirteen – had their eyes peeled for wildlife, and for good reason. If the past twenty-four hours were any indication of what was to come, by trip's end we were likely to have been mauled by the rare Ontario cougar, attacked by Algonquin Park's famous timber wolves, eaten by bears, and, for all I knew, captured and tortured by the little-known Algonquin Park hermit, who, barefoot and mad, took to living in a tiny spruce-bough hut not long before the First World War broke out.

Nothing, at the moment, made sense in the animal world around which I had grown up and thought I knew. The previous day we had come across the largest snapping turtle we had ever seen, drifting in the shallows off the end of our dock at Camp Lake. Its shell was roughly the size of a beer parlour serving tray, its head equal to the folded fist of a brawler. It had come, it appeared, to scavenge something dumped or dropped off the dock during a weekend party held by one of our teenage children – don't ask; I didn't – and was rooting among the rocks for what appeared to be the white of a hardboiled egg, when a second snapper happened along and tried to share the find.

I had watched, fascinated by the astonishing aggression shown by the larger turtle. Humans, of course, are petrified of these prehistoric-looking creatures that can, if bothered on land, snap a rake handle in half; yet every encounter any of us had ever had with one in the water had ended instantly with the shy creature quickly paddling away into the dark depths.

In this instance, the smaller turtle did indeed try to escape, but found itself pinned to the bottom by the larger one. It seemed to me unfair, so I had lifted an oar out of the fishing boat, stabbed it down through the water, and used it to lever the giant off and release its captive.

The big turtle spun away in slow, heavy, underwater motion, and for a brief moment it was upside down, its belly plate a pale, almost whitish green and all seven appendages splayed out from the shell as if bracing to stop its spinning fall.

Seven?

Head, tail, four legs: that's six.

The turtle caught its spin and, with several powerful strokes of its thick legs, pounced back down on the scrambling smaller turtle and pinned it once again.

I used the oar to pry it loose again, sending it rolling off and down toward the rocks.

One . . . two . . . three . . . four . . . five . . . six . . . *seven!*

For a moment I thought I had come across a freak of nature until I realized the only mistake here was mine. How could I not have realized what was going on? It might be two months past their mating season, but where was the law that said they could not practise?

"*C'mere!*" I called back up to the deck, where the others were sitting and reading in the sun.

"*What is it?*" someone called down.

"*Two snapping turtles are having sex!*"

There are a number of things that can bring people running at a cottage. Fire. Quick-melting Popsicles. A bear sighting – even if the race is in the other direction. But all pale against the image of snapping turtles having a go at each other.

They cleared the deck at a full run. They emptied the kitchen, the bedrooms, the shed. They ran down from the outhouse and over from the closest neighbour's. And they all hurried out to the end of the dock at once.

I should have paid more attention to the stampede. This was a floating dock, with additional support from two-inch galvanized steel pipes that had been slid down through metal slots until they reached the bottom and then secured by bolts that screwed in against them. There is always some slippage.

I felt the dock give, ever so slightly. I heard the rasp of metal on metal as the tightened bolts scraped along the pipes. But I was too caught up in this fascinating discovery to do the sensible thing and warn people off. After all, they were my turtles – I had seen them first – and I had the oar, and I was determined to conduct this class in reptile sex education no matter what.

The Harrises were fascinated by the snappers. Their trips into the Far North had produced shivering tales of bear encounters – one spring fishing trip into Prince Albert National Park's Wassagam Lake ended with Don and Marcia hauling at one end of their roped-up pack while a large black bear yanked at the other, a stand-off they would happily have conceded had Don not packed the keys to the truck in with the food – but there is something so primordial, something so under-the-foot-of-the-bed about a large snapper.

Snap! The first bolt gave way. *Crack!* Another gave way.

The dock groaned once and collapsed into the water, hurling the curiosity seekers onto the curiosity.

The cavorting snapping turtles, aware that the lake, if not the earth, was suddenly moving for them, broke off engagement and scattered to deeper waters as the uninvited voyeurs slipped and fell screaming into the lake.

They say one of the characteristics of reptiles is that they are inca-
pable of expression. Do not believe it. I have seen shock in the eyes of
the largest snapping turtle that ever ventured into our little bay.

That evening, while we were sitting around the campfire by the
cottage and some of the kids had gone inside to root around the
pantry for marshmallows to roast, a small, elegant red fox came ten-
tatively down the path from the outhouse.

Our son, Gordon, was sitting there, poking at the fire, when he first
noticed it. Animals are hardly unusual around the cottage. There are
chipmunks panhandling at every corner, squirrels scolding from every
tree. We have pulled porcupines – ever so carefully – from beneath the
building where they have settled in to eat the place as if it were some
gingerbread concoction rather than treated lumber and indigestible
nails. We have seen deer on the path and have watched moose pound
through the crust of late winter snow. We have found bear droppings
and seen mink darting about the shoreline and watched beaver spreading a long, lazy V over the smooth evening water of the bay. And we
have seen fox every year, fox slipping into the underbrush, fox kittens
sitting foolishly on an evening road while they soaked up the heat, fox
eyes sparkling like floating emeralds in the sweep of the car headlights.

But at the campfire, with people sitting around? Never.

"Don't go near it!" the parent in me shouted to Gord.

He laughed me off. "There's nothing wrong with it."

The fox sat. We stared. It had a beautiful, high summer coat, still
thinned out but glossy along the shoulders and sides, puffing out lux-
uriously along the flank and tail. There was no aggression to him, certainly no frothing at the mouth or anything else that might suggest
rabies or distemper or even fox sleepwalking sickness.

Gord had a hot dog in his hand. He broke off a piece of the meat and
tossed it to the fox, who jumped straight into the air as if he had mastered yogic flying. Not a muscle had appeared to move. And when he
landed, it was without a sound. He backed off, leaned forward, darted,
and picked up the piece of hot dog, scooting back up the hill while he
chewed briefly at it, then swallowed with a lunging motion of his neck.

Gord broke off another piece and held it out, waiting.

"Don't be stupid," I warned.

"Don't *you* be stupid," he answered back, in a voice so calm I took it, even though coming from an eighteen-year-old, less as insult than advice.

The fox advanced, sat, advanced again, sat again, checked the layout, then darted forward and plucked the small piece of wiener out of Gord's hand.

"See?" he said.

I did indeed. I was stunned. Fox, it is said, are the least tameable of all the woodland creatures. Deer can be tamed, wolves can be partially tamed, even bears will eventually give in to handouts and man-made accommodations, but never fox. So high-strung are they that professional fur buyers claim they can tell whether a fox has been under stress merely by running the back of their hand over a pelt.

Gord got up and went into the cottage, came out with another wiener, and fed it to the fox in small chunks. Each time the fox would back off, chew and swallow, then advance cautiously. It seemed as if Gord could reach out and pet the creature if he wished.

The Harris boys, Brandon and Vaughn, took turns feeding the fox. After cautiously approaching each boy, slinking in and darting back, then slinking in again, it took the food from their hands as well.

A second and third wiener finished, we stopped feeding the fox, yet it stayed. We watched as it danced up onto the deck – never once hearing a sound from its high-stepping paws – and around the campfire and chairs and back up the curling trail toward the outhouse. It moved in total silence, the darting red, brown, and grey creature trotting so lightly it almost seemed to be floating.

And then, after one more friendly approach to Gord – almost as if asking to have its sleek narrow head patted – it was gone. Into the balsam and poplars up toward the outhouse and gone forever. Never seen before that evening; never to be seen since.

We bandied about theories, dismissing most, and finally concluded that someone, somewhere had been feeding it; a dumb thing to do but, then, we had done it as well. We had been out-foxed.

The following morning we were up by dawn, packing up the food barrels, strapping on the canoes, tying down the packs, and getting the kids up for the race to Opeongo and an early start on what was surely to be a long day. It was a glorious morning, the far high hill just now gilding over with the start of a bright new day.

We drove fast along Highway 60, heading east through Algonquin Park, the sun stabbing at the top of every rise and the day warming quickly. I wore sunglasses and a baseball cap with the visor down as I sat up as high as I dared, occupied entirely with the blinding sun, and missed what had caught Ellen's attention.

"What's that up ahead?"

I had no idea. Up ahead, the hill would crest again. Up ahead, the sun would strike the eyes like acid. But she was leaning forward, looking at something even lower than the morning sun.

"It's a moose," she said.

I slowed. It was indeed a moose. A large one. A large cow moose on her side.

And very dead.

"Someone must have hit it," she said.

I slowed some more, eyes now searching for anything but the morning sun. There were no tracks, no skid marks, no guard rails out. I checked both sides of the road and saw no sign of a vehicle careering sideways; the dirt and rocks and mud and daisies and devil's paintbrushes of the Algonquin road shoulder would have shown exactly where the car or truck had spun and flipped. There should be a car wreck somewhere, but there was nothing.

Few realize this, but running into a moose at night is often not much different from running headfirst into another vehicle heading in the opposite direction. A bull moose can go 1,600 pounds or more, but even more destructive than its weight is its size. They can stand, at the shoulder, well over six feet tall and can reach, from tip of tail to nostril, ten feet in length. Hit broadside, they can rip the roof right off a car. Hit dead on, the massive rack of the bull moose is more alarming than a light standard crashing through the windshield.

The most amazing moose accident story I know concerns Stan

Darling, the eccentric and much-loved Member of Parliament for Muskoka–Parry Sound. Every Friday night for decades, Darling took the long drive back to his riding from Ottawa, often the only driver on the road in winter as he passed through the forty-mile stretch of Algonquin Park. Each year, he would buy a brand-new Cadillac for the run, and one early spring evening, with the days still short, he hit the park boundary just as darkness fell. Moments later, he slammed so hard into a small year-old moose the new Cadillac rode right up on top of the poor creature, grinding it into the pavement. Creature and brakes slowed the car sufficiently to keep it from plummeting into the rocky ditch. The car spun down the shoulder and stopped in a mass of dead moose, soft bog, and moss. A passing logging truck stopped and took the feisty MP back to Whitney, where Larachelle's garage dispatched their tow truck to retrieve the car. The mechanic on duty confirmed that the new Cadillac had come out of the encounter far better than the moose, but he advised the elderly politician that there was no way anyone could drive it. The moose had become so ground up in the undercarriage and engine that no one, Darling was told, would ever be able to handle the smell. Knowing that he had several constituents' birthdays and wedding anniversaries to head out to first thing in the morning, Darling insisted on being handed his keys. He then went into the garage, purchased two of those little cardboard pine-tree air fresheners that people hang from the rear-view mirror, stuck one up each nostril, got back in the Cadillac, and drove up Highway 60 to his appointments.

"Must have been hit by a logging truck," I said as we looked at the moose, already beginning to bloat from the rising heat of the day. It would have been a glancing blow, leaving the carcass intact, but probably enough to kill the poor creature instantly.

Oddly enough, in a half century of living in and around the park and driving through it dozens of times a year, I had never before seen a moose dead on the side of the road. It didn't feel right.

It is unusual today to travel the entire corridor road without at least one moose sighting. Forty and fifty years ago, it was unusual to see a moose, the deer then so plentiful that spotting two dozen or more along the sides of the road would not have been out of keeping. Feeding and photographing the Bambi-like white-tailed deer was the park's top tourist draw. Today it is the deer that are rare, and the visitors come more to photograph each other. More than anything else, the scarcity of white-tailed deer is explained by lack of fire. So adroit have the patrol planes and early-warning systems become – as opposed to the tall, remote fire towers of yesterday – that fire, and the resulting new growth that is so vital to the deer, are now rare, and so the deer have moved out of the park and closer to civilization, where suburban housing projects and farming does work comparable to what fire and logging managed in the past.

Nothing, however, could ever explain what we had seen on a pass through this same roadway in early June 1995. My father, Duncan, a rather colourful and eccentric logger who had worked his entire life in the park, had died just short of his eighty-eighth birthday, been buried in Huntsville – a quiet ceremony which, for once, he had been unable to disrupt with an appropriate remark or, as he did at my Uncle Roy's funeral, a loud, wet leak into a nearby juniper bush while the priest was giving the final gravesite benediction – and the family was driving home to Ottawa when the kids began listing the animals we passed by that sunny, late spring day.

They counted twelve deer, six of them, including two young bucks with soft budding antlers, in a single group at the turnoff to Rock Lake, where Duncan had lived and worked for so many of the fifty-one years he spent in the deep Ontario bush. They counted nine moose. Four red fox. One black bear, a small one, that climbed up out of the ditch and ran alongside the car when we slowed down. And one timber wolf, yellow eyes blazing, that came and sat on his haunches at the side of the road closest to the old man's beloved Mosquito Creek, where he claimed God kept his personal stock of speckled trout.

The children's grandfather would have been pleased. A terrific turnout under the circumstances, he would have boasted, as if somehow word had reached the animals of Algonquin that one of their own, the chain-smoking beer-swilling bush eccentric, had passed on and required a four-footed honour guard. I had never been much for ascribing human characteristics to wild animals. Besides, Duncan MacGregor had no particular fondness for wolves, knowing his cousin, Sandy, had been set on by wolves while timber cruising not far from here and never recovered; and he never, ever forgot that bitter January morning when he stood helpless on the steps of the Rock Lake bunkhouse and watched a pack of park wolves cut off the little Labrador puppy Blackie as the two of them meandered down from the cookhouse and literally tear the dog to pieces before slinking behind the wood piles and back into the bush.

But an "honour guard" was the way the kids chose to interpret what they saw, and I have never bothered arguing the point with them. It seemed then, and still seems, a fitting end to one forest dweller's life.

We reached the Opeongo turnoff just as the sun was growing tolerable for driving. We turned north on a twisting road I had taken dozens of times as a child but rarely since. When we were young, the treks in to the Fisheries Research Laboratory with the old ranger were one of the great highlights of summer for barefoot, sunburned youngsters obsessed with capturing and studying small fish and minnows. Here were huge stainless-steel tanks of trout fry and speckled trout fingerlings and minnows of several different species, from smallmouth bass to creek chub. They also did bizarre experiments that seemed more a child's torture chamber – *how many mosquito bites will a man's arm suffer in fifteen minutes of unprotected exposure?* – than the work of scientists. This was where some of the friendliest rangers stayed, like big George Heintzman and our grandfather's deputy, smiling George Holmberg.

The road was filled with memories, most pleasant, but one of them still stinging after thirty-five years. George Holmberg's son, Hartley, had been a god to some of us youngsters back in the 1960s, a laughing, generous, handsome young man who worked at the fish lab and scooted around the park on a big Indian motorcycle. He was our James Dean, and he died on the worst turn of this road when the powerful motorcycle hit a loose rock and threw him into the unforgiving Canadian Shield.

It had been windy on the lake for most of two weeks. No surprise there. It can be calm the next lake over and whipping on Opeongo, which seems specially constructed for unpredictable wind. Sixty years ago, John D. Robins, an English professor at the University of Toronto, came to this part of Algonquin and ended up publishing a small book about it, *The Incomplete Angler*. It became a surprising bestseller as it somehow tapped into the mood of a country desperate to escape the gloom of the Second World War. A friend of Robins's who was familiar with Opeongo had warned him that the lake "is animated by a sinister Spirit which broods unsleepingly, malevolently, over the three great arms of that majestic water."

The long arms of Lake Opeongo give openings for the wind to build, and the many random islands lend a pinball-machine effect to the gusts, which makes this lake unlike any other in the park. But there is also something different about the islands of Opeongo. Perhaps it is because the lake is so much larger than its neighbours. Once one comes to the shores of Opeongo, perspective changes dramatically, the sightlines so much longer and deeper that the curiously named islands – Wishbone, Hurricane, Squaw, Twin Sister, Wolf, Bear (tellingly renamed Sand in later years), even a Cape Breton – seem to rise so dramatically on the horizon that, at times, they seem tilted on their sides. Perhaps it is because, on a calm bright day, they seem impossibly emerald, seductively inviting.

Calm days are rare on Opeongo. On Canada Day weekend earlier in the summer, the winds had been so wild they had raised six-and-a-half-foot waves on the lake, making it impossible not only to canoe but also for the large canoe-carrying water "taxis" to make it down the arms to drop off or pick up canoe trippers. The blow had lasted three days, and, given our visitors' limited time, I had taken some friendly advice to book the taxis to the end of the North Arm and begin the journey from there.

I had booked the cheater reluctantly. I doubted, very much, if Lieut. Henry Briscoe, who came through here in 1826 in search of a route safe from American attack between the Ottawa River and Lake Huron, had been able to throw his birchbark canoe onto a metal rack and lean back while a ninety-horsepower Yamaha tore across the lake in twenty minutes instead of the usual four or five hours required to paddle.

The first person to recognize that people might like to come to this "sylvan retreat" for sheer pleasure was James Dickson, who in 1886 published Canada's very first wilderness recreation guide, which he called *Camping in the Muskoka Region*. Dickson "moved" Lake Opeongo sixty miles to the west and slightly south deliberately, as he knew that the wealthy of Toronto – the only people with the money to get here and the holidays to allow them to – were aware of Muskoka but nothing beyond. And the lake's actual location was definitely beyond. It was so beautiful, however, that Dickson believed anyone who made the effort to come would forgive him, and even thank him.

While the timber barons were regarding the area that would become Algonquin as nothing more than a garden to be stripped of its pine, Dickson, a Scot, was already thinking tourism. "It is a matter of surprise," he wrote, "that so few tourists and seekers after romantic scenery visit the head waters of the Muskoka, Petawawa and Madawaska Rivers. They are only a short distance from settlement and easily accessible by canoes, and the portages on the Muskoka are of a trifling character, while every bend of the river unfolds some new beauty of mountain, forest or stream; while the lakes, though not as large as those further down, are unrivalled for beauty of scenery, and it may literally be called a sportsman's paradise, the woods abounding with moose and red deer, bear, wolves, and the various fur-bearing animals, the lakes and large creeks with the largest and palatable varieties of speckled and salmon trout, which can be had in abundance either by fishing with the hook and line, or by setting the night line, at all seasons of the year."

Dickson made it far enough along the Madawaska to portage over to Opeongo, which he kept referring to as "the hitherto unknown wilds of the upper Muskoka," and he promoted the excursion as a retreat where "we will be completely cut off from the busy haunts of man." He ridiculed those wealthy early trippers who insisted on bringing with them all the creature comforts of home – "the demijohns of gin and brandy, bottles of old rye, and boxes of cigars" – and hiring guides to do all the work while they later claimed to have been "roughing it."

We unloaded the cars and noted the water was calm enough for paddling. But then, the water is always calm enough on Opeongo to start out. An hour from now, fifteen minutes from now, we could be bottoms up and gagging while four-foot breakers slapped our faces and tossed our packs around the South Arm.

We moved the vehicles over to the long-term parking area, loaded our canoes and gear onto the water taxi, and set out with a curly-haired young local who had once worked at the nearby McRae mill with my father, had delighted, as everyone always seemed to, in the old man and his odd ways, and seemed eager to please a son who also had long ties to the park.

"Could we swing around Bates Island?" I asked him.

"Sure," he said. "No problem at all."

We set out, the ripple of Sproule Bay turning into a light chop as we passed Wolf Island and beginning to pound as we headed fast toward the open water of the South Arm and the point of land with the understated name of Windy Point. He swung the boat hard to the east and headed straight for a large green island with rocky outcroppings that I had not seen since childhood, and which – unlike any other point of land within sight – had changed dramatically in the years since.

"There's Bates," he shouted over the hammering and spray of the waves.

I nodded, knowing. He looked at me, now realizing why I had asked for this small detour.

I had only the vaguest recollection of the man the island was named for – John R. Bates, a pipe-smoking, stocky, loud American who was, for reasons I could never fully comprehend, once the only cottager on huge Opeongo. Bates was said to be fabulously rich, an automobile dealer from somewhere in Pennsylvania, and it sometimes seemed as if everyone we knew in the park worked for him in some capacity. The Bordowitzes, who ran the general store in Whitney, brought in groceries. Sandy Haggart, who ran a truck out of Whitney, carried in building supplies. George Heintzman, the lanky ranger who was connected to my family by marriage, did odd jobs and drove Bates's massive Packard-powered speed boat, *Vagabond*.

It was said that John R. Bates was "connected," that he knew the big politicians in Queen's Park down in Toronto, and he must have had some clout, for they let him set up on the twenty-five-acre island as the only cottager for miles. The park authorities even let him build a garage on the mainland to house his fancy Packards. On the island he put up a large cottage, boathouses, docks, and had a wind-powered generator to run his short-wave radio and power the washing machine. In Algonquin Park in the 1930s, this was unheard of. The locals called his place "the estate," with good reason. No one had wealth to compare to that of John R. Bates, who, it was rumoured, made his fortune in the stock market crash. He was, for that reason, also considered brilliant.

Bates always received preferential treatment. According to S. Bernard Shaw's fine local history, *Lake Opeongo*, Bates's leases would always be extended, his rent minimal. He was allowed, for some reason, to stock speckled trout in a little pond he called Secret Lake just off the North Arm of Opeongo. But he was not resented. He spent freely and was generous. He also spent an inordinate amount of time at the cottage, a rare winter cottager in the days long before electric heat and pink insulation. He and his wife, Belle, would spend stretches at the cottage that might run to three or four months. It was astonishing to the few locals that an American businessman could afford to spend so much time away from his investments. Some said he did his trading by the short-wave radio, which only increased his mysterious aura. Belle, however, seemed the salt of the earth and was beloved by the locals. She was warm and sociable, enjoyed playing cards, and would sometimes go down to the icehouse, chip a block to pieces, get out the rock salt and the wooden ice-cream maker, and make unimaginable summer treats for the rangers' children.

Now, nearly forty years since either John R. or Belle had last come to Opeongo, the "estate" has vanished. There are still, for those who know where to look, a few foundation markers, and, in a sheltered area on the northeast tip, you can see where the men he hired built piers for the docks.

But few today know anything of John R. Bates's story. All they know is that Bates is the first large island heading out into the South Arm, and that not so long ago it made international news.

We headed hard toward the southeast shoulder of the island, the water calming in the shelter that lay between Bates and the near shore. We flew by rocky bluffs and soft cedar shoreline until, suddenly, the shore opened onto a campsite so charming – rocky shelter, a long slanted rock to haul up on, soft brown pine-needle ground covering, tall pines and shade – that it might have served as a postcard advertisement for the serenity of Algonquin.

"There's the infamous campsite," he said.

I nodded again.

"This fall's the tenth anniversary," he added.

On this spot ten years earlier, on a Thanksgiving weekend, Raymond Jakubauskas and Carola Frehe were just beginning to set up camp on the island when, without warning, a black bear tore down that idyllic little trail heading into the woods and, with a single blow each, broke the necks of the Toronto couple. The only sign of struggle was a broken paddle found the following week. The 308-pound male bear then dragged the two back into the dark woods, covered them up with dead leaves and broken twigs, and over the next five days returned regularly to feed off their bodies.

The Algonquin authorities called it a rogue bear. Chief naturalist Dan Strickland, a good and wise man, now retired from the park, said at the time that the attack was "right off the scale of normal bear behaviour." Not only had he killed and fed off the campers, but when police arrived, having been alerted by worried relatives that the couple was missing, the bear was still there, defiantly standing guard over his twig-covered cache.

"It is extremely rare for a black bear to attack anyone," Strickland told the news reporters who came to Opeongo to report on the deaths.

"People are 42 times more likely to be killed by a domestic dog than a black bear," wildlife biologist Lynn Rogers told *The Globe and Mail*, "120 times more likely to be killed by a bee than a black bear, and 250 times more likely to be killed by lightning."

Statistically, yes, it is rare – but it does happen. Thirteen years before the Bates Island attack, a black bear had come across three young boys walking back to camp from trout fishing on the eastern edge of the park and had attacked and killed the youngsters. Authorities believed it had been attracted by the small speckled trout that the boys had stashed in their jackets for easier carrying.

And apparently the attacks are becoming more frequent. Since 1906, the first year it is believed the numbers were accurately kept, black bears have killed forty-eight persons in North America, about half of that number over the past twenty years. One quarter of those forty-eight deaths were recorded in the interior of British Columbia and nine in Central and Northern Ontario. Stephen Herrero, an environmental science professor at the University of Calgary and a recognized expert in bear behaviour, has said that the number of bear attacks has mysteriously doubled over the last decade.

Some believe it is no mystery at all. Human and bear populations have exploded – bear thanks to more restrictive hunting – and the recreation movement of the last quarter century has brought more and more people into bear habitat. Some black bears might feel more threatened, some might feel less intimidated by humans; whatever, the end result has, in too many cases, been tragic for both sides.

My own experiences with bears have left me ambivalent about them, fascinated by their size and strength and habits, fearful of their unpredictability. Don Harris, who is as good in the wild as any Canadian I know, has a definite fear of them and goes nowhere in the deep bush without two canisters of bear spray hanging from his belt, one on each side, for whichever hand might be free on a portage trail. Two of my cousins, Tom and Jake Pigeon – Tom a former park ranger and Jake a park outfitter and guide – prefer to walk through open woods with an axe in one hand, just in case.

And yet Tom and Jake, like me, are grandchildren of tiny Bea McCormick, who, on first sight of a black bear daring to come around her little Lake of Two Rivers garden, would grab a frying pan and a metal pot and hurl her entire ninety-five pounds out the kitchen door and straight up the path at the startled beast, the little Irish pepper-pot yelling and pounding the pans against each other until the bear turned tail and ran in the opposite direction, its rear legs threatening to overtake the front.

There were always bears around when we were growing up. We saw them whenever we hauled our garbage out to the dumps that are now sealed off and closed. We saw them, less frequently, along the roads, and when we'd hike in to isolated lakes to fish. They were always around the mills where our father worked, and though he had been given permission to keep a .30-.30 Winchester in the bunkhouse in case one of them got too frisky, he never used it once. Instead, he gave the bears names – The Boss, Mother, Three-Leg – and took to talking to them when there was no one else around.

My most vivid memory of bears in the park is from when I was eight years old and accompanying my grandfather on his rounds as chief ranger. He'd been called down to the Lake of Two Rivers dump, where, more and more that summer of 1956, the tourists had been gathering each evening to watch the bears come down out of the hills and forage for half-empty jam jars and rip apart newspaper bundles in search of fish heads and guts. There was a large fence erected between the parking area and garbage pit to keep tourists and black bears apart, but the campers had taken to feeding the bears through the chain-link fence – a favourite trick being to lodge an open bottle of sticky, sweet Brown's Cream Soda in the fence and watch the cubs race to drink from it while everyone snapped pictures of the frenzy. Some of the campers were even breaching the fenced-off area to get more "real life" shots of the scavenging bears. A child had come too close to one of the cubs, been swatted away by a mother bear, and the parents, of course, had gone to park headquarters at Cache Lake to complain about the animal's behaviour.

The solution sent down from headquarters was not, unfortunately, to also swat the child's parents for being so foolish, but to deal with the situation in the most politically efficient manner. A call had been made to Tom McCormick, and he had made the only move open to him. Now we were off, the eight-year-old and the old ranger, in his green Dodge to survey the results.

By the time we arrived, the dirty work had been done. Three rangers were putting their rifles back into the Lands and Forests truck as they turned from their distasteful task, looking sad and sheepish. One ranger came over quickly, told the old ranger it was all over and done with, and then the two of them, with me trailing behind, went to look at the damage. Seven bears, two of them cubs, lay dead in and around the garbage pit, slumped over where they had fallen. I could see the holes the shells had made as they tore through their sides, huge black holes like they'd been drilled, the point of entry almost bloodless but the fur beneath, where the bullet had exited, thick with what seemed like oil, and the ground around black with dried blood and, in some cases, red where the blood still oozed from the terrible wounds. One of the cubs had fallen against its mother, and I remember wondering which had been shot first and whether the mother had been running to it or the cub to its mother. I could still smell the "bear" on them, skunk-like and gagging, and at one point had to walk away, afraid I'd throw up.

I do not know if I ever saw the old ranger more upset. He felt compelled to explain to me that the little cubs could never have survived on their own. I nodded that I knew this, and he never said another word, not all the time he walked about checking the animals, not when the larger Lands and Forests truck showed up to cart the dead beasts away, not once on the drive home and the long walk in through the woods to his log home on the point at Lake of Two Rivers. He spent the rest of that day splitting wood, the underarms of his ranger's shirt turning as black and sticky as the bear fur as he pounded his axe into block after block of hardwood.

But if I am ambivalent about bears, so, too, has been the park itself. In fact, at one point or another, it seems almost every species in the park has found itself on the wrong side of the authorities. In 1893, the year the park was established – at the time, the largest *national* wilderness reserve in Canada – the government brought James Wilson, then head of the tame and cultured Queen Victoria Park in Niagara Falls, up to Algonquin for him to look at the area and offer up some wise advice. In Wilson's "Advice to the Commissioner 1893," he called for an all-out war on the creature that more than any other would come to symbolize northern escape: the common loon.

Wilson believed the future of Algonquin lay in attracting trout fishermen, wealthy Canadians and, more importantly, American and British sportsmen, to the cold-water lakes and rivers of the highlands, and he saw the loon as far more dangerous to the precious trout reserves than any possibility of over-fishing.

"Large numbers of the young of these fish are annually destroyed by gulls and loons," Wilson wrote, "and it might be advisable to consider the propriety of waging war upon the latter, as neither bird is of much commercial value and their depredations largely outweigh other considerations."

Peter Thomson, the park's first superintendent, agreed with Wilson's bizarre report and added a remarkable twist of his own: "Bears and foxes should also be destroyed without mercy."

Tinkering with nature is nothing new to Algonquin Park. At times it seems almost impossible to believe that the park's initial purpose was to preserve wilderness. Even the visionary who led the charge to establish Algonquin, Alexander Kirkwood, the Ontario chief of crown lands in the latter part of the nineteenth century, once cast his imagination ahead to when forestry production in his "wilderness" preserve would sustain a local labour force and population of "a million or more people." By the 1950s there were fewer people living in the park than in the 1900s, by the 1990s far fewer still than in the 1950s, and today, on a cold January morning as I write, the total human population of the park – an area significantly larger than the province of Prince Edward Island – might reach one hundred, more than ninety of them merely using Highway 60 to get through to the other side.

They did not ultimately elect to remove the deadly bear and killer fox, the marauding loon and the heinous gull. They did, however,

almost wipe out the local raven population when they took to poisoning wolves and leaving the carcasses out on the frozen ice for the
scavengers to pick at. And they did shoot 650 deer in 1918 and ship the
meat south to alleviate wartime shortage in the cities. And they did at
times try to *add* to the park: smallmouth bass for the fishermen inca-
pable of catching trout; fruit trees that bloomed once and promptly
died; wild rice, which soon vanished; pheasants, which failed; and even
a small herd of elk that was never seen again after 1949. I have in my
possession a long and curling elk antler, which was found at the western
edge of the park near our Camp Lake cottage, possibly dropped as the
last remaining beast ran for its preferred open terrain, in which it might
be able to see a wolf pack in time to take evasive action.

Thomson's desire to eradicate fox was likely due to distemper and
rabies, two afflictions spread easily by such creatures as skunk and fox.
And his distrust of bear was tied, surely, to an event that took place a
dozen years earlier, in the summer of 1881, on this very lake, Opeongo.

In one of the more curious tales of Algonquin Park, Capt. John
Dennison, a military veteran who had helped quell the 1837 Rebellion
in Lower Canada, had decided in his sixties to forgo the relative comforts of Ottawa, then called Bytown, and take up farming in the Upper
Ottawa Valley. When two of Dennison's sons, John and Harry, decided
to push even further into the wild – believing they could carve out a
farm on Lake Opeongo that could supply the various lumber operations moving in to harvest the park's glorious white pine – the old
man decided to come along.

At one point the Dennison families had cleared some sixty acres
on the peninsula that cuts off the East Arm from the North Arm.
They sold some produce to the logging camps, but their ambitions
must have sprung from the belief that the railway would come
through the park and they would benefit from the settlement that
would follow, for Dennison's sons soon became discouraged with the
thin soil, the harsh climate, and the lack of business that Opeongo
afforded. Harry left for Manitoba to look for new land and did not
return for years, during which time two of his five children died

without his even being aware of their illness. When he did return, having failed to find much promise out West, he took to trapping to supplement his meagre farm income.

In June 1881, the eighty-two-year-old patriarch took it upon himself to head up the North Arm to check out one of Harry's bear traps – the warm bear coats, once they were tanned and cleaned, being much prized by winter sledders – and took along his eight-year-old grandson, Jackie. They would have canoed along exactly the same route we now roared over in the water taxi, and there must have been a good chop on the water as they moved through the west narrows, for we know the water splashed over the gunwales enough to dampen the charge in Captain Dennison's old muzzle-loading double-barrelled shotgun.

The trap was set on the portage in to Happy Isle Lake, very near to where we were headed. It was a ten-mile paddle through bad water, remarkable for an eighty-two-year-old man and an eight-year-old boy, and when they arrived the old man told his grandson to stay and rest in the canoe while he went and checked the trap. He took only his axe with him, knowing the old shotgun would be useless until it had a chance to dry out again.

The boy waited, until he heard his grandfather's scream and then one single shout: "*Jackie! Go home!*"

Terrified, the eight-year-old youngster did as he was ordered, launching the canoe himself and paddling, all alone and sick with fear, the entire ten miles back to the farm in search of help.

I cannot come here without thinking of that child. Ten miles up the North Arm, then ten miles back, alone and in heavy winds, the last bit travelled in falling dark. He was, remember, *eight* years old, and yet he handled that canoe in some of the toughest waters known to canoeists. He had to know something terrible had happened. He had to know, too, that no matter how hard he paddled, he could never get help in time to save his grandfather. The sons at the farm did not even set out immediately, knowing it was useless. They paddled up the lake the following morning to make the disturbing, but expected, discovery: Captain Dennison had been set upon and killed by a bear caught in the trap. The old man had been mangled and partially eaten by the desperate animal, which had then, with enormous strength, somehow managed to pull the trap free of its moorings and drag itself off into the woods, where it was eventually tracked down and shot by Harry.

Jackie Dennison would not enjoy nearly as many years as his grandfather had, dying just ten years later in a hunting accident.

They make much of Captain Dennison's story in the park. He appears on the historical map of the canoe routes. His grave can be found on the site of Harry Dennison's farmland, on the west shore of the East Arm, and sometimes campers will tromp in and try to locate the copper "At Rest" sign that marks where the old man was buried.

I would make more of Jackie's story. I suspect I am so stirred by it because I find myself trading places with him, for I, too, was once an eight-year-old travelling all over the park with a very old man. Once the old ranger retired, he seemed driven to visit every camboose camp, every log drive, every portage he had ever known, and he would always take one or two of us along with him on these day-long adventures. I lived in absolute terror of his keeling over from another heart attack. I would try to memorize turns in the trail and landmarks, asking him to put fresh blazes in the trees with the axe he always carried in his left hand – *was he, too, afraid of bears?* – in the hopes that if he died I not only would get back for help but be able to guide the men back into the bush to find him. If little Jackie Dennison loved his grandfather as intensely as I loved the old ranger, then I know only too well what that little boy must have felt as he paddled that ten miles carrying the worst news of what would turn out to be a life of bad turns.

The water taxi moved easily through the narrows and up into the open water of the North Arm, past Hurricane Island, past the island the rangers all called Bear but the maps now call Sand, and on toward the portage that would take us in to Proulx Lake, the first stop on our search for the last great stand of white pine in Algonquin Park.

The North Arm ended at a small freshwater "cove," accessible only by revving the outboard hard, tilting it up as the boat lurched forward on the crest of the waves, and hoping that the force was enough to push the hull through the sand and silt buildup that threatened, always, to close off the little cove entirely from big Opeongo.

Straight ahead was a long, difficult portage up hill and down, and at one point over a mud lake so muck-ridden and shallow that most passing through had long since given up on it and staked out a "bypass" over a steep hill to the south.

To the west was Happy Isle Creek, where little Jackie Dennison had lit out alone in his grandfather's canoe 120 years earlier. Beyond that lay Secret Lake, John R. Bates's beloved speckled hole that he always claimed was not on any map and known only to him, the great secret he kept from all the Opeongo rangers and guides.

It would turn out, however, to pale in comparison to another secret he was keeping.

We unloaded the water taxi – canoes, packs, paddles, fishing rods, food barrels, rain gear, more gear, and extra gear – and waved him off. The now-lightened boat skimmed easily over the sand shoal at the mouth of the cove, back out into the rising whitecaps of Lake Opeongo, and was gone. No one had seen us cheat and, with luck, if any other trippers came along the portage route, they would think we had paddled the four hours up from the charmingly named Fishgut Bay, where we'd put in. They'd also have to think we were in super-human shape, for none of us had yet broken a sweat on this hot August day.

First down the portage were two Japanese trippers. On most summer days, and on every fall day when the colours are at their best, there are more Japanese and Japanese-Canadians in Algonquin Park than any other people, the open space and spectacular vistas endlessly fascinating to them. It is rare, however, to meet Japanese off the beaten path, for they stick to the corridor road and, usually, within an easy sprint of the tour bus. The visitors who come all the way from Japan are not, in the easy generalizations made by locals, considered to be "bush" people, and have been known to fall for some of the silliest, as well as cruelest, pranks: the classic being the time an outfitter, a man who would himself become hopelessly lost on the Tokyo subway, placed an entire tour group in pairs at opposite ends of canoes, *facing* each other, and then stood on the end of the government dock rocking with laughter as the unwitting canoeists fought each other in a vain attempt to paddle about the bay.

These two young men were far more daring. They had rented a canoe and all their equipment and were, when I came across them, attempting to take a "brag photo" of one of them completely covered in packs and fishing rods and cameras and paddles as he pretended to stagger down the portage. I stopped and offered to take a picture of the two of them under their enormous loads, the canoe included, and after we had set them up – everything carried at once for the photo, enough for two trips in reality – we carried on an awkward conversation in their limited English and my non-existent Japanese.

The night before, coming along the Crow River, they had somehow headed down a wrong branch, got briefly lost, and eventually much delayed. With darkness falling, they'd finally stumbled upon a campsite, set up in the dark, not bothered to eat, and crouched in their tent to await the morning light and a better look at their map. Both were awakened several hours later.

"The earth moved!" one said, failing to see the English humour in his observation.

"Our tent was . . . shaking!" said the other.

"I looked at my watch," said the first, holding his elaborate wristwatch out for me to see. "2:45 A.M. – *time to die!*"

They lay there, they said, shaking and near tears as the huge beast walked back and forth in their campsite, the ground trembling, twigs snapping, mud sucking. Both were certain they were about to be eaten by one of the dreadful black bears they had read about at the park entrance.

"In morning," the first said, "we find big holes in mud" – and he made a large circle with his hands – "that big."

"More big," the second corrected.

"Big *bear!*" the first said, shaking and laughing at the same time, the thrill of survival still surging through him.

"*Moose*," I almost said, but I caught the word before it popped out and ruined their story. There was no doubt in my mind – the ground vibrating with its steps, the "big holes" in the muck by the river edge, the fact that their packs had not been cuffed around – but I realized in an instant that this was their adventure, not mine, and that the story of the bear in the camp was, in its own way, also a "brag photo." Not quite true, but great in the telling.

A bear, even an imagined one, gave something to their short canoe trip that they needed: an *edge*. When an expedition into the bush comes with a *frisson* of danger – whether real, as in whitewater running, rock climbing, surviving a vicious storm, or imagined, as in the bear that spent the night roaming through their campsite – it takes on added value in the telling and remembering. We speak of escape from traffic and telephones, but there is also escape from too much comfort and safety, even if, preferably, it happens mostly in the mind.

We left the bear-attack survivors and continued on. The portage in to Proulx Lake was fairly long, 1,450 metres, and also fairly busy. Not Main Street, as the extremely popular route north of Canoe Lake is known to veteran trippers, but certainly a busy side street. The North Arm portages off Opeongo lead to most of the better treks the park has to offer: west to Big Trout Lake and the Otterslides, north to Hogan and Lake La Muir and Burntroot, east along the Crow River to the superb fishing lakes of Laveille, Dickson, and White Partridge.

The contrast was fascinating. The Japanese were followed by a summer camp tripping group, the bearded, tanned guides with their proudly tattered packs, their bad hats, and their bravado, followed along by listless teenaged girls carrying paddles so loosely in their arms that they could not go a dozen paces without one slipping out and onto the ground. Then came a three-generation family, the grandfather with his beloved old Chestnut canoe from the 1940s, his totally disinterested and grumbling son – wearing the "full Algonquin Park" of Tilley hat and Eddie Bauer clothes so new it seemed the price tags should still be dangling from them – and a seven- or eight-year-old grandson for whom this once-in-a-lifetime trip was obviously being undertaken. The rapport between child and old man was obvious; the distaste and impatience of the father in the middle palpable.

The encounter reminded me of a poem by Robert P. Tristram Coffin that I had come across some time ago.

> A father is a strange thing,
> He will leap
> Across a generation and will peep
> Out of a grandson's eyes when unexpected
> With all the secrets of him resurrected.
>
> A man is taken by complete surprise
> To see his father looking from the eyes
> Of a little boy he thought his own
> And thought he had the breeding of alone.

The gear of various groups was fascinating to watch parade by. Much of it brand-new, some of it old, but all of it, with one exception, appropriate. The one oddity was the property of a flabby man, also in a Tilley hat, who trailed a group on one of those one-night guided trips sold at the outfitting stores. The guide, racing ahead with the full pack on his back and the canoe on his head, fit the scene perfectly. As did the two German women walking along uncertainly with their new packs. The man, however, pulled one of those small-wheeled airport luggage bags, the handle extended and the little wheels sending up dust and tripping on every root along the portage. It looked like he was dragging a reluctant animal.

"Which terminal are you looking for?" I asked.

He made no reply.

There is a wonderfully romantic notion that all one needs in the bush is a paddle and the clothes on your back. I like to think that Pierre Trudeau once portaged this same route when he was a fifteen-year-old and had been shipped off from Montreal to Taylor Statten Camps on Canoe Lake. His mother sent him here to improve his English and, hopefully, somewhat ease the pain of losing his father, Charles, that spring. The wealthy Quebec businessman had died of pneumonia he had contracted in Florida as he watched spring training for his minor-league baseball team.

It was here, in Algonquin Park, that Trudeau began his lifelong love affair with the canoe, and here where he first picked up the sentiments he would express in a 1944 essay entitled "Exhaustion and Fulfilment: The Ascetic in the Canoe." The future prime minister of Canada talked about the joys of being "stripped of world goods" and sent out in the wild with only the "canoe and paddle, blanket and knife, salt pork and flour, fishing rod and rifle." One knows, of course, that he had no rifle; and one can only presume that he forgot about the Taylor Statten guides staggering under their loads of tent and cooking gear.

Our own gear at least made us look as if we belonged. We carried two of our own canoes, one made of fibreglass tough enough to survive a whitewater wipeout, the other our twenty-year-old Northland cedar-strip that, thanks to Ellen's paintbrush, looks as perfect and unblemished today as the day I picked it up from Albert Maw's little canoe factory on the outskirts of Huntsville, where my younger brother, Tom, once spent his summers sanding and varnishing the cedar strips that Albert would magically transform into the world's one absolutely sensible mode of transportation.

We also had one rented canoe. We had several packs, one of them brand-new and containing the two new heavy plastic food barrels we had turned to after a bad experience on the previous year's trip into the interior. A raccoon, chuckling and groaning, had spent the entire night hanging off my thirty-year-old Woods backpack and digging for a loaf of bread and a bag of marshmallows we were saving for the final night's campfire. There is no scientific study to back this up, but sometime over the three decades between my purchase of the pack and its final trip into the bush, raccoons somehow mastered the Woods buckle.

Now we had barrels that would, we were told, survive a grizzly attack. Fine, we said, but if it keeps out the little raccoon we'll be happy enough.

Inside the barrels we had all the condiments of the modern camper: freeze-dried scrambled eggs, freeze-dried vegetable and beef soups, freeze-dried desserts, freeze-dried instant cheese flavour noodle casserole, freeze-dried chicken mixes, and, for all I knew, freeze-dried brandy for the late-night campfires. Some of it was from necessity: no cans or bottles are allowed into the park interior. But just as much of it was from laziness or curiosity. Total cost of the week's supply of specially prepared, specially packaged tripping food: approximately ten thousand dollars. Or so it seemed by the time my melting credit card was handed back by the grinning young man at the outfitting store.

The mode of transportation might be much the same as ever – the old man's Chestnut canoe from the 1940s was almost identical to our fairly new Northland – but the cargo has most assuredly changed since Professor Robins headed down these same waters and began scribbling notes for *The Incomplete Angler*. Robins and his partner, Tom, presumed to be his brother but likely an amalgam of several canoeing friends, took along the following:

7 lb bacon
½ lb chipped beef
2 lb Klim
6 cans evaporated milk
4 lb sugar
12 large onions
1 lb cheese
6 oranges
1 lb salt
6 lb rolled oats
4 lb butter
1 lb tea
1 can George Washington coffee
3 lb prunes
2 lb beans

1 lb strawberry jam
4 packs pancake flour
7 ten-cent chocolate bars
9 loaves bread

Total grocery cost: $11.63

The oddest supply taken into the bush by Robins and his friend would be the nine loaves of bread. Bread, especially 1940s bread without today's preservatives, could not last more than a day or so without hardening, turning green, or, more likely, being crushed. Robins claimed it was not his idea, but his partner's; he just went along with it despite his reservations.

"I must confess," he wrote, "to a romantic though waning repugnance against carrying bread into the bush. Bread seems to me to smack too much of the effete life I am fleeing, the life of green vegetables, of the raucous radio, of warm bath-water, of newspapers, of fresh milk, of ties and cuff-links, of refrigeration, of pastry and lectures, of art and social intercourse, of citizenship and womenkind, of cleanliness and white linen sheets, of motor-cars and mattresses."

Times change. No one today would take nine loaves of bread into the bush. And it would be most politically incorrect to suggest "womenkind" is part of an effete life that must be fled, an irritation equivalent to ties, cuff-links and "the raucous radio."

We made the carry, and a second carry for some, into Proulx Lake, loaded up the canoes, and set out. Ellen and I in the red Northland cedar-strip. The Harris boys in the heavy fibreglass whitewater canoe. Don and Marcia in the rental canoe. We spread our gear evenly and had plenty of room, our entire needs, including drinking water, within easy reach for the next several days.

Robins clearly felt much the same when he set out, with one italicized sexist exception: "We were off. I suppose that no more self-contained feeling is possible to man than comes to the canoeing camper at this moment. Gathered about him within a space of somewhat less than thirty-square feet are his transportation, his shelter and warmth, his complete wardrobe, all his food except that which he hopes to catch, his implements of the chase, his hospital, his entertainment, his social and political institutions, indeed, the whole of society *except women*."

One thing that will never go out of fashion is the joy of the canoe. I stand with Bill Mason, the renowned filmmaker and lesser-known oldtimer hockey player, who claimed in his *Path of the Paddle*, "When you look at the face of Canada and study the geography carefully, you come away with the feeling that God could have designed the canoe first and then set about to conceive a land in which it could flourish."

We set out with the wind rising at our backs, the paddling easy, and the silence, but for the gentle slurp of the prow, astonishing.

I love to paddle. I was taught not by my father, but by my mother, who could guide a canoe so quietly along a river there wouldn't be a whisper from the craft or her paddle. Helen McCormick and her sister, Mary, were marvellous paddlers, as was their own mother, the little Irish pepperpot Bea, whose skill seems greater still in the knowledge that she could not swim the width of a canoe. There were years when they lived on MacIntosh Lake in the deepest park when her husband was away on ranger patrol for weeks at a time and she would paddle from the small rock island that held their cottage to a nearby island, chop wood, fill the canoe, and paddle back under conditions some of the guides would refuse to go out in – and never once did she tip.

"The movement of a canoe," Sigurd Olson once said, "is like a reed in the wind. Silence is part of it, and the sounds of lapping water, bird songs and wind in the trees. It is a part of the medium through which it floats, the sky, the water, the shores. . . . The way of a canoe is the way of the wilderness, of a freedom almost forgotten."

It is exactly so, on a river. On open water, a canoe can be a number of different animals, bucking at times, racing, drifting, turning unexpectedly on you. The wind was up and we were soon rising and splashing down on the lake, the water spreading like a travelling lawn sprinkler each time we rode one crest and crashed into the next wave.

We were already getting wet, the water pooling in round glistening balls on our waterproof packs, refreshingly cool on our bare knees. We did not have far to paddle, however, soon coming upon a perfect site: a high and flat rocky point, with the wind singing in the pines that grew along the bluff.

The wind picked up again as we set up camp, the jack pines now swaying like drunks along the brow of the point, each caught in its own rhythm. We found easy shelter on the far side, though, and even a calm place to swim in the early evening and fish until it turned dark. It was still blistering hot – the dry spell of July spread deep into August that year – and a regional fire ban was still in effect, so we cooked over a small propane stove and sat around the fire pit, fireless, and talked on into the night. The stars seemed so low it was a wonder the wind did not stack them all to one side of the sky.

In the morning, we packed up and struck out for the creek that would carry us through to Little Crow Lake, then on to Big Crow and our destination: a virgin stand of white pine that lies about a mile south of the Crow River. It was another spectacular day, hot from the first breath and so quiet along the river we twice came upon an osprey diving for speckled trout, its wide dark wings cocking back as it locked in on its prey, the water lightly exploding as it struck in and instantly out, its catch glistening and twisting in its talons as the bird flew up and away.

It is so effortless to paddle such a deep and quiet river, even more so if one happens to be going with the current, which we were not, and so calming and endlessly fascinating, each turn its own new adventure, each corner presenting a new vista. The pickerelweeds were in full, glorious purple bloom as we passed through, as were the white water lilies with their butter-yellow centres. We quietly approached a great blue heron standing statue-still, and he did not move even as we passed by within three or four paddle lengths. We caught the sounds of red-winged blackbirds and bullfrogs, and every now and then, from the trees closest, the haunting whistle of the white-throated sparrow.

It is in moments like this that the sensual pleasures of canoeing come alive. "Water," Olson once said, "reflects not only clouds and trees and cliffs, but all the infinite variations of mind and spirit we bring to it."

There was nothing to do but paddle and listen and think. Not a word was spoken.

I sometimes give Thoreau his due. It is unfair, I know, to laugh at him for his genuine fear of the true wilds, for I must admit to my own silly nervousness about strange sounds and dark shadows. But it is also very Canadian to think the forest superior to the woodlot, to prefer the impenetrable, impossible tangle to the Walden philosopher's well-ordered fields and stone fences. On water, however, he was superb.

"To float this way on the silver-plated stream," Thoreau wrote in his journal of August 14, 1854, "is like embarking on a train of thought itself. You are surrounded by water, which is full of reflections; and you see the earth at a distance, which is very agreeable to the imagination."

Add what Olson said about the quiet river, and the two Americans pretty well sum up what we Canadians felt on this hot August day as we slipped silently north to Little Crow Lake and then through another creek east to Big Crow, where we planned to make camp again.

There were, by now, fewer and fewer trippers to be seen. When we turned out onto Big Crow Lake, however, we could see in the distance one of the summer camp brigades coming down the near shore and heading, as we were, for the mouth of the river. They were chanting as they paddled, their canoes meandering wildly, and soon, thanks to the wind, we could pick up almost every word.

The lead canoe hailed us. They were lost. They had no idea where the Crow began, and the head guide, smiling at the back of the canoe, had no intention of telling them. The bow paddler had a plastic-protected map spread on his knees.

"Where's the river?" he moaned at us.

I raised my hand, about to point out the obvious.

"*Don't tell them!*" the guide shouted. "They're supposed to find their own way!" He was laughing.

"*Shit!*" the lead paddler said, letting the map slip between his legs and dipping his paddle furiously.

"The only thing I hate worse than Canada," a kid with a New York accent barked from one of the canoes behind, "is being *lost* in Canada." He had been sitting mid-canoe, his back resting against the packs, and perhaps he hadn't seen us as the convoy came upon us. Before I could even get angry or dismiss him as a patronizing rich-kid American, he looked over, smiled sheepishly, and waved.

"*Sorrr–rry!*"

They paddled on, the experienced guide shaking his head at us as if we all understood what he was going through. It seemed to me, however, a small price to pay for a summer job that knows no comparison: two months canoeing in Algonquin Park, every day on the water and every night around a campfire, and when summer came to an end and it was time for him to head back to school, a few thousand dollars in appreciation for what he had gone through. I would put up with a million pampered, insolent rich kids for one summer's chance at it.

Near the mouth of the Crow, we came upon the finest site in this part of the park, a glorious campsite that another group was leaving just as we turned the point. We arrived so soon behind them, the waves had yet to erase the marks their canoes had made on the soft sand beach that ran the length of the site. We had the river on one side, the open lake on the other. The campsite, unusually large, had flat areas for a half dozen tents, well spread out, and beyond lay a rough hiking trail that went out along the edge of the bluff to a series of magnificent vistas down the long lake.

Soon, there was no one else within sight or sound, but we were not exactly alone. A black mink came along the shore and darted around the rocks near where we were stacking the gear. It stopped and sniffed the air while looking up at us, then quickly raced back into the water and away.

We set up convinced a storm was coming. A great wool blanket of cloud was already over the western horizon and spreading fast, the thunder grumbling in the distance. We were certain it would hit, and hit hard. Two solid weeks of unnaturally warm weather had the park primed for a particularly nasty pounding, and we were careful in choosing spots for our tents, trying to draw that fine line between desire for shelter from the trees and fear of lightning striking the same trees we chose to camp under.

It is rare for a year to go by in Algonquin without at least one story of someone being struck by lightning, hopefully surviving. Sometimes they do not, however, and I am always reminded of the story of the camper who died when lightning jumped from a tree to a tent pole, and from the tent pole to the gold chain he was wearing around his neck, killing him as efficiently as if he'd been executed. The kids think I am insane, and perhaps I am, but I tell them not even to wear earrings when they go to sleep in a tent.

The storm passed. It spat a few drops, growled a bit, and then the clouds parted again to reveal the sun, now lowering but still so hot it made being in or on the water the only sensible option. We swam and raced the canoes by gunwale jumping – each person standing on the rim of his canoe at the stern and bouncing up and down until either the canoe shot ahead or the competitor fell off – and then decided to head out for an early evening canoe trek, without the packs.

We had seen a glorious white sand beach at the far end away from the mouth of the Crow River, and so we set out to explore what seemed a great rarity – more like an ocean beach – in a land where beaches, rare enough as they were, were invariably a deep brown.

We paddled up on that glass-like calm that seems to come after a storm has threatened and dissipated. The sun was close to setting, the shadows lengthening on shore, and the loons beginning to gather for their evening concert. What, I wondered, if James Wilson of Niagara Falls' Queen Victoria Park had won the day back in 1893 and talked the authorities into "waging war" on the poor Algonquin loons? No calling, no yodelling, no watching them teaching their cork-like babies how to dive, no white-breasted displays of bravado, no haunting calls in the middle of the night that stay with you, more than anything else, all three hundred and sixty-five days of the year.

We reached the beach easily, a bluff to the east throwing shadow onto the white sand but barely dimming it. We drove our canoes onto the soft sand, the bows sizzling as they sliced onto shore, and got out to examine this extraordinary find. The sand was pure white, and fine enough for an hourglass.

But that was not the most remarkable thing about the beach.

"There's been a moose along here," Don said from farther down the sand.

We hurried over. He was crouched over a huge, perfectly formed moose print. Another similar print lay a long stride away, and then another.

"That," Don said, "is one big moose."

"He must come here to drink," Ellen suggested.

"He's not all that comes here," said Brandon from still farther down the beach.

Brandon, too, was crouched over some prints. But not moose. Bear. Large, unmistakable, bear paw prints perfectly preserved in the soft white sand.

"There's little ones, too!" called Vaughn.

He was pointing at miniature bear tracks, all along the sand and over the grass and into the woods and back out again, hundreds of them, many scattered as if placed in haste and ripped away even quicker.

"She must have two cubs," said Don. "And they've been playing. They must have been here earlier today."

We walked up and down the white beach for half an hour, one eye always cocked toward the dark openings under the cedars and jack pines and into the black bush beyond. If they had been here earlier today, they might come again. Out of rutting season, a huge bull moose was of no more concern than a milk cow, but a mother bear with two cubs? No one wanted to come between her and her charges.

The sky was now dark pink, with purple fingers seeming to reach out and hold on. It was time to be getting back. We pushed off and were away, still staring deep into the dark forest in search of something black that might be staring back.

But there was nothing.

All along the canoe route we had seen hints of their presence. They stood out on the brows of distant hills like missed weeds on a closely cropped lawn. They rose majestic – the only word for it – high over the forest cover, towering above everything but, every so often along the horizon, others of their own.

"I've never see anything like them," Don said as we pushed through the low water of the Crow, wading as much as paddling toward Lake Laveille.

"Wait until you see them together," I said. "It'll take your breath away."

We were speaking of trees. Not just any trees, but the legendary white pine of Algonquin, a tree that once covered the entire park and, for that matter, a great deal of North America, a tree that, but for some impassable terrain, would have gone the way of the passenger pigeon.

Today, there are only sporadic white pine to be seen, each one a surprise, as its trunk alone rises a hundred feet, well above the tops of the highest maple and hemlock, before vanishing into lush, green-needle foliage that seems, from a distance – and it is always from a distance where white pine are concerned – to have been painted by a landscape artist rather than created by cell division and randomly sculpted by the wind. Seeing one immediately reveals why they were once in such demand, the wood so light and strong and unbelievably *straight*. Had there been no Napoleonic Wars, had there been no immigration push into the Upper Ottawa Valley, then there might still be wide stands of the glorious tree. But of course there are not.

It seems silly to think of Napoleon Bonaparte when you're miles back in the deep Ontario bush, but his effect is all about. Once, the canopy of these vast forests was twice the height it is today, and might by now have grown even taller, for there is white pine that was around when Columbus landed that still stands, healthy and tall, more than five hundred years later.

Once the French defeated Prussia and closed the Baltic seaports, thereby cutting off Great Britain from its timber supplies, Britain's shipbuilders turned to the colonies, and reports quickly came back that the central forest held trees taller and stronger and lighter than the best timber available from the Finnish and Swedish merchants. Upper and Lower Canada white pine, overnight, became the first choice of the shipbuilding industry. Philemon Wright, the founder of Hull, sent the first raft of squared timber down the Ottawa River to Quebec City in 1806, a raft composed of four-hundred-year-old pines so vast that many were said to have been twenty feet around at their base. It was just the beginning.

The requirements of war and the needs of poor immigrants formed a mutual partnership in these woods. Impoverished Irish were flooding up the Ottawa Valley to escape famine in their home country in the first half of the nineteenth century, only to find that the poor, thin soil of the valley, acidic from so much pine, was little better than the miserable farms they thought they had escaped. Poles fleeing political turmoil and persecution joined them and found that their land, higher up the Valley, where the Bonnechere and Madawaska twist down toward the Ottawa, was even poorer quality than the farms the Irish were damning.

The Poles had been lied to and soon knew it. Many had come, along with the Irish, encouraged by an 1858 prospectus that T. P. French, the crown land agent for the Opeongo Road, had distributed throughout Europe. The offer was made of one hundred acres of free land to any settler, eighteen years of age or older, who would come up the newly opened settlement road into the bush, take possession of his acreage, erect a house at least ten feet by twenty, and have a minimum of twelve acres under cultivation within four years. It seemed too good to be true. The land, the crown agent stated, was of "a sandy loam, in some places light, but in others deep and rich." While French did admit to some "surface stone," he assured prospective settlers that the rocks wouldn't "form any great obstacle to the raising of excellent crops."

A century and a half later they still curse the "surface stones" of the Madawaska Valley, convinced that back-breaking, soul-destroying rocks are all that ever rose up through the ground – a never-ending crop that ultimately made farming impossible.

The lumber barons were only too happy to take these desperate people in. The men could work the bush all winter and still, if they insisted, work their farms come summer. They could fell the trees, cut and trim the trunks, essentially throwing away more than half the tree, skid the logs by ice road and teams of horses to the nearest waterway, and the spring runoff from the Algonquin highlands would then carry the logs, free of charge, with only a few lives lost each year, down the various rivers to the Ottawa, where they were square cut, tied into rafts, and sent down the river to the St. Lawrence, out the St. Lawrence to Quebec City, and by ship from Quebec City to the shipbuilding ports of Liverpool, Edinburgh, and London.

The Poles actually preferred this life. They reached Wilno, the highest point of land in all of Ontario, and decided the rolling hills and thick forests reminded them greatly of Pomerania and Kaszubia, where most of them had come from, and so they built a huge Catholic church at the top of the hill, with a view of the vast bushland and the lakes for more than forty miles. Beyond, as far as they could see to the west, lay the area that would soon become Algonquin Park, and here they would find the work that would allow them to build their homes, have a few cleared acres, and earn enough money logging each winter to be able to sleep at night without worry that all they would find in the morning on those cleared fields was more rocks to carry. It was a world they felt so at home in that, many years later, forty unhappy Polish families that had previously settled on far better land in Massachusetts pulled up stakes and left for the deep Canadian bush, where they knew they'd be made to feel more welcome.

Between 1863 and 1877, the peak of the white pine trade, more than 400,000 logs a year were being rafted down the Ottawa River. It was possible, in late spring, to dance across the floating, rolling logs all the way to Hull from Parliament Hill, a fact that momentarily gave pause to Prime Minister John A. Macdonald one sunny June afternoon in 1871. He dictated a rather prescient note to the premier of Ontario, John Sandfield Macdonald, who was no relation and had, in fact, opposed Confederation. "The sight of the immense masses of timber passing my window every morning," said the prime minister, "constantly suggests to my mind the absolute necessity there is for looking into the future of this great trade. We are recklessly destroying the timber of Canada, and there is scarcely a possibility of replacing it."

Unfortunately, Macdonald never bothered to make it an issue. And neither did anyone else. The supply seemed infinite. As late as 1895 the federal government's own department of agriculture was claiming there were still thirty-seven *billion* board feet of this beautiful wood in Eastern Canada. So confident of future supplies were the rich timber barons of the day that, according to industry standard, if a felled log held more than three knots, it would be left in the bush to rot.

One hundred years later, those who worked with wood were calling the eastern white pine an "exotic."

Times, and perceptions, change. Anna Brownell Jameson, a British writer and early feminist who came out to the colony in 1836 in a futile attempt to save her marriage, noted in *Winter Studies and Summer Rambles in Canada* that "a Canadian settler hates a tree, regards it as his natural enemy, as something to be destroyed, eradicated, annihilated by all and any means."

Now they will drive and paddle for days just to stare up in wonder at the few great trees still standing.

We were headed for the sacred grove of the eastern white pine, a stand on a gentle hill about a mile south of the Crow River. The route is over such undulating, boggy, and difficult terrain that early loggers must have decided to pass on the green giants in favour of pine far handier to the river route back to Opeongo. We paddled through to the old dam and tied up, all of us ready for a long, hot hike in through the trees to see more trees. It seemed silly, put that way, but we knew that once we got there, the hike would have been worth the effort.

The trail was well marked and, happily, well used. We were hardly the only ones keen to see these remarkable giants of the eastern bush. We walked over mud and old corduroy roads, up rocks and roots and past old stumps so wide they could have held a square dance. We passed by raspberry brambles and brilliant red toadstools and Indian pipes and every imaginable tree of the Algonquin forest: trembling aspen and cedar, high hemlocks and thick maple, spruce and balsam, poplar and ironwood, the odd bass tree, and, as we rose higher into the hills, more and more grey, smooth-skinned beech.

"Gun shots," said Vaughn.

He was looking at a wide beech, the smooth bark pockmarked by black holes that looked, indeed, very much as if someone had stood back and emptied a twelve-gauge shotgun into the tree.

"Bears," Don said, free hand instinctively moving closer to his holstered spray.

The marks were everywhere. Some darker and wider and deeper than others – an indication of age – and some trailing scratches so that, if you looked closely, you could see where the black bears, the original tree huggers, had climbed the beech in search of nuts and succulent branches to snack on.

We began checking each beech we came to, and every one of them showed signs of climbing bears or, at the very least, of bears sharpening and refining their claws on the bark. It was chilling to see, the huge trees looking in places as if they had been strafed by machine-gun fire, or sliced by a furrow of carpet knives.

If they could do *this* to tree bark . . .

Robins, the University of Toronto professor who travelled this route sixty years earlier – keeping his food, including his nine loaves of bread, *inside* his tent at night with no trouble – wrote that the black bear of Algonquin was generally considered to be an "inoffensive creature." Today, the park goes to considerable effort to discourage such an attitude, warning campers against keeping food anywhere but hanging high in a tree, and offering endless lists on how to avoid bear encounters.

Grey Owl, the famous Canadian nature writer who turned out to be Englishman Archie Belaney, and who once snowshoed across this part of the park, challenging my grandfather and his fellow rangers to catch him if they could (they tracked him easily, laughing at his vanity), thought the bear utterly harmless. "Your bear is really a good fellow," he wrote in *Tales of an Empty Cabin*, "and will eat almost anything that you give him, or that you may inadvertently leave lying around, just to show you that his heart is in the right place."

Our hearts, however, were in our throats. If, as experts say, there are more than half a million black bears in North America, perhaps 75,000 of them in Ontario, it seemed dozens, if not hundreds, were within sniffing distance of where we stood, staring at the scarred beeches.

Eventually we lost our fascination for the scratchings and what they might mean about bears in the vicinity. The terrain grew even more difficult, down across bogs and up ever-steeper hills and, with the heat of the day penetrating to the floor of the forest, we grew ever more quiet, simply walking along and wondering where on earth the white pine were and whether the authorities had the foresight to erect a sign to tell us when we had arrived.

There was no need. Up through a twisting trail of hemlock and cedar we rose, up past poplar and spruce and thin yellow birch, up past ironwood and beech and maple, and suddenly, without even realizing it, we had come upon a massive trunk with dark brown bark that resembled the cracked soil of a dry creek bed. The trunk was massive, so large that we gathered about it in awe, not saying a word. And then, almost as a group, we looked up.

I have never felt so small and insignificant in my life.

We had found the sacred grove of the eastern white pine. The trunk, so straight it seemed the product of a drafting board rather than a seed, rose up, bare and dark, stabbing through the tops of the highest hemlocks of the forest, and then up straight and unsullied for a hundred feet or more until the branches began, wide, sweeping branches that barely danced in the wind at the top of the hill.

"*There's another one!*" Brandon shouted.

We raced over to check it out.

"*One here!*" called Vaughn.

They were everywhere. It was as if we had left the bush we'd been hiking through and entered a world of giantism, where dozens of stunningly high trees stood over the paltry forests like lords over the common.

John D. Robins had been equally impressed. "They were not monstrous," he wrote, "as if their pituitary glands had misbehaved; they were god-like."

It is important to realize that not everyone is affected the same way by the deep bush. Thoreau, after all, did not like the *real* wild, and raced home from his harrowing excursion into the harsh Maine heartland to the bucolic comforts of Concord and rural Massachusetts. And Rupert Brooke, the great English war romantic, did not appear to be taken at all with the great Canadian bush when he came over to Canada in 1913 and ended up passing several days north of Winnipeg at a hunting and fishing lodge on Lake George.

"I never expected," the beloved poet snapped, "to pass my twenty-sixth birthday with a gun and fishing tackle, without any clothes on, by a lake, in a wood infested by bears, in a country where there aren't ten people within five miles and half of those are Indians."

When Brooke published his *Letters from America* in 1916, he dismissed the terrain so many today worship as "only pools of water and lumps of earth." He found nothing spiritual about the land, convinced it lacked any genuine connection with humanity. "There is no one else within reach," he wrote, "there never has been anyone; no one else is thinking of the lakes and hills you see before you."

I think he rather missed the point.

Like John R. Bates of Pennsylvania and Lake Opeongo, I also had my "Secret Lake," and we decided to take the Harrises into it for an afternoon of fly fishing. The hike would be considerable, some of the bush almost impenetrable, but it would certainly be worthwhile, for I had something else to show them – one man's very private sanctuary.

We carried everything we would need but the canoe. The old rangers and guides of Algonquin Park used to have canoes stashed at every good fishing lake free for anyone to use, the only proviso being that one used it carefully, repaired anything that needed fixing, and tipped it back over to protect it from the weather until the next person happened along. Once this practise became discouraged by park authorities, they took to hiding their canoes, sticking them upright inside the skirting branches of large spruce or hidden in the centre of thick stands of cedar, and I still have cousins and friends in the park who can hike back miles into the bush, reach up into an evergreen, and put their hand on a canoe that may have been there since they were children.

Many of the older rangers used to do this with booze, too, and a favourite story of our family's concerns Uncle Lorne Pigeon, a long-time park ranger, who was still hiking in on speckled trout fishing trips into his early eighties. At the end of one long portage, the group spread out to nap, and one of the company from Toronto turned over a few rocks to give himself extra space and came upon an old, but still half-filled, bottle of brandy, which he immediately showed to the fishing party as a rare and unusual find.

"*Goddammit!*" Lornie snapped. "That's *my* bottle. I left it here years ago. *Now give it to me!*"

He plucked it out of the finder's hand, drank a bit, and then proceeded to place it back – in case he needed a drink next time he happened along this portage.

We hiked in to my own secret lake with paddles, life preservers, rods, packs, and a good lunch. We walked the first miles along an old logging road, a few bear droppings near the raspberry growths and, whenever there was fine sand or gravel and plenty of sun, signs of snapping turtle shells that had either hatched or been eaten by marauding foxes or raccoons. After a while we turned off the logging road into what appeared to be a dead end, trees blocking all passage, but one swing of a paddle against a long spruce branch and a path opened up like someone had just pulled back the flap of an evergreen tent.

Here the going was rougher. We stumbled often, and several times had to breach fallen trees that certainly weren't on the ground the last time I walked to this spot. We crossed a running creek, descended a hill, climbed a hill, and saw water glimmering through the trees off to our left.

"The canoe should be right down there," I said.

It was, turned over and parked exactly as it had been left last time. The only thing we lacked was valet service.

It was a glorious day, hot and sunny, and though hardly ideal conditions for fishing, we found a deep, cold, and well-shaded bay and managed to land a few speckled, which we cleaned and wrapped for lunch.

The boys loved it. One or two could fish from the little canoe while the others fished from the rocks along the shore surrounding the bay or walked out on fallen trees that allowed anyone with good balance a chance to cast. Vaughn climbed a rocky outcropping just over the bay and stood shouting in the sun that he could see the fish, and we all climbed up and stared down, amazed at how, in the clear, clean water of the lake, it seemed the trout were suspended in air.

We fished until they stopped biting, and then we began gathering our equipment for the long hike out. Once we set the canoe back into the bushes – exactly as we'd found it, out of sight but not unfindable to anyone who knew where to look – we picked up everything and began pushing back into the bush and the difficult trail that would take us out to the logging roads again.

"I want to show you something," I said.

"What?" the boys wanted to know.

"A very special place."

I knew of an extraordinary place a group of us had once stumbled on trying to check out yet another tiny little lake off the logging road. We had only *sensed* water would be in there somewhere – the sight-lines through the pines indicated an open space, and there was a small, gurgling creek of cold water – and had hiked in until the creek had opened up onto one of the most amazing places I have ever found.

We came to the creek and I told the boys to go ahead. They raced in, dancing from wet stone to stone, leapfrogging fallen logs, and scooting up a moss-covered embankment to what was clearly open ground and, beyond it, sharp light and open water.

If you could not see what was coming, you could smell it. The air was lighter as we moved closer, the forest must lifting and a fresh, fragrant forest and water smell taking over. It *smelled* like the perfect campsite, and it was.

I have no idea who built it. I have been a half dozen times or more, but never seen anyone here. I did find a canoe here once, an aluminium one, but never again, and, though I looked, I could not find it stashed anywhere. Whoever found and built the campsite must have carried it in and out.

The campsite was all along one side of the tiny, rectangular lake. There were high rocks and then the terrain tapered down to a flat, wet area where one could kneel and wash dishes. There was even a perfect diving platform formed by one large, flat rock, and immediately below the five-foot drop deep, clean water to plunge into and, off to the side, a place to climb out with perfectly aligned hand- and footholds that go back to the last ice age.

The floor of the campsite was completely covered in soft white- and red-pine needles. There were pines everywhere, and yet there was a sense of being in a park, with everything open and all the fallen branches and twigs as carefully removed as if he'd been here only the day before, keeping house.

There was a shelter, axe-hewn cedar logs nailed between two lovely cedars to provide a break from the prevailing winds, and behind that a fireplace constructed of stones the mystery camper must have hauled up from the creek. Hidden behind the fireplace he had a frying pan, and just enough utensils for cooking. I made a fire, using his kindling (which we would replace before going), and we broke out the speckled to fry them up and enjoy a shore lunch.

We all swam while the trout was cooking, taking turns diving off the perfect rocks into the perfect water and using the perfect hand- and footholds to get out. The water tingled on our skin. The smoke from the fire curled around the pines and cedar and ghosted out over the water, and carried with it a smell so delightful and satisfying that, for a short while, this seemed like paradise on earth.

"This place is amazing!" Brandon said as we prepared to eat our lunch.

"You haven't seen anything yet," I said.

"There's more?"

"There's one thing."

After we had eaten, cleaned up, and restored the stranger's camp to exactly the condition it had been in, I led them back down the little point where he'd cleared everything so carefully and then up onto a much higher rock that opened out onto a spectacular view of the lake.

"Outstanding," said Don.

"You don't know the half of it," I said.

I led them along the highest point of this granite lookout. Here, out of piled-up rocks, the camper had constructed an extraordinary outhouse, complete with a real, padded toilet seat.

Each morning, as the sun rose over the far treetops, he could sit and survey his kingdom.

He had no right, of course. Not in the legal sense. He had no permit, no lease, no ownership of the land, but he had made it his own, and no one who has ever been in to see it could have wanted it otherwise.

His secret was safe with everyone who discovered it. It was almost as if we all wished to be a part of this small sanctuary in the bush.

I wondered if this sense of personal sanctuary is what John R. Bates found off the North Arm of Opeongo Lake when he took his big speedboat out, waved goodbye to Belle as she watered her treasured island garden, and headed off alone for his own Secret Lake. He kept it stocked with speckled trout – again, somehow getting permission to do what no other park cottager would ever be allowed – and since he was generous in sharing the fish around, they forgave him the extra discretions he always seemed to gain from the authorities.

Bates bragged so much about his Secret Lake that the people came to call it that themselves, even if they'd never been in to it or knew precisely where it was. It was prized by Bates, and he loved to go there, always returning with trout, and this they perfectly understood.

What they could not understand was that Old Johnny Bates was keeping an even bigger secret from them.

John R. Bates died in 1969, and Belle, through her lawyers, sought to have the lease switched over to her name.

The park authorities were giving consideration to that seemingly obvious change when a letter arrived from another lawyer who also claimed to be representing Mrs. Bates. Only this was one Sarah E. Bates of Johnstown, Pennsylvania.

Johnny Bates was, it turned out, the ultimate escape artist. Sarah thought him an eccentric husband who lived a hermit's life in the park. She knew nothing of Belle. But Belle, we have to presume, would have known about Sarah.

We cannot help but wonder if Belle ever considered Johnny might have yet another wife at Secret Lake – stashed away like a guide's canoe – where he claimed to have spent the happiest days of his life all alone.

In the evening, we were convinced the storm was finally going to strike. The sky at the bottom of Big Crow was the colour of a week-old bruise, the orange and yellow streaks rising off the sunset being erased by heavy cloud moving in from the south. We could hear the rumbles. Periodically we could see flashes deep inside the cloud and, far away, a heat storm moving north; the worst possible kind.

We double-checked the tents. We set up protective tarps to deflect the wind that was already building. We packed away the food after we'd eaten and hoisted the food barrels and the garbage high in a tree overhanging the bay. If a bear leapt for it, he'd drop fifty feet.

Darkness was falling fast. It was beginning to spit, big dollops of rain that seemed to drive in sideways from the lake and smack against the fluttering tarp. Ellen and Marcia were clearing up the area around the campfire and packing everything away so it wouldn't get wet. The wind was building alarmingly.

Don and I went down to shore to turn the canoes upside down and store the paddles and life jackets and fishing gear safely. We also wanted to ensure that the wind wouldn't flip them and run them up the rocks, so we carefully wedged them in tight between aspen and rocks and well up from the shore, where the waves were already building.

"*Bear!*"

I don't think I heard the first shout clearly, on account of the wind. But Don heard, and was already scrambling up the shore, sand flying and rocks tumbling as he raced for the tree where he'd hung his belt with the bear spray.

"BEAR!"

The shouts came from Vaughn, who was running hard back from the toilet area back of the camp and up through the spruce and balsam, where it already seemed an hour or two darker than down at the shore.

Don had his belt down and was buckling it, his head turning fast as he tried to catch sight of it.

Marcia was laughing.

We turned to her, our mouths open. She was pointing into the woods down toward the river. Something very dark and black and very, very large was moving slowly through the trees.

A huge, elongated head came into view.

"A *moose!*" Brandon called. "It's a *moose!*"

"I thought it was a bear," said Vaughn.

I could see why. Unless you saw the head clearly, it looked like a huge black bear against the equally black backdrop of the pine trees and hill. Vaughn's mistake had been understandable. Movement. Black. Big. Must be a bear.

But it was a large cow moose. She took no notice of us as she broke through the spruce and walked, ever so slowly, across our campsite and then down through the aspen and thickets to the edge of the river, where she calmly waded out and began chomping on water lilies.

We trailed her down, keeping our distance, and marvelled as her huge head seemed to bob for apples and came up chewing as slowly and nonchalantly as a milk cow in a warm barn. She was sheltered from the wind by a thick stand of pine along a narrow peninsula, but the rain was still splattering into her – thick drops, widely spaced. She paid none of it, including us, the slightest heed.

She moved farther out into the water. Her hooves on the boggy, mucky bottom caused huge farting sounds that made us laugh. She moved with the determination of a large tractor, so powerful it seemed nothing could stop her. In muck halfway up her legs, in water to her shoulder, she continued to dine as if this were the warmest, happiest place in the park.

We were sheltered here and watched for a long time, took dozens of close-up photographs, and then, with darkness upon us, headed back to our tents and the tarps, now snapping and roaring in the fierce wind that was sweeping down the length of the lake.

I was glad Don had insisted on putting the tarps up to break the wind. Had they not been there, our tents would have been well up the path to the toilet, I feared, and us with them.

Thunder cracked and lightning flashed, and at times the entire sky over the lake seemed to jump with electricity, but even the heavy clouds seemed dried out in this unusual summer heat. They spat, but could never quite dump, and though the storm rolled and boiled and roared overhead, we remained almost dry, the only indication that any rain at all was falling was the periodic snap of a drop into the plastic tarpaulin, almost as if someone were standing on shore firing a BB gun into it.

I slept fitfully and got up once for the usual reason. The lightning was still flashing on and off inside the clouds racing overhead, but no rain, and no bolts. When several clouds flashed at once, I could see as clearly as if it were daylight.

The moose was still there.

She stood, and stared, and then dipped her head. She had moved back to the edge of the campsite and seemed perfectly content, perfectly at home.

Do they sleep? I wondered. Are they like horses and can sleep standing? And why here, why around humans?

In the morning the wind was still up, the tarp unstrung at one end and whipping angrily against the side of our tent. We hurried out, untied it and rolled it up. I looked out over the water. Whitecaps, but not enough to stop us from heading back out.

"*She's still here!*" Marcia called from down by the campfire.

The moose had stayed through the night. A guardian in the storm? Or seeking shelter? Or just hungry for the succulent water lilies that grew at that turn of the Crow River and to hell with anyone who might be in the way?

The moose went back to eating, slurping about the water and making those huge suction sounds whenever she stepped through the muck.

We went back to breaking camp. We tore down the tents, folded the sleeping bags, rolled up the mats, ate a quick breakfast, cleaned up, packed away the food and the propane stove and the pots and pans and dishes and utensils, tied the packs into the canoes, and prepared to set out.

The wind had died now, the water like corduroy with its even ripples. It would be easy paddling.

"Look!" Vaughn called out.

The moose was now moving out the mouth of the Crow. It was shallow, and the sand firm, and she walked out and stood there, drinking and waiting.

We pushed off and began paddling, stopping to stare at her as we passed by.

"*She's* coming, too!" Vaughn called from his canoe.

I looked back. The moose had waded into the deeper water and was now swimming. She headed straight out into the lake, making for very deep water, and seemed not the slightest concerned.

We paddled and she kept up, at an appropriate distance. Out into the heart of the lake, out around the first long point, and then west and south toward the river that would take us back to Opeongo.

It struck me as the oddest sight. Two red canoes, a white one, and a moose, all moving along Big Crow Lake.

Finally, after rounding the point, she broke off and headed for shore. No wave goodbye, nothing. She reached shallow water, walked mightily up the low rocks, and disappeared into the dark of the forest, gone from sight entirely.

I had to wonder. Had she lingered because of us? What else could it be? I was no Ernest Thompson Seton. I did not believe animals had human characteristics. My father would have laughed at her and talked to her as if we were all in this together, but I knew better. Coincidence, obviously. Just as it had been pure coincidence that all those bush creatures had lined the road that day when we were driving back from his funeral.

We hit the river and the wind died completely. Once again we were canoeing over glass, only this time going with the flow, and so it was easy, almost effortless.

It is almost impossible to believe that, for all the mystical talk of canoeists today, the canoe was never understood as pleasure for its own sake until relatively recently. For the Natives who created it and the fur traders who adopted it, the canoe was for transportation, exclusively functional. It then became the choice of hunters, taking them quietly into blinds and transporting them to distant tracts as well as providing the means to draw large carcasses out of the bush.

Some date the adoption of canoeing for its own sake to a journey Quebec writer Raoul Clouthier took in 1928, when he paddled through much of the central and western Quebec wilderness for the sheer joy of it and later published an account that fired the imagination of others.

"It was nothing but the call of Nature," Clouthier wrote, "the love of the great open air, the lure of the wild and deserted forest which seems dormant in the heart of every man and to which every real sportsman is so responsive!

"No man can define the attraction and the disadvantages of heat, thirst, flies, long hours bent on paddle, under rain or sunshine, hard carries over rough portages, all things inherent to such a trip made through unfrequented territories. What urges one to go, knowing well what is in store for him? Perhaps the charm lies in magnificent sunrise and sunset scenes, or in contending with the forces of Nature by one's own physical power. Or is it the soothing calm of the forest, the restful horizons of silvery lakes, the alluring noise of rapids and waterfalls? The question is hard to answer! One goes in spite of it all, accepting in advance whatever may happen. He goes and returns satisfied, even if he only brings back memories of the beautiful panoramas he has had the privilege of admiring, memories of pleasant evenings spent around the camp fire, listening to the mysterious voices of the wild, memories of the freedom he has enjoyed, far from the tentacles of civilization."

We paddled through Little Crow and back down the river toward

Proulx, past a huge bull moose calmly munching on water lilies that he was scooping up and catching, hilariously, on his massive rack. He looked, in the sparkle of the sun on splashing water, like a Christmas decoration, with the long garlands of lily strung around his rack and several gloriously white blossoms hanging strategically from his antlers. We were able to draw close enough to hear the bubbles when he ducked his head under for another large mouthful of the river plant.

By now, the wind was back up, and we stopped, perhaps foolishly, to swim and rest at the high point where, days before, we had set up our first camp. By the time we set out again, there were whitecaps across the lake and the wind was beginning to howl.

We had three choices. One, we could go for it, straight into the wind. Two, we could sort of tiptoe around the edge of the lake, keeping to the sheltered bays and staying as much out of the wind as possible. Or three, we could quit and spend the night. It is not uncommon for campers to be grounded by the wind. It is, in fact, the smart thing to do when any doubt exists.

We had no doubt, however, that if we went right away we could make it. The Harrises had to begin their long drive back to Saskatchewan. We had family coming on the weekend. It was time.

"This moment always comes as a shock," Robins wrote in *The Incomplete Angler*. "Normally, there is a definite time when we must be back on the treadmill, and our movements of the last three or four days are governed largely by that factor. Nevertheless, there is a clear divide. Up to that divide, we have been forgetting, or trying to forget, that an end must come to freedom. We usually succeed at keeping the disagreeable thought of going out so far back in consciousness that it can emerge only momentarily as an unidentified discomfort. Then, at some incalculable point of time, our whole attitude changes. The trip is over. That accepted, we become eager to be out. The joy of loitering is gone. The delight of the eyes is past. Let's get home."

"Adventure is wonderful," Bob Marshall, the founder of the Wilderness Society, once said, "but there is no doubt that one of its joys is its end." There is also no doubt that we were thinking of the ice-cream stand we had seen at the outfitters when we launched. In the intense heat wave of this summer, we had all forgotten what cool feels like.

We set out, paddling hard around the first point that would expose us to the full brunt of the blow. The two boys, paddling the keel-less whitewater canoe, instantly slipped and skidded sideways across the lake into the deep water no matter how hard they tried to stay with us. But both were excellent paddlers and still managed to head across the lake in a long parabolic loop.

We were luckier – able to keep a straight line toward the far shore – but also heavier, and every wave meant water splashing high over the prow and on our packs.

At one point I became convinced we wouldn't make it and would have to let the wind drive us back toward the sheltered point, but Ellen continued to dig in and wisely refused to surrender. Suddenly, mysteriously, the wind died completely, allowing us all to glide swiftly through the centre of the lake before the wind swirled once and came back at us twice as hard. Had this wind been the first we'd encountered, we would have turned back, but already we were coming into the lea of the far shore, and every stroke brought us into calmer waters.

The whitecaps died. The boys moved back into position. All three canoes were across, with only the long portage, the date with the water taxi back down the lake, and the cool ice-cream bars of Opeongo Outfitters awaiting us.

I felt both relieved to have made it across and sad to be going. The trip had been necessarily short, but it had also been wonderful, and could have gone on for days this way, as far as I was concerned.

"*Bear!*" shouted Brandon.

We all turned to look.

All the way across the lake, along the beach, stood a large black dot.

"It's a *stump!*" shouted Don, laughing.

"No, it's not!" shouted Vaughn. "It's a bear!"

We got the binoculars out and, pulling alongside each other in the water, handed them back and forth, arguing as to whether it was indeed a large bear that had come out to the water's edge or just a big black, burned-out stump.

"Bear," the boys agreed.

"Bear," said Marcia.

"I don't know," said Ellen. "I can't say for sure."

"Stump," said Don.

"In my story," I said, "it will be a bear."

Without one, an Algonquin Park story isn't worth telling.

Chapter Four

FAILED ESCAPES

"One of the derivations proposed for the word Canada is a Portuguese phrase meaning 'nobody here.' The etymology of the word Utopia is very similar, and perhaps the real Canada is an ideal with nobody in it."

NORTHROP FRYE

We used to come here for the bears. Ellen's father, Lloyd Griffith, came here to stick his head inside ovens. But no more. Everything changes eventually, I suppose, even the local dump.

Today, halfway along Muskoka Road 8, just as the thin cold-asphalt road falls down hard toward a creek where we sometimes get our bait minnows, there still is a dump. But I doubt Ellen's father, who died in 1980, would even recognize it as such. There is a huge fence around it, and a uniformed security guard to write down the licence number of every car that comes through the gates during the appropriate hours of the designated days. They burn nothing here now; neither do they put the garbage in a hole and bulldoze it over the way they used to. Today they don't call it a "dump" or even a "landfill site" but rather a "transfer centre," and it consists of a fancy ramp leading up to metal dumpsters on each side, with a large area set apart for the appropriate separation of newspapers, cans, cardboard, plastic bottles, and reclaimable metal.

The local summer camp has switched over to paper plates, meaning kitchen duty now consists of driving the old half-ton to take the dirty plates away at the end of the day. Even brush, which used to be burned where you cut it, has its own designated area. And where once it seemed there were old putterers like Lloyd Griffith everywhere – legs sticking out of half-gutted abandoned ranges while they searched for the last good fuse and reusable element, backs bent as they picked through the metal, the trunks of their dusty cars open as if waiting for the grocery bags to skid down the rollers – there is now only the one older man, carrying a clipboard and wearing a badge pinned to the chest of his security service uniform.

Yes, he tells the kids, there was indeed a bear here this morning when he arrived, but it jumped out of the dumpster and away before the government could ticket it or reassign it. No more do the cottagers gather in the evenings, their car headlights on and doors locked as huge black shadows lumber down from the sand hills and begin picking through the garbage. No longer does anyone come, ever, to let the children pick through the castaway treasures of other country dwellers. Even the immediate past, yesterday's trash, is no longer what it once was.

The dump used to be a good place to put in time while waiting for the minnow traps to fill. I would go down to the creek, break a slice of bread – always stale, always white – into the trap, swing the assembled trap like a pendulum from the rope and send it flying out to a knee-deep spot in the lily pads. After I let it settle, I'd tie the end of the rope to the willows and wander about for an hour or two until the trap had lured enough shiners and creek chub to keep us in trolling bait for days.

Sometimes I wandered up to the dump. Sometimes I went to Mizpah.

I have no real idea of what Mizpah was in its best years, but I do know the graveyard. I know, for a fact, that real people once lived in Mizpah and died there. I know that down this twisting road that heads straight into the deep bush along the western edge of Algonquin Park there was once a small, proud community and that this was, for a time, their *place* on this earth. "A place is not a place," Wallace Stegner once wrote, "until people have been born in it, have grown up in it, lived in it, known it, died in it."

Stegner did not explore what becomes of it once they have also abandoned it, but this was the fate of poor Mizpah.

The name is, obviously, biblical. It appears more than forty times in the Old Testament. The word means "Watchtower" or "Lookout," and it is easy to see how early settlers might have felt this as they crested the high hill and began the drop down toward the small, deep lakes that are now all ringed by cottages. Biblical scholars have long debated the actual location of the Holy Land's Mizpah – or Mizpahs, as the case may be – which is rather in keeping with this more modern version hidden on Muskoka Road 8. It was, according to the book of Judges, a town in Gilead where Jephthah, once commander of the Israelites, lived and where his nameless daughter insisted she spend two months in the deepest wild to atone for some never-explained sin – again, not unlike today's cottagers.

Those who settled in Mizpah, Canada, knew nothing of cottagers. At the time of settlement, Muskoka Road 8 was a rough track heading into what would soon be designated Algonquin Park. But no one thought then of tourists and lodges, let alone of city dwellers coming for a mere weekend before racing back to work. Back then, the track led them to virgin land that had been offered to them free – a deal that seemed, at first, almost unbelievably good. Each family head taking up the government's settlement offer would be given two hundred acres, with an additional one hundred acres for each male child over the age of eighteen, and the only obligation was that there must be two acres cleared each year and a home built and occupied at least six months of the year.

Some did not even last long enough to get the first two acres of hard rock and stump and impenetrable tangle cleared. Others, however, thought that they had found a place where life could only get better. They were, in so many instances, escaping from a life with no possibilities to one of seemingly endless possibilities. Poverty here would not matter, for they would be self-sufficient. There would be no war here, because there would be no one to fight. They could be everything they dreamed of being here. Like every other little community, they immediately put up a church. It, too, can no longer be found.

Today, the cemetery is the only evidence there was anything at all here where Muskoka Road 8 suddenly dips down toward the lovely lake Rebecca, another biblical reference. The lake retains its name, but "Mizpah" has long since vanished from the maps, even from local conversation. At best, people might mention "the little cemetery by the dump," as if the dump had primacy, which now indeed it does.

But I, and others, go there to walk and think and wonder. There are small paths around the various stones, and some of them are animal-made, not human, for they continue beneath the undergrowth that has encroached on the little graveyard over the passing years. There are several old stones, difficult to read, and there was, until just a few years ago, a faded old wooden marker that said "An Indian – 1884." That's all. Just "An Indian – 1884."

Local historian Barb Paterson, who has retired to a year-round cottage nearby, has long been fascinated with the little graveyard. The Indian, she believes, was an old man who camped each summer along the nearby Big East River, died one summer, and was buried here because no one knew where he came from or whether he had family. No one thought to inscribe his name on the little cross. One woman, an area cottager, has kept the little grave cleared for years and, at times, has even strung beads from the cross in his memory. A new wooden cross has recently been erected over the site.

Barb Paterson says that Mizpah was but one of several now-lost communities in the area with biblical names: Antioch, on the shores of Bella Lake, was named after the city in ancient Phrygia, now part of Turkey; Bethany, after the town on the southeastern slope of the Mount of Olives, near Jerusalem; Mount Horeb, where Moses received the stone tablets containing the Ten Commandments. All, Paterson says, were founded by the Methodist New Connection, a fundamentalist breakaway group of Methodists that believed in spreading the word through the establishment of circuit missions. They built small communities and always a church but failed to realize they would need some sustenance beyond prayer. The farms failed; the families, even the most determined, gave up and moved on. Paterson has traced the families of Mizpah to Michigan, to northwestern Ontario, and to Manitoba; only a handful of the original settlers stayed on, and none at all on the original homesteads, which now amount to a few stone fences lost in the tangle around this little cemetery on the hill.

There are few details on Mizpah at the nearest library, in the town of Huntsville. The township, Sinclair, was surveyed in 1876, and almost immediately a group of related Methodist families arrived from Durham and Victoria counties in the more settled parts of Ontario. A school went up on land belonging to William Nelson – a stern-looking man with a high forehead, a full beard, and the eyes of the true believer – and the area became known as "Nelson's Appointment." They began collecting contributions from Methodist churches throughout Ontario, and on January 5, 1896, a small frame church, "Mizpah," was dedicated, with not one, but *two* long sermons delivered by the Rev. J. E. Wilson of Huntsville, with outside temperatures plunging to thirty degrees below zero.

According to the *Christian Guardian*, which reported on Reverend Wilson's "two impressive sermons" and the frigid temperature, the building was "a neat frame structure, nicely finished, both inside and out, and although in this new district the people are not overburdened in wealth of pocket, they have abundant wealth of spirit, so that willing hands and hearts were ever ready to help with the good work."

Five years later, however, the great promise of the Mizpah community was already dissipating. The *Huntsville Forester* of September 6, 1901, reported: "Mizpah appointment is growing small by degrees. . . . The congregation was greatly thinned by the departure of the Hart, Hammell and Nolan families, and about a fortnight ago Mr. Tunis Hart left on the harvest train. Surely some others will march e're long to fill the gaped rank and snatch the fallen banner up."

The little Mizpah church was closed in 1907, spent another twenty years being used by passing hunters and loggers for shelter, and then, in the early 1930s, was dismantled and moved down the road, where it became the Limberlost School and was used by area families until 1945, when the local school board decided to start busing the local children to the larger Huntsville schools. Shortly thereafter, the once-church, once-school was turned into a private cottage, and all that remained of Nelson's Appointment, or Mizpah, was the little cemetery on the side of the hill next to the dump.

A half century ago Mabel Brook of Billy Bear Lodge began cleaning up the little graveyard, and others, like Barb Paterson, have continued the work. A few years back, a handful of locals dedicated to the preservation of the area history erected a simple sign between the dump and the cemetery:

> Here lies some of the stout pioneers of this community who carved their homes and their lands from the forests.
> Here lies Alvin Hart (1866) and his family, McGineses, Neilsons, Halls and An Unknown Indian with a Blanket for a Shroud.
> Brave men, dauntless women and little children who "Builded better than they knew."
> Tread softly, and give thanks for this is hallowed ground.
> Therefore was the place called "Mizpah." For he said, "The Lord watch between me and thee when we are absent one from another."

I do not know which phrase I like better: "Builded better than they knew" or, simply, "Tread softly." Certainly, nothing they built remains in its original form. What buildings did not get swallowed back up in the surrounding wilderness became, like the church, twisted into hunt camps and even cottages, eventually unrecognizable through years of additions and renovations. I doubt very much that's what is meant by "builded better than they knew." Had they known, perhaps they wouldn't have bothered.

Tread softly I do. It is such a beautiful spot, the hardwood forest dropping down that steep slope to a creek filled with water lilies and green arrowheads, the water so clear that you can stand on the road and watch minnows dart among the stalks of the green, green plants. In early summer you can hear the creek rolling through the culvert; in late summer there are juicy blackberries growing in the ditches.

Once, I came for minnows and found a huge snapping turtle lying upside down in the fast water of the creek, a .22 rifle slug lodged in its shattered skull, but every other time has been a pleasant, rewarding experience, never complete without a quiet walk through the little cemetery to the last grave at the edge of the abutment, where the hill suddenly gives way to a view over the creek and the surrounding hills.

Here is little Thomas Alvin Hart's grave. He was all of three years and five months when he died on September 15, 1886. The stone is blackened and rough, but you can still make out the chiselled words if you take the time.

"We loved them in life – let us not forget them in death."

We do not forget, Thomas.

Your small grave at the end of the ridge is a constant reminder, for those who care to look, that things do not always work out.

The poet Tennyson once stood at this precise spot at 14–9–1–W2, near Moose Mountain in southeast Saskatchewan. Perhaps the sky was much as it is this late spring morning, overcast with a faint, almost imperceptible rain, the sun slicing through in golden shards to the west with the promise of the afternoon to come. Perhaps it was here that he was struck with that magnificent prairie line about how such skies seem God sent, "To tell the world it need not yet despair."

We are speaking, it must be admitted, of Bertram Tennyson, not Lord Alfred, the poet laureate of Victorian England. Bert Tennyson was the great man's nephew, who came out to nearby Moosemin when the flat prairie was still known as the North-West Territories of Canada, twenty years before Saskatchewan and Alberta were admitted to the Dominion as full provinces. The Canadian Tennyson came to Moosemin to practise law but ended up driving a stagecoach, which he much preferred as a way to earn a living. But even more than driving the stagecoach, he liked to play cricket and pass his evenings writing maudlin poetry. "A clever and amusing chap," a contemporary once said of Bert Tennyson, "but oh, so lazy!"

Bert Tennyson was, however, the ideal choice for poet laureate of Cannington Manor, the little piece of Victorian England that rose at 14–9–1–W2 in the final years of the nineteenth century. Cannington Manor was Capt. Edward Michell Pierce's ambitious scheme to bring British class structure to the bald, bleak Canadian prairie. Cannington Manor would have its cricket pitch, tennis courts, servants, valets, and fine dining; the landed gentry of Cannington Manor would stage original dramas and establish choral groups and paint and write and even ride to hounds. And Cannington Manor society would have its own Tennyson, its own poet laureate, who, in 1897, would reach the pinnacle of his publishing career when the *Moosemin Spectator* agreed to publish his opus *The Land of Napioa*.

It is still possible to find Cannington Manor, or at least its survey coordinates. Getting to it requires a long drive over gravel roads south of the Trans-Canada Highway and east off Highway 9, which runs through to the thriving farming community of Carlyle. It is an easy drive through rolling cattle-grazing country and low prairie bushland alongside the Moose Mountain Native reserve. There are government signs to bring you to this historical curiosity but few of the curious here, which is unfortunate, for there is much to be learned from Cannington Manor about escaping to Canada and what one might expect on arrival.

The morning rain has turned the paths to mud and left large puddles that spread out onto the freshly mown grass. There are magpies swooping in the trees and curious prairie dogs standing for a better look, but only one human visitor walking along in search of a world that flourished briefly more than a century ago and then, just as suddenly, ceased to exist. There are stones to indicate the outline of the hotel and the flour mill and the parsonage, and you can still find where Didsbury stood, the great stone house where the wealthy Beckton brothers lived and where they brought in two retired British soldiers whose main job was to drag the semi-conscious drunks out of the billiard room, get them into bed, and pull off their riding boots and have them polished up and ready in time for the morning hunt.

Some of the buildings still stand: a couple of houses, the blacksmith shop, the little church where for years they used an old British tennis trophy as a chalice. Some have vanished forever. Nowhere is there sign of the fancy stone structure the Beckton brothers ordered up to house the fighting cocks they imported one fall in the early 1890s. Neither is there any record of a cockfight ever being staged, for the birds all froze to death that first winter.

The little All Saints Anglican church is the best preserved of the few remaining buildings of Cannington Manor. Set back of a stately spruce stand with the wide Saskatchewan sky rolling above and behind it, the lovely church belongs in a postcard: grey-blue clapboard, Gothic windows, a tower, and a belfry, all seemingly in as good condition today as in the summer of 1885, when it was officially consecrated.

Here, too, is another cemetery, also small, but this one dominated by a huge grey stone in the very centre of the grounds, with a stone cross on the top. "Edward Michell Pierce," the marker reads, "born Merriott Somerset England, 27 March 1832, Died 20 June 1888."

Poor man, he would have died believing he had actually carried it off.

Capt. Edward Michell Pierce – always known as Michell Pierce – came from a distinguished and privileged family, with a family arms dating back to 1560. A Pierce had been Keeper of the Wardrobe for Queen Elizabeth I, and the Michells, on the captain's mother's side, were wealthy and upper class too. Michell Pierce had been a captain in the British yeomanry. He was a tall, heavy, and urbane man with an imperial bearing and an abiding passion to make it big in the world. He might have, too, had he only adhered to the conservative bent of his forefathers, but Pierce was also a dreamer with an unquenchable conviction that things would work out in his favour. It made him rash, as when he took his small fortune and invested it in a merchant ship, only to have the ship sink on its maiden voyage. Undaunted, he turned his sights on a new plan, just as grandiose, but one that was landlocked and would, he hoped, involve other people's money.

Michell Pierce was fifty years old when he decided to emigrate to Canada. He was almost bankrupt and had heavy responsibilities, including a wife, Lydia, and eight children. Yet he remained resolute that leaving England for Canada was the right thing to do for his family. He would find land and establish a community where he would, in essence, serve as squire, if not lord, and bring ambitious young men of good British stock and means over to Canada to train them in the art of farming. A handsome fee, of course, would be charged back to his students' wealthy relatives in England. Later, he would establish the young men he had trained on land around a community that he himself would design and control. A little bit of England in the colonies.

According to Ruth Humphrys, descendant of a Cannington Manor family who years ago wrote several articles on the venture in *The Beaver*, Michell Pierce and his son Harvey set out first from England in 1882 and were later that year joined by the rest of the family in Toronto, where they took over a large house and began planning in earnest. Son Duncan was sent west to find suitable land – fertile, plentiful, and, if possible, free – while the captain set about making the social and political contacts he felt might one day prove useful to him in his new life in the colonies.

Duncan found land to his liking forty miles south of Moosemin and sent word back to Toronto. The captain set out to see for himself, astonishing the early settlers of the area with his eccentric travelling style. Before Michell Pierce settled down each night, his "man" would ask him in which direction he wished his head to lay and then carefully roll out and prepare the bedding for his master.

Michell Pierce liked what he saw when he got to Duncan's chosen spot. We have no idea what he thought about the landscape, but we know only too well the sensation of overwhelming expansiveness one feels on the prairies. "Geology stripped bare," Saskatchewan writer Sharon Butala called it in *The Perfection of the Morning*, "leaving behind only a vast sky and land stretched out in long, sweeping lines that blend into the distant horizon with a line that is sometimes so clear and sharp it is surreal, and sometimes exists on the edge of metaphysics, oscillating in heat waves or, summer or winter, blending into mirages and the realm of dreams and visions which wavers just the other side of the horizon. The Great Plains are a land for visionaries, they induce visions, they are themselves visions, the line between fact and dream is so blurred. What other landscape around the world produces the mystic psyche so powerfully? Sky and land, that is all, and grass, and what Nature leaves bare the human psyche fills."

The captain, of course, was already filling this endless space with his vision of a proper Victorian village that he would build, populate with his chosen, and totally control. He determined to acquire the

land, only to discover that this magnificent landscape had been with-
drawn for settlement by the government, which wished to turn it
over to the Natives in the area as part of a reserve. The captain took
the first train back east, vowing to fix things up in Ottawa so he could
have the land he and Duncan thought more suitable for the cultured
and educated British than the wild and uneducated Natives of this
Commonwealth outpost.

Michell Pierce wasted little time. The connections he had cultivated
in Toronto soon had him walking into the office of the prime minister, Sir John A. Macdonald, where he was received graciously and
where Macdonald, himself British-born and a great believer in Queen
and Empire, readily agreed to the wisdom of this scheme to recruit
young "gentlemen of means" and bring a little British civilization to a
region quickly opening up to the poor and desperate of Europe.

These were times of great ambition for the vast Canadian prairie.
The potential seemed enormous, and the rest of the world appeared
eager, often desperate, to follow Macdonald's railroad to the promised
land of the Canadian West. Many believed that the population explosion would be unlike anything ever before witnessed in North
America. In an 1887 address to the Canadian Club of New York City
on "The Future of the Dominion of Canada," promoter Edmund
Collins said, "Alone, the valley of the Saskatchewan, according to
scientific computation, is capable of sustaining 800,000,000 souls."
So, too, one might as well argue, is the head of a pin – but, nonethe-
less, Collins's wild prediction gives some sense of the enthusiasm felt
for the opening of the Canadian West. Macdonald might have been
open to any suggestion that would ensure a small stake of British "civilization" in such an unpredictable development.

Macdonald acted decisively, ordering that rights to the designated
land – five full townships located on 14–9–1–W North-West
Territories – be made available for a single day during which, coincidentally, one application alone would be received for the vast tract of
land and, again coincidentally, duly awarded. Years later, Michell
Pierce would claim he also walked out of the prime minister's office
with the promise that the Canadian Pacific Railway, Macdonald's

great National Dream, would be coming directly through the property, but that is the story of the end of Cannington Manor and we are still only at the beginning.

According to Humphrys, the Pierces left Toronto under a pall, having just lost their second daughter, Annie, to typhoid fever. Michell Pierce established his wife and daughters in Winnipeg before winter set in, and the men of the family set out for Assiniboia, where the first task would be to build a house large enough to hold them all. With hired help, they soon had a sort of "double" house completed to the point of habitability, the two separate structures joined by a long hall, which they boarded and chinked to keep out the wind and the frost. The family came out in January, bringing everything they owned, including a piano, dinner jackets, fancy linens, and a couple of maids. They travelled in cold so bitter they had to rub oil of capsicum on their feet to prevent frostbite. The peculiar winter travellers had trouble crossing the two branches of Pipestone Creek, but made it on the third day and crammed happily into the joined houses to warm up and adjust to the shock of the prairie winter.

"It was all such a change from our luxurious life in England," daughter Lily wrote in her diary. "But we were young and full of life, had the great joy of being all together, and everything seemed a joke, and so we were very happy."

Everything seemed a joke. There was, to be sure, a certain delight to be found in the enormous challenge that lay before them. Beyond the house lay the elements, the howling winter winds and storms that could blow for days, at times obliterating the landscape beyond the rattling, ice-encrusted windows. Inside the house they had to learn new survival techniques. They had hired help, but hardly as they'd had in England. The girls had to learn how to cook and prepare food, how to launder clothes, and even how to starch the men's shirts. They were, fortunately, a completely Victorian family, where to complain about anything was considered bad form. Hard work would overcome any obstacle, even this.

Michell Pierce had his own concerns. He laid out his village by walking out the streets and the various buildings, deciding where a hotel, a church, and the school would stand. He named it "Cannington," after a community in Somerset, England, not aware that there was already a Cannington in Ontario, not far from Peterborough, where Susanna Moodie had first settled. When Ottawa requested something be done to distinguish the two, Michell Pierce added "Manor," and very shortly he began taking out newspaper advertisements back home looking for "people of education and good background" to come out and join in the remarkable experiment at Cannington Manor.

Michell Pierce was appealing to families of wealth with young men, usually second and third sons, who were not in line to inherit family estates or were in trouble or just plain lazy. "Young men with a little capital looking about for something to do," as Michell Pierce put it in his advertisements, "I especially counsel to join their countrymen here. They should, however, before launching into business on their own accord, place themselves with an English gentleman settler abroad for a time, and acquire a thorough and practical knowledge of farming generally, as peculiar to this country, the old world style being of little or no avail in the Great Northwest. This is an English colony, English manners and customs being rigidly adhered to. I shall take pleasure in providing the fullest information and advice, and will secure land and locate young men, if they will correspond with me."

The promise held great appeal to families with youngsters "looking about for something to do" and enough money to do something about it. For a mere one hundred pounds a year, Capt. Michell Pierce would set the young men up with room and board and establish an "agricultural college" to teach them how to farm in the New World. These selected "remittance men," as the advertisements promised, would soon be able to "lead and enjoy an old English squire's existence of a century ago."

Michell Pierce's ambitions went considerably beyond offering some avenue of escape for privileged families with problem sons. He saw Cannington Manor developing as a community that would be totally self-contained, prosperous because of British investment and British know-how, and ever-expanding with the arrival of more and more of the right stock and education. He saw himself and Lydia presiding over the community like benevolent rulers. Lydia even brought along her own silver-mounted horn goblet for the wine that would pour during village celebrations.

Almost immediately the immigrants began arriving. They came in small numbers but with great enthusiasm, and soon Cannington Manor could boast a growing population of educated young men and women who would make this a community quite unlike any other in Canada. As the buildings went up – eventually there would be fifteen structures on the Pierce homestead, ranging from the hotel to various "bachelors' cabins" – so, too, did a social structure emerge under the watchful eye of the Michell Pierces. The musicians among them formed a band, the singers a choir capable of putting on a thirty-voice oratorio. They formed a glee club, a reading group, a theatre group, and a painting group that produced surprisingly accomplished work. Inglis Sheldon-Williams, who would go on to become a War Commissions artist during the First World War, came out of Cannington Manor. They even had a village photographer, and, of course, whenever Bert Tennyson could arrange to drive the stage down from Moosemin, they had their poet laureate. They held their Hunt Ball in the schoolhouse, formal dress required, and it was considered the social event of the year for those the struggling locals derisively referred to as "The Drawing Room Farmers."

The young Englishmen who came to Cannington Manor were healthy and boisterous and were used to lives of leisure. They applied themselves only loosely to their agricultural "studies" under Michell Pierce, but applied themselves fiercely to outdoor pursuits. Pierce laid out a cricket pitch, and they played regularly. They raised thorough-bred horses and built a fancy track to race on. They formed a rugby club that they toured about the territories. They built tennis courts. They brought in riding horses – including side saddles for the women – and rode to hounds, even importing the hounds from the Isle of Wight to hunt down the quick, but now endangered, swift fox.

There are still vestiges of this life to be seen. The fox tails from long-ago hunts are on display. The bachelors' cabins demonstrate that even the young men who lived off on their own had a genteel side, with family photographs and fine china on the mantel. The men had white breeches for riding, shooting jackets for the hunt, caps, and horns. They played billiards and read the latest books and engaged in long political debate at the blacksmith shop during the daylight hours and, in the evenings, at the eight-room Mitre Hotel, with its elegant smoking room and handy bar. A young English solicitor, Lloyd George, came through town at one point, and was supposedly outraged when the barman, a local, turned to spit tobacco juice into a nearby spittoon while serving the future prime minister of Great Britain his evening meal.

In 1890, at the peak of Cannington Manor's odd existence, the village football club went to Winnipeg to play against the best team in the city. The Cannington team picked up the best of the Moosemin players, travelled to Winnipeg, played its game (no score is recorded), and then moved on to the Opera House to watch a performance by Mrs. Abernathy, a well-known hypnotist. The players had obviously been celebrating, so we will presume they had been victorious. They arrived loud and obnoxious and stayed loud and obnoxious, shouting out during the performance and howling with laughter until poor Mrs. Abernathy was all but reduced to tears on the stage. Unfortunately for the Cannington Manor side, the Winnipeg police chief happened to be in the crowd, lost his patience with the wealthy layabouts, and called in reinforcements, causing a huge brawl that resulted in the team spending the night in jail.

The *Winnipeg Free Press* seemed of two minds about the incident. On the one hand, the paper lectured the troublemakers. "The young men," the story reported, "judging by their dress and appearance, certainly knew better than to act as they did." On the other hand, the paper also felt obliged to point out that the brawl "scored an even bigger hit than Mrs. Abernathy's wonderful performance."

While the young men – who came to be known as "the Captain's Pups" – turned their attention to play, Michell Pierce had to concentrate on business. With three partners (H. Bird, R. Bird, and E. N. Maltby), he formed the Moose Mountain Trading Company and opened up a grocery store. They would eventually build and own the entire village,

school and church excepted. They put up well-constructed homes –
at one point most of the Cannington Manor residences could boast
pianos, one a grand piano. The Pierce home, of course, was largest and
fanciest of all, known throughout the area by its Native name, *Gitchee
Wa-Teepee* (Great White House). They built a cheese factory and a
pork-processing plant, then a second cheese factory. They built a grist
mill and hired a brilliant miller in Harold Fripp, who developed
"Snowdrop" flour, which took the gold medal at the 1893 Chicago
World's Fair.

Pierce himself had no interest in farming, despite his claim to run
an advanced agricultural college. Instead, he saw himself as such a
leader of men that his talents might better be spread beyond
Cannington Manor. He wrote a letter to a friend in Ottawa claiming
it was now "the universal desire" of the district that Pierce be sent to
Parliament as soon as the districts were incorporated. "There is a pile
of work to be done here," he continued, "of which I am more fitted to
undertake than grubbing up the land around me for grain growing."

Michell Pierce managed to attract some established Brits as well as
the "Pups" to come to his growing "agricultural" community. James
Humphrys, a well-off marine architect and ancestor of author Ruth
Humphrys, chose to retire there, built a lovely home, and took over
direction of the choral group. Henry Hanson, a banker from
Constantinople, came and freely offered his international financial
advice. Dr. John George Hardy gave up a large practice in England and
left the life of a wealthy country squire in the hopes that the clear, crisp
air of Canada might cure his asthma. He soon became the most
renowned surgeon of the Territories and also served as justice of the
peace, though little was required apart from enforcing the law from
time to time on the nearby reserve.

"We had a very fine class of people in and around Cannington,"
North-West Mounted Police Sergeant Geoghegan reported after his
arrival in 1888, "although a number of them were not fit for what they
came out to do – farming – which they did in a haphazard way. Most
of them had a remittance, a jolly good time, a pack of hounds – and
to hang with the farm."

The most intriguing of all the young men Michell Pierce attracted to Cannington Manor were the three Beckton brothers, Ernest, Billy, and Bertie, who were all wealthy, good-looking, blond, and, it appears, somewhat arrogant, bragging that their family tree went back to the thirteenth century and that they were pure Saxon, free of the evils of either Irish or Scottish blood.

The older two Becktons were sent out by their families when Ernest was nineteen and William eighteen. Their maternal grandfather, who had made his fortune in cotton and was a former mayor of Manchester, thought the boys lacked purpose and liked what he read in Michell Pierce's advertisement in the local *Guardian*. The boys took to life at Cannington Manor instantly and, in 1887, when their grandfather died, they returned to collect their portion of the family fortune and also their younger brother, Herbert, who had just turned nineteen.

Now there were three Becktons, all with money, and they set about becoming the heart of this curious community – particularly after Michell Pierce, who had been growing increasingly ill, died of a massive stroke on the last day of spring 1888. So free were the Becktons with their money that neighbouring farmers found it more profitable to ignore their own land and go to work for the brothers, building their stables and outbuildings and, eventually, taking on the task of constructing the massive stone edifice that the brothers would call Didsbury, after their ancestral home in Manchester.

It is difficult to blame the farmers for quitting their own land for this work. The Becktons usually paid in English sovereigns, which were much prized in the Territories. Michell Pierce would have approved, for British currency often seemed the common coin in the little "English" village. There is even a tale told of Major Phipps's young daughter, whose godmother was Victoria herself, receiving from the queen a birthday gift of a ten-pound cheque in the mail. When she took her godmother's generous gift to the Moosemin bank to cash, the paper was pushed back at her by a wide-eyed clerk who said, "Next you'll expect me to believe the old lady is here herself." She was not, of course, but Victoria's spirit was everywhere.

The Becktons' stone home was completed in 1899 and featured twenty rooms, but even that was not enough for the society-loving brothers, who later added a bachelor wing of five bedrooms with its own separate entrance. They put in a magnificent billiard table and brought over two retired soldiers to serve as valets. For the remaining years of Cannington Manor, Didsbury would be its centre.

The brothers dreamed of becoming horse breeders and so established "The Didsbury Stock Farm" – known to the locals as "The Ranch" – as a breeding operation intended to make them famous throughout the world. Both the house and the barn were built of a beautiful grey-blue granite. They outfitted the stables in mahogany and brass, which they insisted be polished daily. A brass nameplate was set above each horse's stall. They brought in a renowned groom from Lord Yarborough's stud farm back in England and ordered that their horses be kept in "show condition" at all times. The brothers even built their own steeplechase course and held an annual "Race Week," sending out invitations far and wide and triumphing when French counts Rousignac and Jumiac, both living near the village of Whitewood, came by four-in-hand coach, footmen in livery, tall hats, and cockades. The brothers thought they had another sure attraction with their games house, but the grand scheme of staging cockfights for the wealthy aficionados was abandoned, as we already know, when winter showed the imported cocks who was the only sure winner in this country.

Ernest Beckton married Michell Pierce's daughter Jessie in the fall of 1889, and they were soon the premier couple of Cannington Manor. Ernest even had his master craftsmen build a special cart for Jessie that could be hauled about by dogs as she conducted her royal tours of the little village. She loved it. She called her new home Aladdin's Palace and wrote, "I had nothing to do but to enjoy my liberty from the monotonous chores, my pretty rooms, books, and unrestricted leisure."

It was not the same for everyone. The summers were irrepressibly hot for those used to the more temperate climate of England; winters were often unspeakable, keeping residents housebound for days at a time, and from time to time dangerous. Ashton Lyons, one of the young remittance men, was lost in a vicious storm. Frederick Robert, who was warden of the little Anglican church and the son of a well-known canon back in England, died trying to make his way in a sudden, blinding blizzard.

Eventually, the British stiff upper lip began to tremble. The land was far too harsh for such genteel living. The Becktons' dream of becoming world-class breeders foundered largely through isolation; they produced plate winners, but few farther east than Winnipeg knew of the ranch. The servants kept quitting, the maids eager to marry local farmers and begin raising their own families, the male servants keen to take up their own land or, perhaps, just keen to get away from the insufferable "Pups" and their indolent lifestyle.

It all began to fall apart in 1896, when William Beckton went back to England and returned with a bride in tow. She could not bear it in the colonies, begged to go home, and, within the year, had persuaded William to return to Manchester. "For another year the other brothers carried on as before," Jessie Beckton later wrote, "but a broken atmosphere and divided interest brought about the inevitable break. We too went home." It was 1897; Didsbury, the social centre, was boarded up.

The pork-packing plant had closed down, the cheese factories failed. The residents were older, sicker, and dying, and the easy layabout lifestyle had lost its charm. People died in the harsh winter, buildings burned to the ground, crops sometimes failed completely. In winter they had chilblains and frostbite to worry about, but winter seemed a blessing compared to the mosquitoes and no-see-ums that swarmed in the spring and early summer.

Despite the Victorian middle-class trappings and the bravado, conditions in Cannington Manor were tough, if not impossible. In 1900 the dream broke entirely on the announcement that the railway Michell Pierce had always promised was not going through Cannington Manor but some ten miles to the south. There was drought, low grain prices, tough winters, and increasing disenchantment. Some of the young men wandered off to fight with the British forces in South Africa, several headed for the Klondike, where there was word of gold. Some families left for British Columbia, where the climate was said to be so much more agreeable.

In a way it was just as well Michell Pierce had died a dozen years earlier. Even his own offspring were abandoning the grand dream. His sons Harvey and Jack left to seek their own fortunes in the Klondike, and as their sister Lily later sadly noted, "We never saw them again."

By 1905, the year the territory became the province of Saskatchewan, Cannington Manor had turned into a ghost town.

Today, the few remaining buildings, the church, and the cemetery have been declared a provincial heritage site, the village sparkling with life on my visit only when the sun breaks through at the end of the late spring rain.

The new light picks out the grave numbers surrounding Capt. Edward Michell Pierce's final resting place, one simple stone speaking for Michell Pierce's grand dream as well as for those who followed it here:

"Just asleep."

My father wanted to visit another old cemetery. He had come to Ottawa for one of his infrequent visits, and my brother Tom and I had decided to take him for a long Sunday afternoon drive up into those parts of the Valley where his people, our people, had first come when they fled the Scottish highlands and Irish potato famines and Canada seemed like the only escape possible.

He was already well into his eighties by then. He had to use a cane, his bad leg the result of a logging truck that had skidded on an icy hill at the mill where he worked, slammed into him, and crushed his hip and pelvis and finally forced his retirement at age seventy-three. He still chain smoked Players tobacco roll-your-owns, still drank to excess if we let him, still preferred his toast burnt and so much salt and pepper on his meals people sitting three seats over would start to sneeze, but he got around because he wanted to, and was as sharp this day as any day of his life, including the very last one.

He wanted to see Burnstown, the little village along the banks of the Madawaska River where his people had come thinking they would farm and ended up, like so many others, abandoning the land to the bush. He wanted to see White Lake, where a branch of the family lived, and where, sometme around 1924, he figured, he had come one day to bury an uncle.

We found the White Lake cemetery by asking at the general store and then turning right just as we passed the rundown garage with the flaking Canada Dry sign, the pavement running out immediately. We drove out along a gravel road under a hot September sun, the dust rising like a mustard rooster tail behind our back bumper as we passed by rock fences and abandoned fields and grazing cattle. He was nodding by the time we reached the gate, as if 1924 were somehow opening up again and the horse-drawn hearse would be waiting under the shade of the high, faintly blushing maples, waiting for the graveside service to end.

We walked up the gentle rise from the road and entered the cemetery at the high end. A jersey cow stared from just the other side of the fence. There were crows in the trees loudly berating this invasion, the three of us, one hobbling, slowly making our way down toward the old end, where the broken and faded stones lay about.

He knew exactly where he was going. The ground was heavy with grass and rutted from runoff, but he picked his way down through the ages and arrived just opposite a dark red stone, where he stopped, pointed his cane, and announced that we were there. I stood staring at the final date on the stone, 1924, thinking not of the old man who'd been laid in the grave but of the young man who'd been a pallbearer that fall day. My father would have just turned seventeen, younger than any of our own children are today, and he would have been thinking, surely, how he was a man this day, doing a man's duty. He would have seen himself so differently then – about to leave high school forever, about to look for work in the bush – but in no way could he have imagined himself a broken old man, hobbling back here with a cane and two sons, who, to a seventeen-year-old, were now old men themselves.

He was not, however, in any mood to feel sorry for himself. He was struck not with the quick passing of time, but the length of time. Here was where he had stood in 1924, and, by God, he was still standing here now, when all the rest of them who'd gathered here that day were gone. He talked about the family and the history, so little of it known, and how the people here had come to this part of the country thinking they were escaping something for good when, in fact, it turned out worse than ever for many of them.

He took Tom and me up into the northwest corner of the little cemetery and showed us a grave that for decades went unmarked but was known all the same to all around. Now there was a marker, a small dark stone placed by the local historical society, that identified the grave as belonging to "Granny" Fisher and her child, Allan Dhu, who was listed on the polished marker as the "Son of Chief MacNab."

Archibald, the thirteenth Laird MacNab, also had a vision for this huge, unsettled country, which in some ways was similar to that of Capt. Edward Michell Pierce. What MacNab wanted to do when he arrived in Canada in 1823 was recreate a highland "clan" system in the colony and use it to restore the inherited fortune he had frittered away by good living and hard drinking. In Upper Canada, he saw not only an escape from his many debtors but also an opportunity to restore his name and title to the grandeur he believed the MacNab clan chiefs had enjoyed for centuries. As he said in a letter home to Scotland that year, "I will not rest content until I see around me my people . . . under the control of their own Chief."

His method was simple. A huge man of impressive bearing and possessed of a title, the laird first beguiled the socialites and politicians of Montreal so thoroughly they threw him a huge "testimonial" dinner and helped him make the necessary contacts to locate and gain control of suitable lands. Through an influential Montreal bishop, he was able to arrange in late 1823 for a special land grant of 81,000 acres, an entire township, near where the small Madawaska River empties into the Ottawa. Only one government official, apparently, expressed any concern over MacNab's plans to charge "rent" to his settlers, but no one else in authority seemed the slightest concerned that he had any but the best and purest intentions. The government was eager for settlers, and MacNab had promised to deliver in exchange for this extraordinary land grant.

The following year he visited his land and began preparations while contacts back in Scotland recruited potential settlers from the area he had departed from nearly as broke as they were. On April 19, 1825, eighty-four Scottish emigrants left for the colony. They arrived in Montreal more than a month later and were met by MacNab, towering nearly seven feet tall with his clan bonnet and three feathers, accompanied by pipers, and treated to a long and drunken highland party. They believed they had reached paradise.

MacNab painted a glorious picture of the fertile farmland he had already selected for them, of the wide and bountiful Ottawa and the lovely Madawaska, along which much of his land grant lay. His pitch seemed heartfelt and generous, but it also came with its own special twist: though most were illiterate and had no comprehension of contracts, each settler would be signing his name to a paper that, in effect, vowed total allegiance to the overbearing laird. The contracts essentially placed MacNab in control of their lives and property and even appeared to bind settler families to him for generations to come.

It was, in a word, serfdom.

It is a tribute to MacNab's powers of persuasion that the Canadian government not only permitted these unusual conditions but encouraged MacNab to recruit more and more of the poor and desperate being "cleared" from the highlands. His "constitution," largely made up as he went along, made him magistrate and priest, the one who performed marriage ceremonies and baptisms, the one who handed out and collected fines, the one who, alone, could decide who went to jail and for how long and for what crime (daring to step outside the township boundaries was one). They were free to clear the land and farm, so long as they paid their dues to the laird, and he, of course, would own and control all resources, timber being the most significant.

"This land," he once declared, "is mine and all the people on it!"

By 1830 he had more than sixty Scottish families signed up and on his land, all committed to paying him so much a year in produce, even though some of the families were themselves reduced to subsisting on potatoes. It was, says a historical plaque unveiled several years ago, "believed to be the last successful feudal system in North America." But successful only to a degree. The laird was in charge and the settlers worked the land and paid their dues, but their resentment was so huge that eventually the people began to revolt. They complained that the land they were forced to work was unsuitable for any agriculture. Some wanted to go off and work in the woods, but they first needed the laird's permission. Some even questioned whether or not they owned their own land, which they had been led to believe they would. They turned to the courts for help against MacNab's tyranny, but his connections, particularly with the Family Compact, denied the settlers the justice they craved. Instead, he increasingly took them to court. He threw others he believed were challenging him in jail. He once even turned Catherine Fisher, his loyal housekeeper and the mother of his illegitimate son, out into the cold.

Catherine Fisher, known as "Granny" to all, came from unknown origins; she simply arrived with the laird after one of his drunken trips to Quebec City. According to Joan Finnigan's *Giants of the Ottawa Valley*, Granny could match MacNab "drink for drink and blow for blow." Her son, Allan Francis, apparently delighted the laird, whose wife, Margaret, left behind in Scotland to fare for herself, was said to have produced eight children before her husband's departure, none of whom survived infancy. Allan Francis was much less a delight to the locals, however, who dubbed him "Allan Dhu," "Black Allan." Though he was never charged for any crime, Black Allan was thought to be a rapist who preyed on local Native women. Some locals even maintained he had murdered several young women who had resisted his advances.

It soon became clear that MacNab was losing his grip on the settlers. When the Canadas briefly rebelled in 1837, he grandly offered up the services of "his clan and the MacNab Highlanders to march forward in defence of the country." He ordered his settlers to assemble in his presence and, once they had reluctantly gathered, shouted out for volunteers to step forward. Only two trembling settlers of the one hundred and fifty men standing before him moved, sending the laird into a furious rage. He could not induce any more to come forward.

MacNab's reputation was now preceding him. Despite the Highlanders' eagerness to escape their situation in Scotland, few were willing to join him in Upper Canada. Increasingly, he found it difficult to recruit new immigrants to satisfy the arrangement he had made with the government. Even the officials who had once been so happy to strike the deal with MacNab were now beginning to question the wisdom of their actions.

When a majority of the settlers petitioned the governor to look into their plight, the authorities of Upper Canada finally sent an investigator to the Madawaska River, and a report was eventually filed by the government land agent accusing MacNab of "wanton oppression and outrages on humanity."

"MacNab," the government investigator reported, "has conducted the affairs of the township in the worst possible manner for the interest of the settlers or the country; there is not a grist mill and many have to travel fourteen or sixteen miles to any mill, through roads which in any part of the country as long settled as MacNab Township would be deemed disgraceful."

The report went on to accuse MacNab of having "an arbitrary bearing and persecuting spirit, checking all enterprise, paralyzing the industry of the settlers." The laird, it suggested, "could not have followed a course more calculated to produce discontent and disaffection amongst a people. The devotion of the Scottish Highlanders to their Chief is too well known to permit it to be believed that an alienation such as has taken place between MacNab and his people could have happened unless their feelings were grossly outraged."

MacNab had enough political smarts to sense that he could not win this. He quietly approached the government in search of 9,000 pounds in return for his giving up all claims to the land and settlers. He went to Toronto to negotiate and settled for a mere 2,500 pounds. He remained convinced, however, that he would still be given his due by the courts, where he was seeking damages for defamation of his good character by the investigation.

It appeared for a while as if the settlers would exact frontier justice from the disgraced MacNab, at one meeting angrily shouting that they should go out and "seize him" and that "death is too good for the likes of him." But in the end, cooler heads prevailed, and they decided to wait to see what the Toronto courts would do.

The trial was a farce, with the settlers stating how they had been defrauded by the laird, and MacNab arguing in reply that his good character had been defamed by the investigation. The jury brought in a verdict that stated damages for his "loss of character" must be paid to MacNab, but set the amount at five pounds, a decision that made him the laughing stock of the city.

MacNab was also ordered to remove a sawmill he had illegally constructed on land he did not own and to dismantle a small dam he had constructed on nearby Waba Creek to drive a grist mill competitor out of business.

MacNab left his township in disgrace, lived a while in a cottage on the grounds of kinsman Sir Allan MacNab, who had constructed an ambitious castle in Hamilton. He continued his wild ways, drinking heavily and often disturbing the peace with his impromptu parades and bagpipe ceremonies. In 1843 he left Canada for good, returning to Scotland and the Orkney Islands, where he had come into a small estate.

By 1846, despite MacNab's absence, conditions had not much improved in his old holdings along the Madawaska. The missionary record of the Free Church of Scotland described the township as one of the "most destitute localities in Canada." The Highlanders who were still attempting to clear their land and scratch out a living "understand little else than Gaelic," the missionary record stated, and "vast numbers of people are in a deplorable state of ignorance, and all but wholly destitute of the means of grace."

As for the laird himself, little more is known. In 1859, having reduced his inheritance on the Orkneys to nothing, he retired to France on a small pension granted him by the wife he had left behind in Scotland. He died in France a year later, at the age of eighty-two.

It is hard to know what to say about this Scottish chief and his wild plan to escape to Canada, where unsuspecting, illiterate fellow countrymen could support him like a feudal lord. Perhaps our father said it best that September afternoon, standing at the foot of Granny Fisher's and Black Allan's graves in the little White Lake cemetery.

"*Tsk-tsk-tsk-tsk-tsk.*"

It is the middle of a late fall day, yet barely light enough to read the map as the rented car makes its uncertain way down a narrow paved road whose surface appears to have been papered, badly, by large, wet, brown and yellow maple leaves. Closer to the eastern coast of Vancouver Island, the fog is rolling in off the Strait of Georgia, making this side road into tiny Cedar-by-the-Sea simply vanish at times into thick, damp cloud.

It is hard to imagine it was here, or at least somewhere along this shrouded strip, that Edward Arthur Wilson came in the 1920s after having been struck with a heavenly "Invocation of Light." Somewhere along here, too, there should be Wilson's infamous Tree of Wisdom, but if it is here, it is concealing that intelligence among the hundreds of sagging, shedding broad-leaf maples that line this part of the coast just south of Nanaimo.

This is where Wilson – by then calling himself Brother Twelve – planned his City of Refuge. And to the east over the water, out beyond the fog and the mist and the spitting rain of this typical November day, lie little DeCourcy Island and the long, thin island of Valdez, which runs just south of Gabriola, where the remainder of this story of misdirected escape took place.

And yet if the precise location is difficult to determine so long after the fact, that is nothing compared to tracking down the truth of this remarkable story. In many ways the tale of Brother Twelve and his City of Refuge is much as portrayed by Jack Hodgins in his brilliant novel *The Invention of the World*. Hodgins cast his tale around a bizarre religious leader and a cult called The Revelations Colony of

Truth, and near the end of the work Hodgins has a central character note, "His story has returned to the air, where I found it." It is in the air again, this fogbound day on the coast of the Strait of Georgia.

There was a time, however, back in the late 1920s and early 1930s, when a great many people believed, as Brother Twelve preached, that it was not only possible but wise to seek to build an impenetrable "Fortress to the Future" as a refuge from the evils of the world. The most horrific war in the history of the world had been followed by sickness that had wiped out millions more, and just as the 1920s produced its frivolous, carefree generation, it also produced a far more searching side that gave serious thought to the world as it was and the world as it could be.

Many embraced theosophy, the mystical movement founded in 1875 in New York City by Helena Petrova Blavatsky "to form the nucleus of a universal brotherhood of humanity, without distinction of race, creed, sex, caste or colour." She attracted followers from around the world, including the poets Aleister Crowley and William Butler Yeats, who were key members of the Order of the Golden Dawn, a legendary branch of the movement. The Theosophical Society embraced belief in the "Universal Soul" of Buddhism and Hinduism but also included in its tenets world philosophy, science, and a discretionary amalgamation of the best of the world's religions.

It was what is now commonly referred to as "New Age" thinking, decades before Shirley MacLaine was even born – or, as she may prefer, *reborn*. Brother Twelve, in fact, claimed to represent "the first Trumpet-blast of the New Age."

There had been Canadian branches of the society since 1891, when several highly educated and privileged Torontonians came together and began calling themselves theosophists. That first group would include Dr. Emily Stowe, Canada's first woman doctor, newspaper editor Albert Smythe, and, later, Smythe's son, Conn, who would become famous as the owner of the Toronto Maple Leafs and remain a practising theosophist throughout his life. Other well-known Canadian members around the time of Brother Twelve's rise on the West Coast included the likes of painter Lawren Harris and other members of the Group of Seven, as well as the critic William Arthur Deacon.

It was not just Canadians who were entranced by Brother Twelve and came to the City of Refuge. Some were British but most were Americans – often rich, searching women who were seduced by the hypnotic Wilson, a feral-looking little creature, barely five-foot-six, with bright, hypnotic eyes, a Lenin goatee, and, long before Pierre Trudeau came along, a fresh rose each day in his lapel.

He was once described by a follower as a "little brown leaf of a man," but it would be wrong to presume he was without substance. Among those who came to sit and listen beneath the moss-covered maple he called the Tree of Wisdom were Robert England, who had been a United States Treasury agent; James J. Lippincott of the famous New York publishing house that bore his name; Maurice Von Platen, a Chicago lumber baron; Ohio publisher Joseph Benner; and Will Levington Comfort, a popular American novelist. Intelligent, successful middle-aged men, they seemed not the slightest put off by the vanity of a little man who could claim, "As Mercury dwelleth near the Sun, so I abide in the heart of the Lord. My feet run upon his errands, and by my mouth are His words spoken."

The story of Brother Twelve is well known on Vancouver Island and has been told, in various forms, by the likes of Pierre Berton, Howard O'Hagan, and John Robert Colombo. The best account is a book-length treatment by Vancouver journalist John Oliphant, *Brother Twelve: The Incredible Story of Canada's False Prophet.* It remains, however, a story the locals have never embraced and, in fact, appear to dislike.

Jack Hodgins discovered this almost immediately when he happened to come across vestiges of the tale in the 1970s, when the then-unpublished novelist was teaching high-school English in nearby Nanaimo. A student lived in Cedars-by-the-Sea and claimed to have one of Brother Twelve's gold vaults in the family basement. Hodgins thought there was a superb non-fiction book to be had in this true, and truly remarkable, tale.

"Once I started doing research," says the award-winning author, "I quickly discovered that people don't want to talk about it – not even now, after all these years."

There is, admittedly, some sensitivity toward *any* such discussion in British Columbia, for no part of Canada has attracted as many idealistic, and sometimes ideological, escapees as has the West Coast. Journalist Andrew Scott, the author of *The Promise of Paradise: Utopian Communities in B.C.*, analyzed 150 years of alternative settlements in his province and eventually came to the conclusion that much of it was predictable. British Columbia, after all, was the last truly hospitable place on the planet to be colonized by the Europeans.

"To the European mind," Scott wrote, "the province was a vast empty space on the map, a blank slate where any number of ambitious schemes might take root and flower. The age of exploration – at least for the temperate regions – ended here."

Even so, it is still somewhat surprising that any British theosophists would find their way to Canada, considering Aleister Crowley's impressions of the new country following the contrary poet's 1906 tour. "Vancouver," Crowley wrote in his autobiography, "presents no interest to the casual visitor. It is severely Scotch. Its beauties lie in its surroundings.

"I was very disappointed with the Rockies, of which I had heard such eloquent ecomiums. They are singularly shapeless; and their proportions are unpleasing. There is too much colourless and brutal base; too little snowy shapely summit. As for the ghastly monotony of the wilderness beyond them, through Calgary and Winnipeg right on to Toronto – words fortunately fail."

Even so, it was to British Columbia that so many came in search of Utopia. Anglican missionary William Duncan came to Vancouver Island in 1862 to build his isolated coastal village, where he believed he could keep the native Tsimshian people far removed from the alcohol and violence of most trading posts, and where he succeeded in doing so for many years. Here is where so many Scandinavian settlements – Swedish, Finnish, Danish – sprang to life in the hopes of promoting high morality and pious belief in communities that tended to flourish briefly and then vanish. And here, of course, is where the Doukhobors came to escape oppression, having left Russia in 1898–99 to gain religious freedom and, three years later, abandoning homesteads in what would soon become Saskatchewan to escape government interference. In British Columbia they found relative peace, with the significant exception of the radical Sons of Freedom sect, which still periodically turns to arson and nudity to protest interference from the secular world.

None, however, of the scores of various "paradises" founded in British Columbia ever drew as much attention as Brother Twelve's City of Refuge, and yet there is not even a mention of it in a tour of the quaint museum in nearby Nanaimo. The museum did mount a temporary exhibition a few years back with the relatively few surviving artifacts – a "No Trespassing" sign among them – but today there is only a thin booklet in the museum gift shop to tell visitors of the area's most famous, or infamous, resident.

"There are a lot of people from around here who will not talk about it," says Rick Slingerland of the museum. "There are old grievances that persist to this day concerning Brother Twelve."

That such grievances should persist for three-quarters of a century is astonishing, but then so, too, is the tale of Edward Arthur Wilson. He was, apparently, born in England around 1878, though others claim he was born in Wyoming, Ontario, to a strict church family that banished him when at fifteen years of age he impregnated a local girl. Some accounts have him born Julian Churton Skottowe, son of a pious church missionary and an exotic East Indian princess, while another has him born as Skottowe and then changing his name to Wilson when he went to work for the Dominion Express Company in Calgary and, later, Victoria.

The confusion is understandable. There was, after all, even an "authoritative" biography of Wilson, *Canada's False Prophet*, published in 1967 by Simon & Schuster and purportedly written by his brother, Herbert Emmerson Wilson. This Wilson, the book flap maintained, was a Baptist minister and veteran of the Boer War, during which he had befriended Winston Churchill. Better references would be difficult to come by. Herbert Emmerson Wilson claimed that Edward had once operated as "Swami Siva" in New Orleans and had later headed for the South Seas to study the occult and sexual rites. The brother's account is, by far, the most exciting and tempting, but alas, the title is not the only place the word "false" can be used here. As John Robert Colombo much later discovered, the "authoritative" biography was in fact written by Thomas P. Kelley, a well-known Canadian writer of pulp fiction.

The authors of *The Brother XII: The Devil of DeCourcy Island*, Ron MacIsaac, Don Clark, and Charles Lillard, later traced death certificates to conclude that Brother Twelve was indeed Edward Arthur Wilson, born in Birmingham, England, on July 25, 1878, the son of Thomas Wilson and Sarah Ellen (nee Pearsal) Wilson, which strongly suggests there was no Indian princess involved in the birth. The authors of the slim volume, published in 1989, researched all the available writings on Wilson and concluded, rather aptly, that "everyone who's touched this story has mauled it in one way or another."

No matter where Wilson originated, however, it is clear that by the mid 1920s he was on Vancouver Island and going by the name of Brother Twelve. The name, he claimed, had been bestowed on him in a vision in which he was also given his assignment. He was to establish the City of Refuge on the island so that the great minds of the world might come and exist in harmony and safety, with no obligation but to think about how a world sinking under the weight of its own excesses might be bettered.

We have to presume that Wilson was, as advertised, a spellbinding speaker. Pierre Berton, for one, has dismissed the popular theosophy of the time as "gobbledygook," but it is surely significant that Wilson attracted so many well-educated middle-aged men, as well as those women who seemed to fall under his hypnotic spell. This is not, as it might at first appear, the story of an older man with evangelical talents attracting a following of the young and the naive and the gullible. He obviously had great intellectual attraction for many, and a number of wealthy people, particularly women, seemed only too eager to send him money for his grand scheme.

Naturally, the flood of money soon attracted local attention. Early on, Wilson's chauffeur-driven car seemed to be making almost daily trips from Cedar-by-the-Sea into Nanaimo so that Wilson, always immaculate and dapper in his suits despite the rustic nature of his new home, could make large deposits. His growing wealth was soon the talk of the island.

The devoted were arriving regularly, eager to give up their worldly possessions (to Wilson, of course) and move into the community, where they were expected to do all the physical labour and then be content simply to sit beneath Wilson's fanciful Tree of Wisdom and listen to the great man. At times he would read from his seminal work, *The Three Truths*, which enjoyed some international success and which revealed the story of the vision that began his strange quest.

"About 9:30 P.M., October 19, 1924," Brother Twelve wrote of an experience he claimed to have had in Italy, "I was not well and had gone to bed early. At this time, I wanted to get some milk to drink, so lighted the candle which stood on a small table at the side of my bed. Immediately after lighting it, I saw the Tau suspended in mid-air just beyond the end of my bed and at a height of eight or nine feet. I thought, that is strange, it must be some curious impression on the retina of the eye which I got by lighting the candle. I closed my eyes at once, and there was nothing there. I opened them and saw the Tau in the same place, but much more distinctly; it was like a soft golden fire, and it glowed with a beautiful radiance. This time, in addition to the Tau, there was a five-pointed star very slightly below it and a little to the right. Again I closed my eyes and there was nothing on the retina. Again I opened them and the Vision was still there, but now it seemed to radiate fire. I watched it for some time, then it gradually dimmed and faded slowly from my sight.

"The next day I made a note of the matter, and recorded my own understanding of it, which was as follows: 'The Tau confirmed the knowledge of the special path along which I travelled to initiation, i.e., the Egyptian tradition and the Star of Adeptship towards which I have to strive.' Now, today, the Master tells me that is true but there was also another meaning, hidden from me then, but which he now gives us.

The Tau represents the age-old mysteries of Egypt and the Star of Egypt is about to rise; the mysteries are to be restored, and the preparation for that restoration has been given into our hands. In the great Cycle of the procession, the Pisces Age has ended, the sign of water and blood has set and AQUARIUS rises – the mighty triangle of Air is once more ascendant and we are to restore the 'Path of Wisdom and the First Path' – knowledge."

The book went on to prophesy that "destruction cometh upon many" – but not those wise enough to escape to the City of Refuge. Those who came were to listen to Brother Twelve's words, for, as he put it, "I am the Messenger of the Fire, the Messenger of the Whirlwind, the Messenger of the Day of Adjustment."

Sometimes the faithful followers were commanded to watch from a distance and marvel as Wilson entered his sacred House of Mystery, a cabin where no one else was ever permitted, where he would leave the door partially opened while he slept and supposedly went into wild, thrashing trances.

In one of Wilson's more remarkable "visions" he received the inspiration to found a third party in American politics, one that would put the concepts of *The Three Truths* to work in the U.S. political system. He himself would personally determine who would be the next president of the United States.

He and key followers set out by train for Chicago, where they intended to found this new party, and on his way Wilson met, and seduced, Myrtle Baumgartner, a lovely young woman recently married to a New York doctor. The political movement foundered even before it was launched, but Wilson chose to return in triumph to Vancouver Island, announcing to startled followers that Myrtle, who had come along with him, was the reincarnation of the Egyptian goddess Isis and had graciously agreed to join the little colony. As for Wilson's wife, Elma, she was no longer welcome.

Wilson had such a strong hold on the little community that few, if any, challenged his newest pronouncements. Not only was pretty Myrtle really the goddess Isis, he told them, but he was himself the reincarnation of the Egyptian god Osiris. The two of them together,

Edward and Myrtle – or, if you prefer, Osiris and Isis – would produce the next saviour of the world, whose name would be Horus, and "He" would rise up in the world to save the true believers in the year 1975 as "a second Christ."

When Myrtle, who was already pregnant from the train ride hijinks, produced a girl, not a word was said, though Wilson stopped speaking of the unborn child as Horus, the next Christ child.

Wilson was already showing signs of paranoia when he decided to depart Cedar-by-the-Sea. He had money to do as he wished, at one point receiving a cheque for $25,580 from Mary Connally, a wealthy North Carolina socialite who had met Wilson for all of three hours before deciding to throw her lot, and her fortune, in with his madcap scheme. He soon moved operations to little Valdez Island and, later, expanded to a lagoon at the south end of larger DeCourcy Island. The lagoon, with its twisted arbutus trees and wind-and-water-sculpted sandstone cliffs, seemed only to add to the supernatural feel of Brother Twelve's odd colony. It was on DeCourcy that Wilson built his farm, having the disciples clear the land and build greenhouses and plant and harvest the crops. "Build thou the City of Refuge," he would tell them, "it shall hide thee in the Day of Adversity."

The islands suited Wilson, for here he could control everything, including passage to and from the mainland. He was having problems with Myrtle, who wasn't finding it so easy to separate her old life as a doctor's wife from her new one as an Egyptian goddess who had failed to produce the requisite male heir. Already unstable, and likely pushed by the manipulative Wilson, poor Myrtle went off the deep end and was sent away, never to be heard of again.

She was replaced, almost instantly, by a new partner for Brother Twelve, a woman named Mabel, who came from Florida to join the colony. Mabel changed her name to "Madame Zee," and began a life of cruel domination, terrifying the lingering true believers as she marched around the compound, barking orders and occasionally underlining her commands with the crack of a bullwhip.

The unfortunate disciples felt they had no choice but to follow her orders, for Brother Twelve had told them, "She is my eyes, she is my ears, she is my mouth. Whatever she says, you are to take as coming from me." Madame Zee seemed to take particular delight in harassing poor Mary Connally, the North Carolina socialite, who by now had handed all her fortune over to Wilson and been reduced to a life of scrubbing floors, chopping wood, and building outhouses, and who very nearly died from fatigue and lack of nutrition.

Money was still pouring in to what Wilson called the Aquarian Foundation from those true believers lucky enough not to live in the City of Refuge. And more and more disciples continued to come to the islands and agree to Brother Twelve's first rule for discipleship, "The Surrender of Personal Possessions."

Some, however, found it hard to understand the necessity for fine linen and china in Brother Twelve's lodgings when their own existence was so spartan. Rumours began to circulate of Brother Twelve and his cruel mistress dabbling in black magic, and local gossip soon came to include everything from sex orgies in the City of Refuge to pagan animal sacrifices.

A few of the early, and by now disenchanted, supporters tried to take Wilson to court on a charge of misappropriating funds intended for the Aquarian Foundation, but the trial, which was held in Nanaimo in 1929, quickly fell apart when Brother Twelve supposedly used his "black magic" on the courtroom. The key witness vanished mysteriously and was never seen again (the widespread assumption being that Wilson had had him murdered), and other witnesses found themselves unable to stand when they looked into the glowering gaze of Wilson. Some even raced to the washroom to throw up. When the plaintiff's lawyer took his feet, he found he was unable to speak, could not, in fact, even remember what it was he had intended to say. When the most crucial witness, poor long-suffering Mary Connally, told the court that the money Wilson had supposedly misappropriated from the colony had, in fact, been a personal gift to him from her, the case fell apart and the charges were dismissed. Not surprisingly, the legend of Brother Twelve only grew.

He was, by now, utterly paranoid. And perhaps with reason, for there were dozens of outraged former followers out to put an end to his cultish colony. Wilson became an early "survivalist," packing in food supplies and buying guns and ammunition. He had his disciples dig rifle pits and build a stone fort in case of invasion. He kept his two small ocean-going craft, the elegant *Lady Royal* and a refitted tug called *Kheunaten*, ready to launch at a moment's notice. He set up night patrols and ordered his "guards" to fire on wayward boats, many of them merely curiosity seekers come to Valdez and DeCourcy to see for themselves if the rumours of a crazed cult were true.

Wilson, convinced the world was out to get him, sent a letter to one of his followers, Roger Painter, which contained detailed instructions on a number of "assassinations" Brother Twelve wished to be carried out. The list included the provincial attorney-general, a Vancouver lawyer Wilson felt had offended him, and a rich couple from the United States who had made sure their money was beyond his grasp even as they fell under the spell of the cult.

Wilson began removing his considerable fortune – estimated at $430,000 – from the banks in twenty-dollar gold coins, stashing them in Mason jars, and then ordering the colony carpenter to pack the jars in specially made wooden crates. He stored the crates at first in vaults, but soon was periodically and randomly moving them about the islands and secreting them in various hideaways. To this day there are fortune seekers checking the coves of the strait islands, convinced that somewhere an abandoned crate of gold coins is still to be found.

A new court challenge was mounted in 1933, and finally Brother Twelve snapped. He decided to run, but first he and Madame Zee set out to destroy the City of Refuge, burning down some of the buildings and blowing up others with dynamite, before setting off in the tug *Kheunaten* for destinations unknown. They apparently took the gold coins with them. Workers who came to the island to clear up the mess soon found the underground vault, but it contained only a small roll of tar paper with a final message from Brother Twelve chalked onto it: "FOR FOOLS AND TRAITORS – NOTHING!"

After that, the story trails off. Wilson died, apparently, in Switzerland on November 7, 1934, but there are those, not surprisingly, who believe that, too, was a hoax. Sightings of him – in Europe, San Francisco,

Canada – continued for many years after, but there were no more books produced by him, no more colonies founded. The City of Refuge, despite Brother Twelve's claim he had created a utopia, was in ruins.

"He may have had Utopia for himself," says Rick Slingerland of the Nanaimo museum. "He had his money pouring in and he had his wives and mistresses – but I doubt it was Utopia for anyone else."

It is difficult to know what to make of failed utopias. The word itself is a problem, taken from the Greek word for "nowhere" and popularized by Sir Thomas More, who ended up losing his head in a collision between fancy and reality. It is simply a concept that exists in the pursuit and dies in the discovery.

Often it hardly matters. The very rich can afford their fantasies. There is a ranch in southwest Alberta that proves escape is frequently better in the imagination than in reality. In 1919, Edward, Prince of Wales, was twenty-five years old when he came on a royal tour of Canada and stayed, briefly, at the Bar U Ranch in the foothills of southern Alberta. He fell madly in love with the West – just as, years later, he fell madly in love with the American Wallis Simpson – and before leaving the country he decided to buy his own ranch. He renamed it E. P. for "Edward, Prince," and left for home, declaring that "I think this western spirit must be very catching, at least I know I've caught it very badly."

E. P. Ranch became a grand enterprise. On Edward's orders they brought in the best crystal and china, inset the initials E. P. into the huge stone fireplace, brought in breeding stock of shorthorn cattle, Percherons, Clydesdales, and Dartmoor ponies. It was to be the prince's magnificent escape, but he came only rarely and, by the mid-1930s, was anxious for the Canadian government to take it over. Just prior to his 1936 abdication so he could marry the divorced Wallis Simpson, he was desperately trying to sell it outright. He did bring Simpson, now the Duchess of Windsor, to the ranch in 1941, but not before ordering that wallpaper samples be shipped to their residence in the Bahamas so that the duchess could be involved in remodelling the home she had never seen. The duke by now had changed his mind about selling, and with war raging in Europe, he began to regard his fanciful escape in a more realistic light.

"The present trend of events has materially changed my attitude towards selling the ranch," he wrote to the E. P. manager, "and unless I get a really good offer, I intend holding on to it because I now regard it as a great asset in these difficult and uncertain times."

The duchess, however, was unimpressed with everything, even the new wallpaper, and she never returned to the ranch. Edward kept ownership of it even so, right up until 1962. Forty-three years in his possession, a few visits in the 1920s, one in 1941, sold in 1962.

And yet, oddly enough, in a 1950 interview, the Duke of Windsor, who had lived in Buckingham Palace, in a Paris mansion, in Cap d'Antibes, and Government House in Nassau, would say that the E. P. Ranch was the only home he had ever owned.

Perhaps he preferred it for its possibilities rather than the reality.

There is, even in failure, something inexplicably beautiful about believing there is sanctuary and happiness somewhere over the mountains, around the turn, at the end of the river.

I sometimes stand in the little cemetery at Mizpah, checking my watch to see if the minnow trap might be ready yet, and wonder what those who lie here believed would happen to them as time went on.

Two years before the local "correspondent" for the *Huntsville Forester* himself decided to give up on this impossible farming, move into Huntsville, and find work at one of the mills, he filed a column for November 8, 1901, that is filled with optimism.

"This," he wrote, "is a wonderful romantic season, abounding in the most picturesque scenery, to delight the eye of the artist and fill with rapture the soul of the close student of nature.

"After giving the matter careful consideration, I believe it will not be long e're this region will be known for pleasure seekers and if the day should come, as I believe it will, when an electric railway will be in operation between Huntsville and the Big East River connecting

Rebecca, Bella and other beautiful lakes to one string, this district will enjoy patronage unrivalled by any other. A good mail service between civilization and these land locked lakes, coupled with comfortable accommodation for passengers, is most needed to bring into note this 'rural paradise.' "

There is no electric railway and people drive into town for their mail. But the "pleasure seekers" do come, and many would call it a "rural paradise," more treasured, surely, at the turn of the twenty-first century than it was at the turn of the twentieth.

Perhaps Mizpah never became what they dreamed. But if we do "tread softly" enough, there is a distinctive sound in the high pines that grow on the side of this hill falling down toward the creek.

It is likely just the wind.

But it may also be the spirit of little Thomas Alvin Hart, who was loved in life, who was part of a grand dream, and who asks only not to be forgotten in death.

Chapter Five

WINTER

"I begin to think this is the height of folly in a man to reside in a country of this kind deprived of every comfort that can render life agreeable."

SIR ALEXANDER MACKENZIE, EXPLORER, 1764–1820

There can be, surely, no other country in the world where hardly anyone who lives there knows the words to the national anthem. But that does not stop two Canadians from trying on this cold, grey February evening, when the ice seems thicker than the auger and the only lights on the south shore are ours, flickering down through the bare trees to wash over the surface of Camp Lake Gardens.

We have shovelled for nearly two hours. The rink is approximately half the size of a regulation National Hockey League ice surface. It has packed snow banks for boards, no ads for McDonald's or Molson, no red line and no blue line, three-eighths-inch plywood for nets, no scoreboard, and, for once, the only disagreeable music at this original *Hockey Night in Canada* experience comes from our own throats.

But we love it. We are here to play the Camp Lake Classic, a treasured tradition that is observed certain March breaks, weather, ice conditions, and personal inclination permitting.

There is no need for a program. There are, after all, only two players – three, if we count the dog, Bandit, who keeps wandering off to slurp cold black water out of the fishing hole we have drilled with the manual auger and then cleared of slush with a large spoon with holes in the bottom for the unfrozen water to drain back into the lake. Bandit is a black-and-white mutt, fair at checking but useless as a playmaker, which means she is more trouble than she is worth. But so long as she doesn't run off with the only puck and drop it down the water hole, she is welcome to stay and run and skid and slip and go crashing into the snow banks for as long as she wishes to do so.

Gord is eighteen years old. He has played organized hockey right through midget and was coached by me through most of those minor hockey years, so being on the ice together is hardly a new experience for us. And yet there is still something about this moment – a light north wind blowing in off the island, the ice so black and shiny it seems freshly painted, the heartening sound of puck on the rough board of the net – that makes house-league championships and even weekend tournament trips to the United States pale by comparison.

Here on Camp Lake, on a cold February evening when we are the only people on the lake, let alone the only skaters on the Camp Lake Gardens ice surface, he is once again the hero of the schoolyard rink, the champion of the basement, the Stanley Cup winner of his night-before-the-big-game dreams.

I feel it myself. I have passed the half-century mark, and soon it will be fifty years since my mother helped me pull on older brother Jim's hand-me-down Canadian Tire skates and tied them so tightly over several pairs of grey woollen socks that the eyelets nearly overlapped. A half century since I walked, penguin-like, across to Munroe's, where Brent's father, Maurice, had built a large, lighted, slightly sloping rink between the two huge white spruce that towered between their old farmhouse and the barn that lay between their property and ours on the edge of Reservoir Hill in Huntsville. I have never seen ice so slippery since – perhaps it was the slope, perhaps the unfamiliar skates – but it should be noted that my very first hockey moment brought tears to my own eyes, not those of any amused parents who happened to be watching, when I fell straight back and struck my head on the ice with a sound not unlike two rocks colliding underwater.

Two years later, when I was eight, I pasted my first hockey memory – and likely the high point of an extremely modest career – into a fifteen-cent, red Empire Scrap Book. "Goals by MacGregor Give Auxiliary Tie with Hay & Co. 2–2," read the headline of the little clipping from the *Huntsville Forester*, which I still have and treasure:

The Legion Auxiliary's Roy MacGregor turned two spectacular solo rushes into a 2–2 tie with Hay & Co. Saturday morning.

A highlight of a Huntsville Hockey League Squirt playoff game, MacGregor's goals marked the second time Auxiliary had battled from behind a one-goal deficit.

Young defenceman Michael Allemano was especially good for the Hookmen, breaking up many Auxiliary rushes. Both of the Hay & Company goals, by Brent Munroe and John Newell, were scored on power plays.

There is a beauty to this game that has no relation to truth. I can show someone this clipping and say nothing, convinced that in their head (presuming a certain naivete about squirt hockey and gracious small-town reporting) I am picking up a puck behind my own net, head up, shoulders squared, and then soaring down the ice like a dipping, accelerating osprey, the puck nursing the end of my stick blade, my eyes alert to openings, chances, opportunities, the defence splitting helplessly and the goaltender, accepting the inevitable, foundering in his crease as I lazily lift the puck over his outstretched hands into the top of the net, the goalie's water bottle flying toward the glass, where screaming fans have long been out of their seats, their arms raised in praise.

It sounds good, and the temptation is to let it stand. But the fact of the matter is, we played half ice in those days, with boards strung along a wire suspended over the red line. Our sponsors were local service groups and businesses, hence we were the Legion Auxiliary (the women who ran the snack bar), and the "Hookmen" referred to the local lumber mill, Hay & Co. The only rush I recall is when one of the players had to go to the bathroom partway through. I swung at one puck and it somehow reached the goal much as a curling stone sneaks up, with heavy sweeping, on the button. The other goal I no longer even recall.

On an ice surface like this, it all comes flooding back. The minor hockey in Huntsville, the road trips, the tournaments, the fantasies, the fun, the game of an entire lifetime. With the rink shovelled off and the "nets" up and the dog barking, I am again on Munroe's backyard rink, again at the Huntsville Memorial Arena, again on Hunter's Bay, where we would shovel off rinks every winter, again on the little beaver pond behind the high school where we sometimes played, again calling on Brent and Eric to shoot tennis balls up along Dufferin Street all day and hope the cars remembered to straddle the chunks of hardened snow that served as goalposts.

Gord, I know, has his own fantasies, and I can almost see them swirl as he kicks the puck off his skate blade to his stick, feints to the right and dips down, tucking the puck back between his own legs and sending the barking, skittering dog off helplessly into the nearest snow bank. That is not a dog he is toying with, but Chris Pronger or Rob Blake, and that is no plywood board he is now rattling the puck off, but Patrick Roy or Dominik Hasek, cleanly beaten by the bullet from Camp Lake.

We play long into the evening. Ellen comes down to watch. Bandit tires and walks back up with her, arching through the deep snow like a dolphin, and we play on, finally quitting with the score approximately 274–273.

"*I won!*"

"*No way, I won!*"

The ice is scarred. Our skate blades have carved the story of our swirling, circling game and then layered it with the snow sprayed up from sudden stops and changes in direction. If shinny were music, it would be jazz. If it were a painting, it would look like this: Camp Lake on a February evening, the shadows blue, the sky as black as the spruce trees at the edge of the shore, the light thick yellow through the trees, and along the path back up the hill, boot marks punched into the deep snow, the lunges and the landings of the dog's more erratic path seemingly sculpted by a mad wind that has since moved on.

By morning, the water hole will have frozen so solid the auger will have to be used again to break through the foot and a half of new ice. Periodically during the night there will be sounds like muffled rifle fire in the distance, the ice shifting slightly, groaning, and then suddenly cracking at different levels. There will be other shots as well, trees suddenly snapping or shifting against each other as the thermometer plummets to twenty below, then thirty. It is one of the great mysteries of a winter night in the deep northern bush that it can look so serene and yet sound like the elements are at war with one another.

There may be no other cottagers on the lake on a cold February weekend, no children yelling, no splashing, no motorboats passing back and forth from the government docks, not even a songbird or an aspen leaf to rattle in the wind, but there are sounds absolutely distinctive to the bitter Canadian winter night.

When John and Theodora Stanwell-Fletcher decided to winter in the British Columbia interior in the late thirties and early forties, Theodora, a renowned Pennsylvania naturalist, was astonished by the amount of noise winter made. She had been worried about having no neighbours for miles and the unbearable silence of the winter muffle, but what she would remember, she wrote later, was the terrifying sound of ice seeming to rip entirely across a bay, the sudden crack of trees, and what seemed like shots in the cabin attic as joists and support beams shifted.

She was also struck by the intensity of the winter night, when such a cold could descend from the clear black night sky that it left the little windows "so densely frosted that it seemed as if daylight, even if it were there, could never penetrate the cabin." In the deepest cold of winter, she learned never to touch her bare skin to metal, even a spoon, for her fingers would instantly lock onto the spoon or cup or pot or even fire poker, the skin peeling off if she was so foolish as to try to remove the metal forcefully.

Winter has long been seen as an impediment in Canada, a problem. This perception began not without justification, with the earliest explorers. David Thompson had four of his men desert him as he was going through the Athabasca Pass in the tough winter of 1810–11 and seemed almost sympathetic when he wrote in his journal that they had been broken by the "mental distress" of winter travel. The fur trader Alexander Mackenzie, in a letter to his nephew back in Scotland, showed his growing frustration with the hardest season when he admitted that "I begin to think this is the height of folly in a man to reside in a country of this kind deprived of every comfort that can render life agreeable."

Once the long hurdle of winter was recognized for what it meant to Canada's future – in terms of attracting immigrants and settling the more remote reaches – those with a vested interest often began lying about its very existence, as if the stories of north winds and chilblains and frostbite and slow death by freezing were unsupportable rumours, the nineteenth-century rural equivalent of the modern urban myth. When the main force behind the Canadian Pacific Railway, William Van Horne, was touring Europe in search of immigrants and, more important still, investors, he used to make a great fuss complaining about the cold of, say, Florence, and then say, loudly, "How I pine for Winnipeg to thaw me."

It was hyperbole to battle hyperbole, for there was more than enough exaggeration coming from the other direction. Gladstone, the British prime minister, referred to Canada as a land "of perpetual ice and snow." The Irish paper *The Nation* dismissed the new Dominion as "a kind of Siberia," which was hardly encouraging to those Irish still wondering whether or not to throw their lot in with North America.

In many ways, it was this rush to counter negative impressions abroad that led to Canada claiming its climate was, in fact, beneficial to one's constitution. It began with Lord Dufferin, who was governor general in the 1870s. "A constitution nursed upon the oxygen of our bright winter atmosphere," harrumphed the Queen's representative in Ottawa, ". . . makes its owner feel as though he could toss about pine trees in his glee." The renowned physician Sir William Osler, according to Pierre Berton in *Winter*, took to predicting that "the most virile nation on the continent will be to the north of the Great Lakes."

The Department of the Interior in Ottawa even went so far as to ban such words as "frost" and "cold" from brochures and publications. "Buoyant" became an acceptable word, hard as it might be to imagine one Canadian asking another if it was "buoyant out today."

That morning after the big game it was far from buoyant at Camp Lake. Morning coffee required the auger and the slush spoon before we could even think about filling the kettle. The wind had come up again during the night and had blown large stretches of the lake clear of snow, the ice now gleaming dark blue under the morning sun and the snow drifted into long fingers reaching toward the far bay.

By mid-morning, however, the wind had died down, the day now impossibly white and bright and still, apart from the odd gust that would pick swirls of snow off the lake and send them, spinning, as if the air were suddenly filled with gold dust. I wished I had remembered to bring along the camera.

We always forget the camera in winter. We are no different from most Canadians in this, for family photo albums from one end of the country to the other contend that there is but one season in Canada, summer, or at least one season alone where people line up and smile and happily pose for photographs.

Winter family pictures seem to have been taken simply to *prove* people were outside, an unfortunate attitude to have in a country where, as the New Brunswick poet Alden Nowlan so long ago put it, "December is thirteen months long, July's one afternoon . . ."

If winter is indeed so dominant, why would we waste so much valuable time avoiding it?

"Cottage" has long been synonymous with "summer" in Canada, but I have found each season at the cottage, or cabin, brings its own delight. I love to come here in the early spring on a day when I can roll the car windows down for the first time since fall and let my skin and nose have their fill of air that seems fresh born that day. I like it when the hills are purple with swollen buds rather than green with leaves, and when the dominant sound by day is water trickling down out of the hills and into the bay, when the evenings are ringing with the mad lovemaking of spring peepers. And I love it in the fall, when the maple and beech leaves parachute down and the far shore looks as if it should be in a fire grate. I love the smell of new life in spring, the smell of decay and wood fires in the fall. But I also don't mind it one little bit when, on a cold, cold day in January, my nostrils lock together and I can't smell a thing, in fact, I can't even breathe except through an open mouth. A mouth opened in awe at the toughest season of all.

By the mid nineties we were becoming old hands at "winter cot-taging." We had, like most nearly normal Canadian families our age, passed through the early eighties with young children begging for Disney World. Asking nothing of our offspring other than that they care for us in our old age, we had capitulated and taken that long drive south where every few hours produce a new cheer for the slow north-ward creep of spring. A couple of thousand American dollars later, we had returned, burnt and itching with beach sand, our Mickey and Minnie Mouse ears bent, and the car wretched with the stink of fes-tering seashell collections and ten days on the road for a family of six.

One year, broke, we decided to head in the other direction – and have never looked back. I see from the cabin log that we have not missed a visit in more than a decade of winter cottaging. I see where, after a week of fog and rain and a dull ice auger, someone has scrib-bled "No one wants to leave!" at the bottom of the last entry for the winter visit of 1990. I see where, the first time we came to stay over in winter, in 1985, the eldest of our four, then going on nine years of age, has said, "I like it here even better than in the summer."

I would never go quite that far myself – not even since we cut out that circle of thick felt to haul up to the outhouse those bitter cold mornings – but we do come, when we can, in December, January, and February, and we do love it. By the time study breaks roll around these days, there is a battle for the place, with kids now old enough to drive up, as they prefer, with their own friends.

They have not yet, fortunately, suggested we might rather be in Florida.

There are, we now swear, few places more delightful than a cabin in the middle of winter. Even if you cannot drive to it, even if winter-ing over for a few days or more requires constant work – supplies to haul in, doors to dig out, pathways to clear, toboggans and skis to scrape, fires to stoke, ice to chop, water to haul, an outhouse with hoarfrost on the seat to consider – it feels somehow worth it. As if, in some way, you have travelled back in time and, thereby, gathered in your arms time you thought lost.

This was written all over the laughing faces of two elderly women

– my mother, Helen, then going on eighty, and Ellen's mother, Rose, then going on seventy-five – who hiked over the big hill and into the cottage to visit one winter and ended up falling down the hill when they both lost their footing in deep snow. They laughed until they wept, two women embracing old childhood memories – Helen's from Algonquin Park, Rose's from an isolated Saskatchewan grain farm – and then they began making angels in the snow while their grandchildren cheered them on.

We so often talk about how we feel "more alive" at the cabin than anywhere else. Try winter, where "more alive" becomes a necessity rather than a luxury, where if you can't keep up with the elements, you simply won't keep. Think of it, if you will, as Extreme Cottaging.

The historical record has not been kind to Canada's dominant season. The Vikings bailed out because of winter. Jacques Cartier spent his first winter at Stadacona watching the walls inside his shelter coat up with six inches of solid ice. By spring, twenty-five of his one hundred and ten men were dead.

Even in the nineteenth century, winter was largely something to be waited out. Most early pioneers tried to explore the joys of the season, but the demands of winter soon overwhelmed them, and they huddled indoors with their neighbours around the fire and prayed for an early spring that rarely seemed to come. It is winter, more than any other Canadian reality, that has made Canadians who they are today: private, shy, stoic people who, traditionally, have worried less whether an imaginary glass is half empty or half full than whether the very real wood box is down. "Cold," as Robertson Davies once said, "breeds caution."

We are cautious about winter, very often with good cause. There are roads in these parts where winter travel without a shovel, without a bucket of sand, without an emergency kit of candles and tin cans and blankets is as foolhardy as daring to drive across a freshly frozen lake where there is still open water around the currents. There are nights when, if the fire goes down, you may not get up. There is an *edge* to winter that wisely breeds caution, but there is also a challenge to winter that brings out an equal portion of daring.

It has even been argued that our national game of hockey is precisely the sport that had to emerge from the Canadian landscape. If the American passion for baseball – a leisurely game with sporadic movement and built-in pauses – can be tied to summer afternoons and sun-baked fields, then surely the exertion and constant flow of hockey has something to do with keeping the blood flowing while being out on the ice. The same applies to those watching in the stands, the fans stomping and exuberant to keep warm, especially when the game was played exclusively out-of-doors in the natural winter elements. Fifty years ago, novelist Hugh MacLennan told the American readers of *Holiday* magazine that hockey represented "the counterpoint of the Canadian self-restraint." For players and spectators alike, MacLennan said, "Hockey gives the release that strong liquor gives a repressed man."

I have seen liquor – or at least alcohol – have another effect on Canadians as summer whittles down and the new school year and coming winter begin to loom. It is as if the adults of the lake find themselves as reluctant to leave as the kids are excited. Perhaps it is a symptom brought on by too much wine, perhaps by the giddiness of no more mosquitoes – no matter, the end effect is that many of us are suddenly seized by an irrational dream to stay on long after the north wind starts stinging exposed flesh with snow crystals.

"I'd love to see the seasons come and go," one will say as another glass is poured.

"I'd like to get into the rhythms," someone like me will add, "to see, just once, what it's like to spend the entire year up here."

It is an understandable, if somewhat simplistic, sentiment. Faced with the prospects of salt, snowploughs, and windchill factor, there is something almost overwhelmingly attractive about a blazing fireplace, a steaming cup of coffee, and, finally, time to read that damned *Crime and Punishment*, which has proved longer than summer for the past two decades.

This is not – despite our twenty-first-century desire to escape the "*mouse* race" of inter-office e-mail – a modern ambition. It is, admittedly, one most often voiced by loud Canadian men who have had one too many beers on the dock, but the most compelling realization of this ultimate macho Canadian escape plan may have come from an American woman, who headed into the solitude of the Canadian winter nearly a century ago.

"I am tired to death," Laura Lee Davidson wrote in 1914, as she set up on an isolated island in Ontario cottage country. "I need to rest for at least one year. I want to watch the procession of the seasons in some place that is not all paved streets, city smells, and noise. Instead of the clang of car bells and the honk of automobile horns, I want to hear the winds sing across the ice fields, instead of the smell of asphalt and hot gasoline, I want the odour of wet earth in boggy places. I have loved the woods all my life; I long to see the year go round there just once before I die."

The Baltimore schoolteacher was in her mid forties when she temporarily quit the human race. At the end of the summer of 1914, she was dropped off on the small island with enough supplies and enough wood stacked around the little cabin to get her through the winter. She was still alive, and still sane, when the steamer returned to pick her up sometime after the ice went out.

Seven years later, Davidson published *A Winter of Content*, her account of that brave year. She had, she claimed, regained her vitality, her appetite, and her overall happiness.

"It has given me health," she wrote as she took stock of the year that had passed. "I have forgotten all about jerking nerves and aching muscles. I sleep all night like a stone; I eat plain food with relish; I walk and row mile after mile; I work rejoicing in my strength and glad to be alive.

"There has been also the renewing of my mind, for my standards of value are changed. Things that were once of supreme importance seem now the veriest of trifles. Things that once I took for granted, believing them the common due of mankind – like air and sunshine, warm fires and the kind faces of friends – are now the most valuable things in the world."

It is much easier at the start of the twenty-first century than it would have been in the early years of the twentieth century. Davidson

had her supplies, her woodpile, her stove, her layers of woollen cloth-
ing. But today we have so much more. Pink insulation, Gore-Tex, electricity, baseboard heaters, eiderdown, four-wheel drives, nylon,
airtight stoves, microwaves, and imported cognac have all conspired
to turn winter around for most Canadians. We ski and skate, snowmobile and snowboard, and we tell ourselves that it is winter that
makes our most-treasured season, summer, so very, very special.

This, of course, is our very own peculiar logic, one that certain outsiders have not always been able to follow. "Genius," Francis Brooke
said of Canadians two centuries ago, "will never mount high where
the faculties of the mind are benumbed half the year."

Mr. Brooke didn't know just how lacking in genius, how downright
stupid, some of us can get on a brittle winter weekend. We, for example,
will set out from our Ottawa home in a vehicle stuffed with children,
their wary friends, down-filled sleeping bags, boxes of groceries, thick
jackets and pants, heavy mitts, toques, hoods, insulated boots, and
mandatory changes of grey woollen socks, the roof rack piled high
with toboggans and sleds and skis. We will drive four hours in good
weather, five or even six in poor, before pulling off onto Muskoka
Road 8, which is usually well ploughed and lightly sanded. On a bright
winter's day, tiny colourful redpoll and pine siskins will be picking
through the fine gravel, waiting until the final second before scatter-
ing to escape our front bumper.

The township ploughs only to the bottom of the toughest hill on
the road, meaning the mentally "benumbed" must park in the turn-
around area and hike from there. Often there are trucks and empty
snowmobile trailers already there, and while the snowmobiles will be
cursed in the early morning – "winter mosquitoes," some call them –
they will later be thanked by anyone who has to tie the rope of a
toboggan about his waist and begin the long slog uphill dragging two
hundred pounds of supplies and packs. The snowmobiles pack down
the snow and make winter walking possible.

There may be no scientific proof for this, but every winter cottager
knows that it is colder inside than out. Winter cottagers, on arrival,
often warm up their places by firing up the wood stove and opening all

the doors and windows. I have taken shovel to woodpile, axe to blocks, and cranked the fire box up to the danger level while youngsters have stayed outside and played until they stood shivering on the deck and shouted to see if it was "okay to come inside yet?" as if it were rabid raccoons I was chasing out instead of thirty-below temperatures.

It is perhaps the sweetest time of the entire visit, working and waiting while the cabin warms. The rising temperatures are called out and cheered as if we were on the floor of some rustic, backwoods stock exchange, and the first jacket off is, in its own way, as significant as the first and last dive of summer. Smart people bring slippers, for while the walls are insulated, the floor is not, and we slip and slide like first-time speed skaters as three layers of grey work socks seek purchase on linoleum floors.

There is something so . . . so *accomplished* about that very first winter evening at the cabin. The trek in has been completed. The place is still standing. The woodpile has been located, a water hole has been augered and chopped through a foot or more of hard ice. There is water, unfrozen, in the pail by the kitchen sink. Jackets and boots are off, the fire roars against the snow falling outside. There are books to read and silly board games, which, for some reason, are even more pleasurable in winter than summer. Perhaps there is a hockey game on the radio. If some of us believe the game is better played on natural ice, a small, static-ridden radio is a reminder that it has never been better played than in your own head.

For the next few days, it is like discovering that the place you once believed you knew best has a different personality. When the leaves are down, there are no more secrets in cottage country; winter is a snooper's paradise for those who wondered, a few months earlier, what all the hammering and sawing was about on the far side of the island. There is something naked about the lake: not only can you see so much more, but you can walk along the shoreline far closer to neighbours' properties than you would ever dare paddle in summer. No one is there to catch you gawking.

Just as in summer we have certain rituals, we have now developed them for winter. We walk to the falls, a good two miles or more across the lake and down a twisted narrows. If the snow lies heavily on the ice, we snowshoe, but usually the wind has swept patches clear, and we walk on the thin crust of snow, then "skate" over the clean polished ice. The kids take out the summer inner tubes and build luge runs down a nearby hill, the ride better than anything Disney ever imagined. When they were smaller, they hooked a harness on to the dog, tied on a long rope, and knelt on a plastic Flying Saucer while Bandit, so much younger and stronger then, hurled about the ice. On certain turns, their speed would equal that of a summer wakeboarder with a ninety-horsepower Johnson instead of a barking mongrel. The kids are too big for that now, and the dog is old and arthritic, but she still barks and chases around in the snow as if there was nothing she would rather have than a harness, a rope, and a new kid to fling about.

Some rituals span both seasons. They swing again from the rope that, in summer, sends them far out into the bay, backflipping into the dark, sparkling waters of July and August. In winter, they swing out and then back, spinning into the thick mattress of snow that clings to the rising banks. The flips they save for the deck railing, front flipping and diving face first into the six feet or more of soft snow that builds around the slope heading down toward the dock. In summer it is marshmallows around the campfire; in winter it is hot chocolate around the fireplace.

Arthur Black, host of CBC Radio's "Basic Black," once called the winter silence "unnatural." It struck him as absurd that Canadians spent so much time rationalizing their winter existence and pretending it has value. "Unnatural," he argued, "is the key word. Winter is not natural. There is a perfectly good reason it is silent out there. Anything with legs or wings and two brain cells to rub together has left – that's why it's silent."

He should have been here last night when my brother-in-law, Ralph, arrived with his son, David, from North Bay and we sat around drinking tea and hot chocolate and talking about all the things we'll do this summer that we never got around to doing all those other summers. Finally, my poor benumbed brain – by now down to a single cell, sometimes firing – decided the difficult hike up to the outhouse could be put off no longer. I grabbed the felt seat from back of the wood box, pulled on a heavy coat, my big boots, picked up a flashlight, and headed off on what I hoped would be the only trip of the long night coming.

It was dark, but *blue* dark rather than black, and there is a fundamental winter difference to those shades. The stars were set so deep and precisely that it seemed I was walking through them, not under them. If the moon is full and the snow deep, it is like precious extra time has been tagged on to the day; it is bright enough to play on the ice, bright enough even to read. If there is no moon but the stars are out, standing on thick ice in the middle of a lake is, likely, as close as any of us will ever come to what it must be like when a heavily insulated astronaut leaves the ship and floats freely. An out-of-body experience without the necessity of nearly dying.

And there are indeed sounds, Mr. Black, not absolute silence. An owl in the deep woods on the opposite bay. Wolves howling in the distance. The growling of the shifting ice and the loud snap of the trees that so surprised Theodora Stanwell-Fletcher those winter nights in the British Columbia interior. To those who have lived too long in cities, there is even a sound to silence itself.

I was just leaving the outhouse when my heart all but stopped. There was a sound for which the English language does not provide words to describe. A bit like a train coming through, though there are no train tracks within thirty miles of Camp Lake. A bit like a jet coming in, though there is no airport within a hundred miles. A bit like a heavy-breathing Cyclops, though there are no Greek gods or monsters here, even within reach of the eclectic bookcase.

I stood, listening and wondering. There was a deep, powerful rhythm to whatever was making this extraordinary sound. There was a crashing to it, as if something heavy were breaking, constantly breaking – and the sound was growing closer.

I plodded back down the rutted path and quickly opened the cottage door to a waft of hot air.

"Come out here a minute," I told Ralph.

He was bundled and out quickly. "What's up?"

"Shhhh. Listen."

We stood there, listening to the strange, powerful sound grow. It seemed, now, to fill the entire space around us: the bush, the sky, the lake, the insides of our puny, single-celled, winter-benumbed brains.

The sound seemed everywhere. To the right, the left, up the hill and down. We even looked up into the sky. If there had been flashing red-green-and-blue lights, I would have expected a space ship to settle and take us onboard.

The rhythms and the crashing finally seemed to make sense.

"It's something walking," I said.

"Breaking through the crust," Ralph suggested.

There was a crust on the snow hard enough to hold children walking, hard enough to hold sleighs and toboggans sliding. What could be heavy enough to break through – and not only break through, but *crash* through, hard and fast and steady, as if an inch-thick crust of ice offered no more resistance than an eggshell?

"A *moose!*" we both said at once.

We stood under the black-blue night and listened while the moose made its powerful way along the side of the hill, the crashing, smashing, ploughing, breathing building louder and louder until it seemed we should be able to reach out and touch the massive beast as it brushed by our shoulders.

But we never saw it. We walked, flashlights stabbing, up the same hill where, a few years earlier, the grandmothers had come tumbling down like two elderly Jills, but could not even find the tracks.

In the morning, with better light and, admittedly, better nerves, we searched again until we realized the moose had passed by so far back in the bush it seemed ludicrous that the two of us, shivering at midnight, thought we might be warmed by his breath.

In summer, we would not even have heard him.

After breakfast that final morning, we skated again. Only now it seemed as if Camp Lake Gardens had expanded its boundaries to include the entire lake. The wind had swept and polished and all but freshly flooded the ice until it seemed the entire surface of the lake had turned to thick, dark-shadowed glass.

It reminded me of what the Scots call *verglas*, something the late broadcaster Peter Gzowski once came across when, as a ten-year-old, he woke one winter's day to find that the freezing rain during the night, followed by a sudden cold snap, had encased the streets and fields of Galt, Ontario, for as far as the eye could see.

Gzowski wrote in *The Game of Our Lives* how he and fifty or sixty other Galt youngsters laced up their skates and set out to play a day-long game of hockey on a rink where the goalposts, as if they even mattered, were a half-mile apart.

"I didn't know if that had anything to do with hockey," he wrote, "but I know I'd never been happier.

"At the park's end, yelling excitedly to each other, we flung our sticks over the fence, and headed for the open country."

We, however, headed for the open ice. The snow that had once covered the entire ice surface now lay blown in pockets and drifts, the vast majority of the ice open and clear, a fresh sheet waiting for our skates to write the story of the perfect winter day.

It was beautiful beyond belief. You could look down the lake and see swirling lassos of fine snow everywhere, and occasionally rising waves of snow, sparkling and flashing in the sun. On the open ice you could gain enough steam to drift, the wind at your back, like a human sailboat, arms hunched out, legs apart, nothing required for a turn but a small twist of the shoulders. I skate in the bitter winter wind far better than I sail in the gentle summer breeze.

There was no one there but us. We skated around the lake, the dog slipping and sliding and trying to bite snow as she scampered over the drifts. We skated out to the island and down the far end, in through the narrows, and on into little Flossie Lake, where the old hunt camp has stood on rickety stilts since the 1930s.

We skated right up to the hunt camp and awkwardly climbed the windblown steps in our skates, trying to peer in through a door held shut by nothing more than an old rope.

There was not much to see: some old pots and pans, a few bedrolls strung up tightly for winter, the bare walls of the rundown cabin papered with *Playboy* pinups from the 1960s, their pubic areas airbrushed away and nipples hardened, no doubt, by the bitter north wind that had been rattling the makeshift door these past many months.

We skated down through the narrows and stopped, for breath, on the small peninsula where, in summer, there is a perfect place to pitch a tent and spend the night.

We skated back into the larger lake, chasing and stickhandling and passing the puck back and forth as we split the islands to come in and score wherever we wished.

The wind was burning our faces now, the dog's tongue dragged, and our legs were beginning to turn to spent elastic, but still we skated, determined to finish the entire lake before the day was done or fresh snow arrived to cover up this temporary miracle.

It struck me that I had just skated into Algonquin Park and back. But I knew, instantly, that I was far from the first member of my family to skate in Algonquin Park.

My mother left photographs of her father, the old park ranger, and the makeshift "Zamboni" he built in the 1920s and early 1930s to flood the ice at Brule Lake, where they lived along the old Ottawa, Arnprior, and Parry Sound railway line that was built through the park in the 1890s.

He had taken a rain barrel and fixed it to skis, then ran burlap sacks along a board that he dragged behind him, a pipe syphoning the water back from the barrel to the burlap, where it spread as evenly along the ice as if he were flooding a National Hockey League rink during intermission.

There is another photograph, and this is blown up to life size and hangs in the new Algonquin Park Visitors' Centre just off Sunday Creek along Highway 60, which cuts through the park from Huntsville to Whitney.

It is of my grandmother, Bea McCormick. She is on her skates, cutting a perfect figure over shining ice that we can presume her husband the ranger has just flooded.

She has a woollen scarf thrown daringly around her neck, and she has turned her head slightly to make a face and laugh.

She is not, however, aiming it at the photographer.

She is laughing at the elements.

And when I stand there, staring at her forever alive and on display in the park she so loved, I cannot help but laugh back.

Chapter Six

WHY GOLDIE HAWN CAN'T ESCAPE

"The very name 'tourist' has a charm in Muskoka; even the sunburnt settler children look forward with delight to the time of their arrival and burst out of the little schoolhouse singing, 'The tourists are coming, hurrah, hurrah.'"

ANN HATHAWAY, MUSKOKA MEMORIES, 1904

Her name was Elizabeth Posthuma Gwillim, and the history of Canada should record that she was the first Torontonian who absolutely had to get away for the weekend.

She was also the wife of John Graves Simcoe, first lieutenant-governor of Upper Canada and the British officer who had burned Richmond, Virginia, to the ground during the American Revolution. She was an orphan who had inherited two considerable family fortunes and, at sixteen, married the thirty-year-old soldier, becoming Simcoe's inseparable companion throughout his meteoric career.

If John Graves Simcoe left Canada its largest city – he built Fort York and saw to it that Toronto would become the provincial capital – then it must also be said that Elizabeth Simcoe left Canada its complementary custom of escaping the city in summer to Cottage Country. The strong-willed and rather eccentric Elizabeth grew to hate the muggy summers of muddy York. She first sought relief from the oppressive heat by taking to the little peninsula that would later form the Toronto Islands, and here she ordered so many brush fires set to ward off the mosquitoes that she began to be regarded as a menace to the community. The bugs, she claimed, made it impossible for her to work on her small watercolours and intricate pen-and-ink drawings, and it was this passion for breezy spaces and new landscape that took her farther afield than perhaps the wife of the fort commander would be expected to wander. She took particularly to the higher ground north of the swamps that lay between the Don and

Humber rivers. Here she painted and drew and even went slightly "native," falling in love with the graceful canoe and eventually insisting on using birch bark for her art instead of paper.

In the mid 1790s, Elizabeth persuaded her husband to build her a summer home in the north country. It seemed far more distant then than it does today – she chose a bluff overlooking the Don, roughly where the Castlefrank stop on the Bloor subway line is now located – and here, in the woods, the Simcoes built a massive log home, which they named after their youngest son, Francis: hence, Castle Frank.

It may have fallen rather short of what is today regarded as Cottage Country, but there are locals living in places like Bala and Honey Harbour who would recognize in Elizabeth traits they still see in the privileged who flee to the north but cannot resist bringing some of the city with them. Not happy with merely a log home, Elizabeth had Castle Frank's builder front it with gaudy *faux* Grecian columns. And she complained, bitterly, about the high cost of basic help, and how those she hired for such small essentials as "dishwashing" acted as though it was *they*, not she, doing the favour.

John Graves and Elizabeth Simcoe stayed only four years in what would become Toronto. Their little daughter Katherine, only fifteen months of age, was buried just outside the walls of Fort York in the spring of 1794, and by 1796 the Simcoes were once again back in England. Their son Francis was killed in action fighting for England in the Peninsula War, and John Graves died in 1806 just before taking up his new and much-longed-for appointment as governor general of India. The remains of John Graves and Elizabeth, along with five of their eleven children, are interred in a wall of Wolford Chapel, near the village of Dunkeswell in Devon.

Elizabeth had been looking forward greatly to India, but her heart, apparently, stayed forever back in her lovely country home in the Canadas. Here was where her art had flourished. Here was where her husband had believed a near-utopian world would one day be built. Here was where John Graves Simcoe had breathed easiest, for in Canada he had found the greatest relief from the asthma that had troubled him all his life and would hasten his death. Here was where the Simcoes had buried their precious Katherine, the child who had not lived long enough to enjoy the beauty of the outdoors that so entranced Elizabeth.

Elizabeth had, like so many others who would eventually follow her north, despaired of leaving her precious retreat far from the stinking, noisy settlement of York. Her last Canadian entry in her diary – July 21, 1796 – sounds almost like a Labour Day lament from two centuries later: "I was so much out of spirits. I could not eat, cried all the day."

The first known "tourists" to strike into the territory that would one day be known as Cottage Country, or Muskoka, were James Bain Jr., whose father ran a book and stationery business on Toronto's King Street, John Campbell, whose father owned James Campbell and Son Publishers of Toronto, a man known only as Crombie, and Crombie's dog, whose name has been lost to the history of leisure.

The three men and the dog left Toronto's Union Station on August 5, 1861, aboard the northbound Simcoe & Muskoka Junction Railway. They rode the train to the end of the line at Barrie, where they caught the steamer *Emily May* and crossed Lake Simcoe to Orillia. They then rowed up Lake Couchiching (those who complain today about slow traffic along highways 400 and 11 might like to consider this a moment) and reached Washago in failing light. Under cover of dark, they continued on foot to the little village of Severn Bridge, where they took shelter. The following morning they set out on foot up the Muskoka Road, a new settlement passage that had been cleared only the winter before by the government of Canada West.

The young men travelled fairly lightly. They carried with them straw hats to protect them from the sun, homemade knapsacks filled with food, guns, and powder for protection from any bears or wolves they might encounter, and brandy flasks to ease the mosquito bites and shorten the nights. They could be said to have officially arrived in Muskoka when they walked into McCabe's Tavern, which stood at approximately the site where the gates to Gravenhurst would later be erected. They were immediately treated to the local drink, "stirabout" – a concoction including water, molasses, and, presumably, rum or moonshine – and began asking what might be seen in the area and what they might do there with the few days they had remaining.

No one, apparently, knew what to make of them. The few settlers who had already headed up the settlement road to stake out their grant land were baffled that anyone would come here without seeming purpose. They took the group at first for surveyors, except it was noted they carried no surveying equipment, and then concluded that they must be preachers, yet they carried no bibles and seemed decidedly shy about attempting to convert anyone.

The travellers walked the two miles to Muskoka Bay, where they'd been told they would find, and were welcome to use, a scow to take them out on the water. The scow leaked and there was only one oar, but they took turns paddling and bailing and, with the dog ensconced in the bow, made it out into the Narrows and landed just as Lake Muskoka widened before them. Here they collected botanical specimens, wrapping some of their discoveries in newsprint and storing others in bottles, took a short nap on the rocks, and then paddled back, still bailing.

Back at McCabe's Tavern they supped and talked about their wonderful day, the tranquility of the water and the marvellous finds of plants and wildflowers that so excited them. Those who had mistaken them for surveyors and preachers now must have decided they were insane, for no one there had ever headed out in a boat except to fish or hunt or get somewhere else on the lake. Besides, the settlers saw their task as ridding the land of unwanted wild plants and weeds, not carefully packing them away so they could be carried back to the city.

It would not be the last time a year-round resident of Muskoka would fail to comprehend the mind of the summer visitor.

When the men made it back to Toronto at week's end, they regaled their friends with tales of the wilderness and the exquisite scenery and clean, cool water of the north country. Bain and Campbell were seen by their peers as role models – Bain would eventually become chief librarian for Toronto's first public library, Campbell was a respected theology professor in Montreal – and when they recommended to their friends that they all begin heading north together in the summers, the idea was enthusiastically accepted.

This was the beginning of what, in 1864, would call itself the Muskoka Club. For the nominal fee of one dollar per year, the Muskoka Club would organize and "provide an annual expedition" for its exclusive and limited membership. Bain and Campbell remained the leaders, Bain preferring to be called Finn the Fisherman on the sojourns and Campbell serving both as curate and botanist to the vacationing groups.

The Scottish-born Campbell was the more intelligent but flakier of the two. He had been a brilliant student at the University of Toronto, walking off with gold medals in metaphysics and languages and winning prizes in both English verse and poetry. According to Paul King, writing in *Summertimes*, published in celebration of the first century of the Muskoka Lakes Association, Campbell had even been adept enough at botany to fill in as a university lecturer at times.

If they seemed somewhat precious long before young visitors to Muskoka were *expected* to put on summer airs, it was all fairly harmless play-acting. Peter Robinson, who served as unofficial "recording secretary" to the club for many years, told of a climb the group took one summer in search of a spectacular view of the lake, a climb apparently so exhausting that the young men reached the top no longer able to speak English and fell to speaking Greek for the remainder of the trek.

They had soon investigated all of Lake Muskoka and pushed on into the adjacent lakes, exploring Lake Rosseau over a number of summers and one year determining to push through the north channels into Lake Joseph. The Natives in the area had always claimed Joseph was the most beautiful lake in the district and contained, instead of the tea-like water of Lake Muskoka, water so crystal-clear you could watch trout swim along the bottom.

When they finally reached their destination, the Muskoka Club members saw that the Indians had been right. Lake Joseph, recorded Robinson, was "last, loneliest, loveliest, exquisite, apart." So taken were club members with the new discovery that they established a permanent camp on Chaplain's Island, near the Joseph River flowing out of the lake. They also began spreading their social net, bringing more and more people up from the city on their annual forays into the wild. As the young men married, they began coming up with wives – the first female tourists to journey to Muskoka.

The name "Muskoka" was by now getting some currency in the city, especially in the academic circles in which the various members of the club moved. It meant much more than the lake, though it would be still some time before it would come to signify a particular lifestyle. Variations of the word – usually *Mesqua Ukie* – had been around since Samuel de Champlain skirted along the eastern boundaries of the lake country in 1615, and Muskoka eventually came to designate an area of some 1,585 square miles, with seventeen rivers running through it and roughly 1,600 lakes of various sizes. Winters were harsh, but summers glorious. The lakes and rivers teemed with game fish, particularly speckled and lake trout, and the bush filled with a vast variety of life. One Lake Muskoka wildlife census from a few decades back counted 174 species of nesting bird, 54 kinds of mammals, 36 reptiles and amphibians, 70 butterflies, and 89 dragonflies and damselflies. No figure, mercifully, was ever attached to the number of mosquitoes or blackflies.

Though the earliest explorers, Champlain and Étienne Brûlé, didn't investigate the region, heading elsewhere in search of easier passage through to the Upper Great Lakes, the lakes and rivers of Muskoka do show up on French fur-trade maps from the 1650s. True exploration did not come about until after the War of 1812, when an alarmed government began fretting about possible future threats from the United States and started a search for alternative water routes that might cut through Upper Canada rather than the more exposed Great Lakes.

Lieut. Henry Briscoe came to the area on a surveillance assignment in 1826 and deserves to be remembered as the first visitor to become hopelessly distracted by what he saw. His report infuriated the Duke of Wellington, who slammed Briscoe and his party for commenting on everything "except what they were sent to examine." Briscoe had not found a route to eliminate passage through lakes Ontario, Erie, and Huron. He had found, and reported extensively on, a remarkably pleasant countryside filled with fish-rich lakes and small, charming rivers, all of little practical use.

Briscoe was followed by Alexander Shirreff, sent by his father to check on the lumbering possibilities, and Shirreff became first to use the word "Muskoka," which he took to be the name for an Ojibwa chief who lived around present-day Orillia.

The most significant explorer, however, turned out to be the legendary David Thompson, the world's greatest map-maker and the one who mapped most of the Canadian West. In the late 1830s, he landed a government contract to survey the area that would one day comprise Algonquin Park and Muskoka. He was sixty-seven, virtually blind in one eye from an accident, and may even have been suffering tunnel vision from mercury poisoning from his lifelong habit of carrying and working with the mysterious liquid element each day as he took his location readings with a sextant. He was also impoverished, the victim of several terrible business endeavours by some of his thirteen children. Thompson's motives for taking up the assignment were immediately met with suspicion. Captain Baddely, Upper Canada's commanding royal engineer, wrote to the official in charge of the survey, John Macauley, claiming that David Thompson was no longer "trustworthy as to the reporting of facts." The fear was that the legendary but aging explorer would simply report back what he thought his employer wished to hear.

Thompson set out with an old twilled-cotton tent, mildewed and filled with holes, and a list of supplies that would sink a modern tripper:

450 lb salted pork
100 lb beef
300 lb biscuit
2 bushels peas
1 lb tea
8.5 lb butter

5 gal. whisky
5 lb nails
2 yd towelling
tin mugs
7 lb tobacco
tea kettle
50 fathom net of five-inch mesh

Baddely's concern was what Thompson might have to say from the point of view of military strategy, but just imagine the response if the explorer's paymaster had been the local tourist association. Thompson called today's Lake Muskoka "Swamp Ground Lake" – a name that would have stopped in its tracks any notion of the idle rich heading off to their retreats in "the Swamp Grounds" – and complained that there were few fish the party could trap in its wide-mesh net. The "musketoes," he reported in his 1837 *Journal of Occurrences from Lake Huron to the Ottawa River*, were awful, the lakes barren, and, in a body blow to today's real-estate market, "almost every where the lake etc. is bordered by rude rocks."

Thompson may have been half blind and cranky, but he was no fool. When he came across impoverished Natives and further discovered that the woods possessed few animals apart from the "novelty" of songbirds, he drew conclusions that were decades ahead of their time. "For several years," he wrote, "all these Indians were rich, the women and children, as well as the men, were covered in silver brooches, ear rings, wampum, beads and other trinkets. Their mantles were of fine scarlet cloth, and all was finery and dress. The canoes of the fur traders were loaded with packs of beaver, the abundance of the article lowered the London prices. Every intelligent man saw poverty that would follow the destruction of the beaver, but there were no chiefs to control it; all was perfect liberty and equality. Four years afterward [1801] almost the whole of these extensive countries were denuded of beaver, the Natives became poor, and with difficulty procured the first necessities of life, and in this state they remain, and probably forever. A worn out field may be manured, and again made fertile, but the beaver, once destroyed, cannot be replaced; they were once the gold coin of the country, with which all the necessities of life were purchased."

The Natives were certainly at a severe economic disadvantage as settlement spread northward. In fact, much of their traditional land had already been taken by the time Thompson pushed through with his big canoes. In 1815, the government had purchased hunting grounds under the control of Chief Yellowhead, intending to leave the area from Lake Simcoe far into the north as reserve. But only three years later, another exchange of land for goods shifted the vague, never-designated reserve again. They were pushed back once again in 1836, when Natives living around present-day Orillia sold their choice land between lakes Simcoe and Couchiching.

They sold out cheaply and kept moving, first farther north and then to more isolated, less attractive land. On January 31, 1862, the Muskoka band met with surveyor John Stoughton Dennis in the Native village of Obajewanung – now Port Carling, summer home of designer clothing boutiques – and had Dennis draft a petition, which they asked be sent off to Lord Monck, the governor general. "Father," the band stated, after offering condolences to Queen Victoria on the death of her consort, Prince Albert, "we are in trouble and we come to you to help us out. We believe that your ears are always open to listen to the complaints of your Red Children and that your hand is always ready to lead them in the right path."

The Muskoka Band believed they had been misled, partly by government negotiators, partly by their own leadership. According to a treaty signed in Sault Ste. Marie, they were to go to an island near where the town of Parry Sound today stands on the shores of Georgian Bay. "Father," the little group pleaded from the banks of Lake Muskoka, "our feelings have changed. This place is beautiful in our eyes, and we found we could not leave it."

There was little patience and next to no sympathy for Native complaints in those days. A government report on the Sandy Island band in 1858 baldly stated, "The Sandy Island Indians are Heathen. . . . They have hitherto resisted all the attempts to civilize them, and cling with unaccountable tenacity to the foolish superstitions imbibed from their fathers."

The plea from the little Muskoka Band fell on deaf ears. The settling of the area was already underway, and the government would not intervene. The Ojibwa had no choice but to move on to the reserve at Parry Island. By the early 1870s, all Natives had left Muskoka, a vast territory where they had camped and trapped and lived long before the first Europeans reached North American shores.

The settling began in earnest following Thompson's explorations and, more significantly, the 1837 Rebellions. It was now clear to immigration officials that frustrated newcomers were finding it next to impossible to gain access to land to the south if they had no influence with the ruling Family Compact. The people were still unruly, despite the failures of the two rebellions, and more and more were fleeing the south for the Muskoka region each month. The population of Upper Canada was now 400,000, with new arrivals from the British Isles as well as Germany and the Netherlands eager to take up land. Lord Durham, who had been dispatched to the colony to prevent any subsequent revolts, was adamant that more land be opened up, and north was the only direction open.

The early reports were not encouraging. The government offer most certainly seemed acceptable – two hundred free acres, with another one hundred acres for each male child over the age of eighteen, with a home to be built and only two acres to be cleared a year – but the reality was sobering. Those settlers who did not discover they had hiked in to swamp often found that the soil was poor and so thin that it blew away once the land had been cleared. "In too many instances," an early press report on the Muskoka experiment noted, "the settlers made the mistake of clearing off the timber from the rocks. The result is that the soil, no longer held by the fibrous roots of trees, is readily washed away by rain." And too often when it was not washed or blown away, it was found to be too acidic for acceptable crops, because of years of pine cover. "The country of defeat," the poet Al Purdy once called the land of the Precambrian Shield, "where Sisyphus rolls a big stone/year after year up the ancient hills."

Early settlers learned to distrust much of what was held to be fact. Thomas McMurray of Belfast had been one of many unsatisfied Irishmen who, in 1861, turned out to listen to a Mr. J. Donaldson speak glowingly of the great farming potential in the new Dominion of Canada, and who decided to throw his lot in with others heading for this new land that was just opening up. "In looking over the map," McMurray wrote in a later account of his life, "I was favourably impressed with the position of Muskoka. Its proximity to Toronto, and its unlimited water facilities, led me to conclude that if the soil was that the surveyors reported it to be, that eventually it must become a place of considerable importance."

Like so many others on arrival, however, McMurray found he was "very disheartened by the appearance of the country. . . . At Orillia, many tried to dissuade me from going there: 'If you go there you will die, and there will be no one to bury you.'"

McMurray also suffered the first recorded con job at the hands of a local. He selected his land on the Muskoka River and arranged with a Mr. Hanna to have it cleared and a house built by the time McMurray got back from Ireland with his family. "I returned," McMurray wrote, "expecting my house to be finished, but, while the frame was erected, it was destitute of floors and roof, so we were obliged to make a shake-down, with nothing but the sky for our covering.

"On retiring to rest, all was pleasant, but at midnight the clouds gathered, the lightning came, the thunder rolled, and the rain descended in torrents. There we were out in the wild woods miles from any human habitation. This was our introduction to backwoods life."

McMurray was hardly alone in his shock at the roughness of the country. "Oh, the horrors of that journey!" Mrs. Harriet King, an English settler, wrote in a letter home. "The road was most dreadful – our first acquaintance with 'corduroy' roads. The forest gradually closed in upon us, on fire from both sides, burnt trees crashing down in all directions, here and there one right across the road, which had to be dragged out of the way before we could go on . . . your poor sister had to cling convulsively to the rope which secured the passengers' baggage (ours was left behind and we did not see it for weeks) to avoid being thrown out, and for long afterwards we both suffered from the bruises we received and the strain upon our limbs."

The road itself was often enough to discourage immigrants more used to the easy, natural roads of Europe. "Many settlers," Albert Sydney-Smith wrote in a July 1871 letter to the editor of the *Stratford Beacon*, "after passing through the rocky country between Washago and Bracebridge and still finding rocks staring them in the face, get discouraged or homesick; and, without going into the country to see what it is like, pick up their traps and leave by the first steamer. . . . I must say that the rocks have rather a chilling effect at first sight on those who are not used to them."

So, too, did some of the less-than-natural rocks they encountered. An eccentric Scot, James Cuthbert, built a stone fortress he called Gibraltar near where the Sparrow Lake overpass would eventually cross the highway. He cut logs, blackened their ends, and stuck them through makeshift portholes to resemble cannons and eventually purchased and hauled a real one in to his strange fort, where he would occasionally greet travellers by firing it as they approached.

An Englishman grandly called F. M. de la Fosse answered an 1878 British magazine advertisement placed by an entrepreneur in search of a few select, highly educated young gentlemen willing to pay one hundred pounds a year for the chance to be trained in advanced farming. He signed up for a three-year course and landed in Muskoka, where he cleaned out stables, fed the pigs, cut wood, and had to pry his socks off the frozen floor each winter morning to start his day.

"There was no farm," recalled de la Fosse many years later, "and if we had worked with him fifty years there was not enough good land on his lots to have enabled him or anyone else to practice the art of husbandry. . . . In three or four years, as soon as he had got a few of us settled on our plots, he left the district, and I believe never visited the place again."

It was not uncommon for settlers to leave quickly. Many had expected the rolling fields of the English countryside. Some thought the bush would be the equivalent of a tidy European wood lot. Some, like Englishman Titus Hibbert-Ware, who came only as far north as

Orillia, expected British society to rule in the Canadian wilderness as surely as it had ruled in the gentle countryside outside London. Hoping to cash in as a land speculator, Hibbert-Ware began writing letters back home to family and any "others interested in settling in the wild lands near Orillia." "The greatest inconvenience which a family from England has to submit to in this country," he said in one letter, "is the difficulty of getting female servants and keeping them. Women are in great demand here, so it is a common occurrence for a maid to leave without notice and get married. Another disagreeable situation arises from the equality notions which the servants have here: they believe 'Jack is as good as his master.'"

Hibbert-Ware's cousin Joseph Ware travelled to the new lands to see for himself, but he was unimpressed. "Titus says the problem of getting and keeping servants is very great," his anxious letter read. "And also it is too wild a place for me. I will go to other places, perhaps New Zealand."

Like all farmers, those who did decide to stay and take up their grants held onto hope that soon everything would get better. McMurray found himself surrounded by poverty when he reached Muskoka, but he placed blame on the settlers, not the land. "Such is the exception, not the rule," he wrote back to Belfast. "If the right class will only come, they will do well."

The "right class" would eventually come – but not for the soil.

The settlement road was soon through, and the railroad followed. By 1872 it was possible to travel by train from Toronto to Washago, thereby eliminating the need for a steamer to Orillia and then a smaller craft to get passengers and baggage over the shallow Lake Couchiching. By 1875, trains were coming all the way to Gravenhurst, and once travellers had reached Muskoka Bay it was possible to travel by water virtually anywhere else on the three main lakes and the twisting Muskoka River, which ran north and east to a string of smaller lakes, ending at Lake Vernon, just to the north of the new village of Huntsville.

The first hint of what Muskoka would ultimately become is contained in, of all places, a guidebook that was intended to do something quite apart: convince potential farmers that the land was indeed workable. W. E. Hamilton published *Muskoka and Parry Sound District* in 1878, and while he mostly sang the praises of the land and the transportation system, he also felt obliged to stand up to some of the derogatory comments circulating about the state of farming in the area.

"The rocks of Muskoka which fringe our territory and frown on the incomer are not true samples of Muskoka land," Hamilton claimed. "It is difficult to give an average of the proportion of good land in the district but we are not overshooting the mark when we say 60 per cent. The rest includes swamps, which could be drained to make the most valuable portions of the farm. Much of the so-called rocky portion of Muskoka would make excellent sheep pasture."

It may be that Hamilton himself did not believe such balderdash, for he almost immediately switched topic and, in a single sentence, spelled out what would be the true future of the district he had been hired to promote.

"Muskoka," Hamilton predicted, "is a virgin field for the great army of tourists."

It is a lousy day for a cruise. It has been spitting rain since early morning and now, with a cold wind bullying out of the west, a hard downpour is slapping against the port windows of *Lady Muskoka*. The foul weather has driven the few game tourists from the observation deck of the tourist ship to the galley, where hot coffee is outselling the advertised cold beer. It feels more like late fall than early summer.

For sixteen dollars you get two and a half hours of Lake Muskoka. The daily cruise begins in downtown Bracebridge, heads down the Muskoka River and then out into the wider lake. It is a casual, informational cruise – "Lake Muskoka is eighteen miles long, five miles wide, and goes down to a depth of just over three hundred feet" – but the people here are not along to determine distance. They come to measure wealth.

"That's Rebecca Island," Capt. Tom Brown announces over a scratchy intercom, "the smallest named island in the lake."

Tourists crowd to the starboard windows to stare out through the water-streaked windows. There is nothing within sight but a rock sticking out of the water with a marker on it. It would hold a gull, but not much more. Beyond there is only slanting rain, almost completely erasing the near shore.

"That happens to be the last one that the government still owns – or can afford!"

Everyone laughs. This short cruise aboard the three-hundred-passenger *Lady Muskoka* has been about money since it headed downstream in the Muskoka River and passed the first "For Sale" sign at the edge of a manicured lawn, a relatively nice white-frame house beyond the maples. "The asking price," crackles Captain Tom, "is $799,000."

The passengers are taking photographs of everything the ship passes by. It is understandable, for back home in Japan and the United States and Great Britain and Germany and France and even Toronto, they may be called upon to prove some of the more outlandish claims they will take with them when they disembark.

They have passed through the town of Bracebridge and, with the rain pausing long enough for the passengers to take to the deck, have stared at one another in wonder as the sounds of Christmas songs come floating across the water from Santa's Village. We are at the forty-fifth parallel, "Halfway to the North Pole," and for decades the mouth of the river has been the summer home of Santa Claus, a fifty-acre site where Rudolph is a ride and Santa sweats so hard it is a wonder little children still pile onto his lap for the commemorative picture. It is cold this day, but surely not cold enough for "Winter Wonderland" to be blasting out from under the drooping, windblown maples.

The passengers have then travelled out into the main body of the lake, where the prow slaps through the whitecaps and, every few minutes, the loudspeakers crackle with the latest announcement. The Binder family has just arrived "all the way from Germany," says Captain Tom. And sure enough, the German flag is up and flying over an exceptional island cottage compound that is merely a small hint of what is to come.

The route runs between Eileen Gowan Island and Browning Island, two of the largest on the lake, and then on past a series of exquisite postcard islands, each one charmingly named: Nine Mile Island, Fox Island, Jupiter Island, Old Woman Island, Stonewall Island, Christmas Island, Grandview Island, Columbia Island, Squirrel Island.

The farther out into the lake *Lady Muskoka* churns, the higher the cottages escalate in price. The old ones are of log and sometimes barely visible in the thick growth unless the rustic shutters happen to be painted red. There is money of great discretion at work in such places, no ostentation but the high value obvious in the perfect grounds. It is found in the well-worn paths, in the sturdy, perfectly level, and recently stained docks with their inviting, and fresh-painted, Muskoka chairs, and in the potted red and white geraniums with not so much as a curled leaf to spoil the sense that, moments earlier, a cover photograph for *Town & Country Living* might have been taken at this precise spot.

"Just to give you a sense of the value out here in the centre of the lake," Captain Tom crackles as we pass Old Woman Island, owned by a family from Boston, "this island has about sixteen acres, a nine-bedroom cottage, with room for seven more in the two boathouses.

"That would set you back about five million dollars."

The newer cottages are wood frame, large, and generously win-dowed, almost as if the dwellers have decided it is more important to be able to see in than out. They all seem freshly painted – robin's egg blue, seaside grey, delicate yellows, and soft greens – and all strangely empty, as if they are model summer homes that have yet to sell. Or perhaps the rich just don't bother with Muskoka in poor cottage weather. Either that or, as one man standing on the observation deck suggests, they cannot come because they're working full-time just trying to spend all the money they have.

There is a remarkable tameness to many of the island retreats. They often suggest not so much Canadian wilderness as a strong sense of English *order*. The grounds have been cleared, the trees thinned back, the woods no longer dark and mysterious, as they must have seemed to the first paddlers who travelled along these waters.

Sally Carrigher, an American naturalist who grew up in Kansas City, once wrote about the time her family came to "the Muskoka Lakes" and spent an entire summer on just such a dark and mysterious island. "The trees, vaguely and strangely, were menacing," she wrote in *Home to Wilderness*, the memoir she published in 1973. "Not in any park, cemetery or pasture had I ever been so entirely enclosed by trees. These were massive, like giants. One surrounded by them felt helpless. They spread above, forming together a cavelike dark. They were presences . . .

"I didn't believe consciously that a tree might be hostile," she wrote. "I was just strangely uneasy there in the eerie atmosphere of the grove. One can name this dread and call it claustrophobia, which probably is an ancient fear. A prehistoric man might have felt trapped in dense woods, and recently Sir Francis Fraser Darling, the eloquent conservationist, has said that many modern people are afraid of the wilderness, which is why they are so willing to see it destroyed. Anyway, I was slightly alarmed by that island forest, and although I was rather eager to know what was there I couldn't force myself to continue farther."

It took Carrigher the entire three months of summer to get over her trepidation. For a long while she could walk about the island only if accompanied by the lodge-owner's son, who always carried a rifle.

"Compare a park," she wrote. "Only a few, spaced-out trees were allowed to grow, their dead branches were pruned away, the flowers were all in neat beds, the grass was kept mowed, never allowed to become weeds or 'grasses.' All controlled, therefore safe.

"Here the plants grew their own way and the animals went their own way – one might appear anywhere, any time. No one knew what might happen – did happen, for there were dead broken trees among the live ones. Everything was wild – naturally. That was the meaning of forests of course, that they were wild. Therefore unpredictable.

"Yet the wilderness was a beautiful, even enchanting place with its graceful movement and active life. Even underfoot if one scratched away the brown leaves as the bird had done, one might come upon small, secret lives. But might there be things that would bite? I had heard of tarantulas. With a feeling of cowardice, shrinking back, I wanted to leave, to return to the wide placid lake."

She gradually forced herself to enter the woods. Each morning, alone, she would head out on a small peninsula on the island and sit and stare at her surroundings. "Gradually," she found, "a few moments one day, more moments the next, being there in that small safe woodland began to seem almost the same experience as making music, as the way, when I played the piano, I *was* the music, my physical body feeling as if it dissolved in the sounds."

It took three months, but Carrigher mastered her fear and found that by the end she had come to *prefer* her time alone.

"The sunrise across the wild northern lake seemed a kind of holiness that human chatter was bound to destroy a little," she concluded. "The water, so still and lucent, beyond it the dark mystery of the forest, and the firs' fragrance: for this sacred experience, enjoyed alone, I would get up at dawn every day during that summer."

Lady Muskoka cuts between Squirrel Island and Tondern Island, and Captain Tom speaks a phrase that has been heard at this spot for nearly a century – but which has come, in recent years, to take on a quaint note of understatement.

"We are about to enter an area known," the loudspeakers crackle, "as 'Millionaires' Row.'"

It should, of course, be *Billionaires' Row*, but tradition is hard to shake in Cottage Country, and the misnomer persists long after it has become apparent that if a mere millionaire turned up at one of these grand docks, security would be called.

The area known as Millionaires' Row was also known, at the turn of the twentieth century, as Little Pittsburgh. It is the result of difficult breathing and the lack of air conditioning, for it was here that the rich industrialists of booming Pittsburgh found their summer relief from the smog and sweltering heat of the valley produced by the convergence of the Ohio, Allegheny, and Monongahela rivers. One can appreciate the strong urge to escape when reading James Parton's late nineteenth-century account of the city, where "every street appears to end in a huge black cloud." By day, Parton recorded, Pittsburgh was "smoke, smoke, smoke – everywhere smoke," and by night it was "Hell with the lid taken off." In the days before air conditioning, the wealthy had only the one escape route: out of the city entirely.

It was not just the smog-bound who found it easier to breathe in the new country. Allergy sufferers were also quick to note that the fresh air and cool nights of the Ontario bush offered unexpected relief. "The Muskoka air," a brochure for the Grand Trunk Railway read, "is one of the best alleviations known for that very persistent and annoying ailment, Hay Fever . . . there is entire immunity from the disease here. . . . Owing to the high altitude and pureness of the dry atmospheric conditions, perfect immunity from malaria is also assured."

Excellent train connections to Buffalo, then to Toronto, and then north to Muskoka meant that wealthy families could depart the steel town the moment school let out for the summer, head north with as many trunks as the trains and Muskoka steamboats would allow them to carry, and never have to lift another finger until it was time to call for a gin and tonic before the sun went down over the western hills.

The cruise down Millionaires' Row would be dangerous if *Lady Muskoka* were not so large and stable, for the tourists race from port to starboard as the Gatsby-like summer homes reel by. They take photographs and point and stare, tongues hanging out like docks reaching into the channel that runs between Squirrel and Tondern islands. It is hard to grasp the grandeur, the genteelness, the quietly arrogant wealth of Millionaires' Row.

Captain Tom points out the Mellon Estate on the right. Mellon, as in Mellon Bank of Pennsylvania and Pittsburgh's heart-of-the-city Mellon Center.

"Notice the brown building up between the two boathouses," he advises.

The tourists hurry toward the railing on the starboard side, some pointing, others already photographing the gorgeous, understated cottage on the rise beyond the two massive boathouses.

"That's the summer home of *the caretaker!*" Captain Tom cackles.

"Applications are available at the snack bar!"

The cottages tend to palatial, but quietly so, as if the builders were honouring the design standards set by the dramatic rock outcroppings, the rust-coloured pine-needle floors of the islands, the soft cedar and the high-spreading maples. So discreet, so *hidden*, are many of the homes, that the boathouses have become the focal point of this part of the lake, with two bestselling photographic books published on the boathouses alone. No one has ever effectively penetrated the natural tree cover, the security, and the overwhelming desire for privacy that many of the rich have brought to their summer retreats hiding well back of the boathouses. One gets the impression that the cottagers would happily hide their boathouses too, if they could. It can hardly be a pleasant way to spend a summer afternoon, sunning on the dock as a three-hundred-passenger tour boat washes past your shore, your name, your private business, and your cottage's value echoing through the static of the public address system.

The summer residents are not out, it suddenly occurs to me, not because of the weather or because they are too busy trying to figure out how to spend their money. They are not out because, obviously, they know the tour schedule.

Millionaires' Row would have been inconceivable to Edward Prowse and his brother-in-law John Wilmott when they first came up this channel on October 16, 1873. They had come from England to start new lives in Canada, the Prowses with their four children (four more yet to come) and the Wilmotts with their nine, and travelled by ship, train, stagecoach, and, finally, the steamer *Waubamik* to reach Tondern Island, where they hoped to farm.

They were not the first to reach the island. An Irishman, Paul Dane, had purchased the 338-acre island in 1868 from the Crown for $101. Dane died three years later and the property fell to his nephew Maurice John McCarthy, who then sold it to Prowse and Wilmott for $1,560 – nearly fifteen times what Dane had paid for it only five years earlier.

It can therefore be regarded as Muskoka's first property flip.

Prowse named the property Beaumaris Landing, presumably drawing on Beaumaris Castle, which Edward 1 had built in 1298 to ensure English domination over the Welsh. With Wilmott, he set out to clear the land, using oxen, but Prowse already had larger plans for an entire community and, he hoped, a handsome resort that would cater to well-off travellers. The Prowse and Wilmott families were themselves very well off by Canadian standards. They had landed with trunks filled with fine linen and china, quality dining furniture, and complete bedroom suites. There was even an upright piano for evening entertainment.

By 1880 Prowse had completed his hotel, while Wilmott had applied himself to clearing the land and trying to get a farm under-way. The new hotel, called simply Beaumaris, was large enough to serve as many as two hundred guests and offered cricket and lawn tennis, dancing, billiards, bowling, boating, and fishing, as well as evening concerts around the piano. The daily rates, meals included, were set from $1.50 to $2.00.

For decades Beaumaris reigned as the resort of choice in an area that would soon have many world-famous resorts: Windermere House, Cleveland's House, Elgin Lodge, Lake Rosseau Resort, Pratt's Hotel, Prospect House, and the Royal Muskoka Hotel, where Prime Minister Sir Robert Borden was frequently a guest. Beaumaris set the style, even having its own travelling cricket team and, at one point, boasting William Lyon Mackenzie King, who would succeed Borden as prime minister, as a player. The grand lodge of Beaumaris survived when others failed in the 1920s and 1930s, and was still a going concern when it was burned down on July 21, 1945, by a nineteen-year-old arsonist who was described as a "borderline case mentally" and sen-tenced to two years in prison.

There were already a number of fishing and hunting clubs at that end of Lake Muskoka when Beaumaris opened for business in 1880. The various clubs were made up of wealthy professionals from Toronto and Hamilton and Pennsylvania. They were often a curious amalga-mation of the traditional hunting or fishing camp and the "muscular Christianity" movement of the day. Spirits were rare around the lake, even the lodges were dry in these temperance days, and there was a strong belief in the healing powers of fresh air and moderate exercise.

"The health of the entire club had been most excellent," a Captain McAdam reported from the Garfield Hunting and Fishing Club, a Pittsburgh group then camping near Bala falls. "Men become attenuated and return robust, whilst the doctor declared that not a symptom of ennui or even low spirits is to be now found in camp.

"The bill of fare announced for the breakfast in the camp was boiled trout, roast porcupine, venison steaks, and stewed ducks with bread, coffee, and the usual accompaniments. No wonder with such a menu, such air, and such surroundings, dyspepsia, languor and low spirits take flight at once and the nervous invalid of a few weeks before finds himself boating, fishing or hunting with a new lease on life."

Some, like the Sharon Social Fishing Club, have been on Lake Muskoka for more than a century, though the original landscape has changed so dramatically that today the once isolated and rustic Sharon Club is in the very heart of Millionaires' Row. The club that inspired Sharon, the Solid Comfort Camp, is quite the opposite story. Solid Comfort was founded by Pennsylvanians who became the first Americans to buy on Tondern Island, and in 1883 they put up a permanent camp, paying a mere $107 for a four-acre site near the Beaumaris wharf. The Solid Comfort group, despite its name, tried to keep matters as simple as possible, putting up only one simple cottage and housing most members in three large tents. Soon, however, the tents seemed an oddity, out of fashion with the growing ostentation of the area.

By 1905, the Solid Comfort Camp was finding Lake Muskoka just a little too "touristy" for its members' taste. "While these cottagers were first class people and splendid neighbours and friends," Quincy Gordon recorded in the camp's official history, "the character of Beaumaris had so changed that the call of the wild, which has always appealed so strongly to this Club, could no longer be satisfied here." The camp sold out that year and moved on to the more isolated French River.

In a single generation, the thirty-odd years since Sproule and Wilmott disembarked on Tondern Island and decided to call their little find Beaumaris, the landscape had been dramatically altered by the single most intrusive force since the last ice age had rumbled through: money. An extraordinary building spree was underway – fifty-eight sprawling cottages would be built in the Beaumaris area between 1895 and the start of the First World War – and they all adopted names that contained their own euphemistic boast of old money and high standing: Treetops, Pudding Point, Grandview, Westwind, Tanglewood, Rockmount, Outlook, Baypoint, Ramatola, Grumblenot.

The "summer settlers" were, for the most part, wealthy Americans, many coming on the invitation of friends and then deciding to purchase, or build, their own summer retreat. More than a century later, the flavour persists. Beaumaris, *Equinox* magazine noted in 1985, "is the only place in Canada so removed from the U.S. border where such a concentration of Americans has lived for so long and with such dedication."

Back when it first began, cottage life in Muskoka was often a comedic combination of determined luxury and necessity. Many wealthy cottagers would bring their own bathtubs back and forth with them, but seeing as the best defence against the mosquitoes and blackflies was thought to be to cover one's skin with a stinking mixture of pork fat and carbolic, the tubs had a practicality to them.

The wealthy showed no inclination to dress the part of rustics living off the land – the style of the day requiring collared shirts and ties even for fishing – and in the evening they behaved much as if Beaumaris were located in the toney heart of Toronto's Rosedale rather than at the end of a choppy lake in the heart of the Ontario bush.

Even so, according to a report carried in the Toronto *Globe* society pages, "Elaborate evening toilets are very sensibly eschewed up here at Beaumaris, and the girls are quite as pretty in their light muslins, with perchance tams or fancy hats on their heads, as they would be were they more gorgeously attired, while the men in their white ducks or white flannel suits look as if they were, indeed, enjoying a summer holiday most thoroughly."

The wealth was mind-boggling to the poverty-stricken settlers who were finding it more profitable to work the lakes than the land. The Kuhns of Bell Isle, for example, had a "Big House" so large that it required eight maids, two German butlers, a housekeeper, and a chore boy. The family also employed two handymen, as well as a captain and full crew for the boat. The main cottage was built in 1902 by Pittsburgh industrialist James Kuhn and his wife, Ella, and featured a massive stone fireplace, stuffed mountain goat and deer heads on the walls, and port and cigars for the men at the end of the evening meal. One summer, the steamships from Gravenhurst unloaded more than thirty massive trunks on the Bell Isle dock containing nothing more than the Kuhn family essentials.

It was genteel living at its best, the mosquitoes excepted. The enterprising locals realized early on that any service that made summer living even easier would be rewarded handsomely, and soon there were supply boats working the large family compound docks so that the vacationers would not have to think about sending their own help to the local markets. Twice weekly the *Alporto* would arrive carrying fresh produce and a butcher with slabs of fresh beef on ice blocks, awaiting only instructions on the size and type of cut required.

It was a lifestyle of enormous charm for those fortunate enough to have the money and leisure time required. "There may be a prettier place than Muskoka in the world," Pittsburgh astronomer John Brashear wrote in a memoir published in 1924, "but in all my travels I have never come across it."

It was the beginning of the glory years for Muskoka, when rich Americans flooded into the little Gravenhurst and Bracebridge and, later, Huntsville train stations and then set out by steamboat for whatever lodge they had booked. The king of the Muskoka waters was A. P. Cockburn, whose Muskoka Navigation Company would eventually have a fleet of one hundred and forty boats of various sizes working lakes Muskoka, Rosseau, and Joseph, as well as another fifty working the waters around Huntsville and Lake of Bays. Tourists would arrive at Toronto's Union Station and catch the daily Muskoka Express headed north, many of them just to catch "The 100-mile Cruise" to the top of Lake Joseph and back, but most to stay for stretches that varied anywhere from a long weekend to the entire summer.

For years, the summer cruises were the delight of the idle rich. The style of wear was rather formal – black suits for the men, white, ankle-length dresses and fancy hats for the women – and the happy cruisers would board the likes of the ss *Wenonah, Sagamo, Nipissing, Cherokee,* or *Segwun* and strike out for their resort destination while taking tea in the glassed-in dining room.

It was, ironically, the lesser cottagers who killed off the steamships. As more and more crown land was opened up and the Canadian middle class began rimming the lakes with their simple cottages, a local service industry emerged to cover everything from building supplies to groceries. A growing local population and demand for goods soon resulted in new roads about the lakes and, eventually, the familiar steamboats were put out of business by ground transportation.

By the 1950s only two of the elegant steamers, *Sagamo* and *Segwun,* were operating on the Muskoka lakes, and both were retired from service on the same Labour Day weekend, in 1958. Sixteen years later, when Prime Minister Pierre Elliott Trudeau came to Gravenhurst for the relaunch of *Segwun* as a dinner-and-dance tour boat, 6,000 people showed up for the ceremony. The prime minister, for once, was not the main draw.

No one foresaw exactly how this new land called Muskoka would evolve; they certainly did not anticipate that the land would be bought up by so many who wished only to "settle" there during the best weather. Muskoka became a world where the poverty of the permanent settlers contrasted dramatically to those who could afford to build on the finest properties and visit only a few weeks of each year. And yet a strong relationship quickly developed between the two: the wealthy cottagers had needs, and the needy locals had supplies and services to offer in exchange for a small bite of that wealth. The first wave of cottages created such a boom in the building industry that, for a while, there were seventeen sawmills operating along Gravenhurst Bay alone. Summer was becoming a year-round enterprise.

Tourism was soon the main industry of Muskoka. The logging was essentially over, except for those willing to haul from deep back in the bush. Farming was sustenance, at best, and more often futile. Whereas previous settlers had become discouraged and fled the land for the bush, or the gold fields, or Australia if they could not get into the United States, these settlers who stayed on turned to the water and a new source of income the likes of which Canada had not known before. They began to sell to the very rich who came for the summer – "The summer outing is robbed of half its charm," an early advertisement read, "if music is made impossible by want of a piano" – and even to the lesser classes who came for the day. No better example of early enterprise exists than the farmers who gave up trying to clear their land of impossible bramble and tangle and turned, instead, to building twig furniture, the first uniquely Muskoka tourist offering.

There is no record of the first tourist trap, but it may well have been the phoney Indian village set up in Port Carling to be part of the Muskoka Navigation Company's 100-Mile Cruise. Two "Indian Chiefs" – Chief War Eagle and Chief American Horse – were brought in from Upper New York State. With their wives, they set up an "Indian" encampment with about twenty other Natives, put up teepees, made and sold handiwork and birchbark souvenirs, and even put on "Indian" costumes and danced when the cruise ships docked. No one ever noted that the "Indian Village" had been erected on the very ground where, in 1862, the Muskoka Band had met with the government representative and vainly petitioned the governor general to be allowed to stay on at this place which "is beautiful in our eyes."

The vast wealth of the summer visitors created other businesses that otherwise would not have looked twice on the marshland and rocky outcroppings of Muskoka. Craftsmen began moving to the area to build the exquisite mahogany watercraft that the rich cottagers preferred. As early as the 1890s, Muskoka was considered the custom-boat capital of the world. Names of local builders – W. J. Johnston, Bert Minett, Henry Ditchburn, C. J. Duke, Thomas and Ernie Greavette – became famous for the boats that are, today, prized possessions, the annual antique boat shows drawing thousands to various wharves to drool as they imagine what it was like to be very rich and very idle on Lake Muskoka.

It became fashionable for the wealthiest families to have their own private steam yachts, the most famous being the sixty-eight-foot *Naiad*

– modelled on J. P. Morgan's beloved *Corsair* – and directed about the lake by Senator William Sanford of Hamilton. By 1915 there were 329 gasoline-powered boats scooting over the Muskoka lakes, most of them small. The *Rainbow VII*, however, which was built by Ditchburn for Harold Greening in 1928, featured two 517-horsepower Liberty V-12 engines and could carry fifteen passengers at sixty miles per hour.

For four decades, the most popular boats on the Muskoka lakes were the curious products of the Disappearing Propeller Company of Port Carling, the little highly polished DPs – or, as they were also known, the "poor man's launch," with their smaller size and adjustable propeller for shallow waters – meant that the cottagers no longer had to rely exclusively on the big steamboats, which were quickly being reduced to mail and supply work.

Mobile cottagers with money and endless free time also meant opportunity for businesses providing entertainment. Dunn's Pavilion soon went up alongside the village wharves in Bala, and Saturday night would see as many as 2,000 showing up, most arriving by water, to dance to the likes of Louis Armstrong, Duke Ellington, Stan Kenton, Tommy and Jimmy Dorsey, Les Brown, and Woody Herman. For thirty years Dunn's operated successfully without a liquor licence, something that present-day visitors to the establishment – now known as Key to Bala – would find hard to believe as their shoes suck and stick to a floor that seems to have been swabbed nightly with beer.

The glory days of Lake Muskoka have long since gone, even if today Cottage Country is busier than ever, real-estate prices are still going up, and the Sea-Doo and its various hyperactive cousins have become the modern version of the Disappearing Propeller boat.

Muskoka today is so active in summer it bears little relation to what Commander John Cheyne found in the summer of 1888, when the British navy veteran came to Lake Muskoka to recuperate from an unspecified serious illness. In a booklet he later published, the commander advised readers "where to find a quiet vacation at a moderate expense away from the cares and anxieties of business life."

He recommended the very place now washed by the high wake of the 104-foot *Lady Muskoka* as the cruise ship leaves Beaumaris and heads back across the open lake to Bracebridge and the end of the two-and-one-half-hour voyage.

"A place," Cheyne called it, "where you are so secluded from the busy world that you cannot be found unless you so desire."

" 'The tourists are coming, hurrah, hurrah,' " the little settler children sang as they burst out to greet the summer visitors in Ann Hathaway's charmingly naive little 1904 novel *Muskoka Memories*.

Ann Hathaway, the pen name for Fanny Cox, was witness to a pivotal time in Cottage Country. The grand resorts were up and running, the smoke from the steamboats trailing over the lakes, and such a building boom was underway she felt compelled to remark, "Isn't it wonderful how rapidly the houses are increasing on these lakes? They appear to be springing up like mushrooms on every island and point."

The cottages did, indeed, seem to appear, like mushrooms, overnight. They came in an extraordinary and colourful variety. And while most were harmless, there was always a risk that everything was not quite as it seemed on first sight.

"For the past few years," Hathaway continued, "the population of Muskoka has been gradually dividing itself into two classes – tourists and settlers, otherwise capital and labour, pleasure and toil, butterflies and bees . . . and between the two there is a great gulf fixed. . . . One thing is sure, each class would be badly off without the other."

Nearly one hundred years later, it is astonishing how close Ann Hathaway came to defining the split personality of Cottage Country. *Two classes: tourists and settlers, capital and labour, pleasure and toil, between the two a great gulf fixed . . . each class in need of the other.*

I grew up in Muskoka. I was born in Whitney, on the eastern side of Algonquin Park, but went to school and lived in Huntsville, the northernmost town in Muskoka, so I know something of what I speak.

The rhythms of Cottage Country are such that those who grow up here eventually get used to living two lives. A split personality develops almost out of necessity, for the people, particularly the young, feel obliged to fit the changing landscape. For three seasons of each year,

Muskoka is provincial, for one season cosmopolitan. Both visitors and locals carry themselves differently in summer, as if everyone is on display for the next two months or so.

To fully appreciate the "great gulf" Hathaway talked about, it is perhaps helpful to look at this summer arrangement in colonial terms. There is a sense among the locals, mostly blue-collar or rural families, that the purse strings are controlled elsewhere, a sense among the visitors that the locals are there to serve, that the locals are somewhat quaint but, all the same, less. It is an intriguing echo of the history of Canada as a whole: the early French resented the court, the early English resented British Parliament; early fur traders had decisions cast for them in London, later manufacturers were told what to do by American head offices. Even when the symbiotic benefits are obvious – and what can be more obvious than an economy created by tourism? – there is still an undeniable, abiding emotion that sticks in the craw of those whose livelihood depends on outsiders. Especially so if those outsiders tend to view the locals as support staff.

The defence mechanism, for those who live here year round, is to look down on those who come before the visitors can look down – as surely they are doing – on those already here. The tourist sees the local as some innocently charming fauna, wily if not worldly, obscurely philosophical and endearingly quick to provide humorous anecdote for dispersal on return to the city. Locals, of course, have to stay on once the lake turns and the first leaves fall.

Tourists, in this strange, bipolar world where both sides view the other as somewhat lacking, are held not to be particularly bright by the locals. They don't know a snapping turtle from a painted turtle. They would pay, if they could, to see a dump bear rooting around in a rusted dumpster filled with broken green plastic bags – the black bear, in his natural element. They don't know where the fish are or how to get down to them. They sit in the wrong end of a canoe. They tick the gunwales when they paddle. They don't know how to mix their gas. They wear short pants into raspberry bushes. They have an endless supply of clean khaki, don't appear to own socks, and – the No. 1 telltale sign of the modern Muskoka outsider – they wear Tilley hats. The No. 2 telltale sign, despised by the locals, is that they refer to this part of the country as "The Muskokas," a phrase that has never passed the mouth of a single soul who has passed through a November or March in Muskoka, no "s."

Hathaway also wrote that, despite such an obvious gulf, "each class would be badly off without the other." It is as true today as it was in 1904. What the soil could not deliver to Muskoka, the tourists brought: a living. In some cases, particularly around the three most prosperous lakes, Muskoka, Rosseau, and Joseph, it can be quite a good living. Rich Toronto cottagers and American vacationers and Japanese tours have created a curious seasonal economy that can, in the extreme, mean that the guy who replaces the leathers on the water pump in July might spend his winters in Australia.

The cottagers and tourists pay their bills, usually promptly, and if much of their own reliability is based on the fact that they recognize they are themselves at the mercy of the locals as much as the locals are obviously at the mercy of the visitors, then so be it. That, after all, is the definition of a symbiotic relationship.

As Ann Hathaway noted so long ago, they *need* each other. They may not always like each other, but they dare not show it. They are, invariably, polite to each other, even if the locals are as quick to duck behind the canoe racks and howl with laughter as the cottagers are to sit around their campfires regaling each other with passable imitations of local accents and tales of workers who show up, if at all, when they damn well feel like it.

Cottagers soon learn that "next week" means, at best, "next month" but can even mean "next summer." Attractions are rarely as fabulous as advertised. And bargains are impossible to find. It is, however, the local economy. And has been now for generations.

The *Lady Muskoka* cruise is drawing to an end. The rain has stopped completely, and the tourists and their cameras are back out on the observation deck as the ship draws near enough to the mouth of the river to catch fragments of the latest tune bouncing about the trees of Santa's Village.

Captain Tom has told a great many stories, but not them all. He has not mentioned, for example, that the original Wilmott log home back in Beaumaris is still standing. It is now the Johnson & Daniels real-estate office, and the deals brokered by that company and many others about Lake Muskoka over the past decade and more make the original land flip of Tondern Island look like that rarity in Muskoka: a bargain.

On the July 1st weekend 2001, there were sixty properties on the three main lakes listed for between one and five million dollars. One-third of those cottages were newly built by speculators. Those unable to buy were lining up to rent, one "cottage" in the area, going for $1,400 a *day*, getting snapped up by a family that elected to come and go by seaplane to avoid the traffic snarls coming up from the city.

"If your home is your castle," Muskoka realtor Anita Latner told a reporter that summer, "your cottage is Camelot – and in Muskoka nowadays you're going to need King Arthur's treasury to buy it."

There were, surely by coincidence, three separate properties listed for $4.9 million. One had 710 feet of frontage on Lake Joseph and was merely "a golfcart ride" to the nearest course. "If you deserve the summit in graceful living amidst nature's beauty," the advertisement read, "you must see this." Another $4.9 million property on Lake Joseph was described as "a natural beauty," and, if that failed to have one dialling for one's favourite Hong Kong banker, it was also deemed "too nice for words." The third, on Lake Rosseau, boasted a wraparound verandah, a four-slip boathouse, separate sauna, separate guest cottage, separate sleeping bunkie, a caretaker's house, and was, as might be expected, a "meticulously maintained olde Muskoka property."

This was a new buzzword for the new century – "*olde* Muskoka" – as if a mere $4.9 million could conjure up mahogany boats and supply steamboats and cricket whites and put an end to the riffraff that dared think it had rights to the water and shoreline. The second buzzword was "nature," as if these monstrosities had somehow managed to preserve the shoreline precisely as Campbell, Bains, Crombie, and that poor forgotten dog found it when they pushed out from shore in that leaky scow back in the summer of 1861.

An advertisement in *The Muskokan* of August 9, 2001, showed a massive stone-and-glass home that might have been drawn up for Microsoft magnate Bill Gates, the huge home somehow squeezed, presumably by crowbars and airbrushing, onto an island so small it must certainly have sunk moments after the shot was taken. The ad proclaimed the over-the-top structure to be "At Home With Nature."

The cottage of the mind is rarely found any longer in Muskoka. Rustic, small, with an outhouse, no running water, not winterized, perhaps without electricity and certainly no telephone – if it exists at all, it is as a "handyman's special" on the real-estate pages. The two great rituals of cottage life, the Closing Up and the Opening Up, have virtually been reduced to the same weekend, thanks to ploughed roads, electric base heaters, and, in some instances, central heating systems that can be fired up from a cellular telephone while the driver is still battling rush-hour traffic on Highway 400.

Some would say the development of Cottage Country has been offensive, but let us be a little more polite and call it attrition, for it has largely snuck up on people, evolving so slowly it has barely been noticed as the summers slide by – a sort of innocent *wearing away* of good intention that, by the time it is finally recognized for what it is, may already be too late to prevent.

In our own small cottage it is not so many years since we installed a telephone, purely, we thought, for precautionary reasons. Ellen's father had died suddenly of a heart attack, and her mother was insisting on carrying on the cottage tradition, even if it meant felling her own trees, cutting up her own wood, carrying her own water, clearing the brush, shovelling the roof in winter, and chopping holes in the two-foot-thick ice to get enough water to boil for her beloved tea. She might fall, we worried. She might need help.

At first it was a party line, then a private line. Then Bell Canada informed us the old rotary dial telephone would have to go, because, well, Cottage Country was turning to "pulse" dialling so that people could use their computers up North. In my work, this seemed heaven-sent at first, for computers and modems meant a journalist could work from anywhere.

Soon there was a new light in the sky, very low on the northern horizon, and bright red: the top of a communication tower. One of the neighbours discovered if he hiked up the tallest hill on the south-east side of the lake and turned just so, he could use his cell phone and keep up with such critical summer matters as the afternoon market performance of the Nasdaq.

In a matter of two or three short summers I was about to discover that going to the cottage – even this rustic little place on Camp Lake, with no running water and an outhouse – was no longer "getting away from it all." Work could track me down. I could now check my e-mail, and I found myself, at times, torn between the cold beer in the ice box and workplace paranoia. Before long we found ourselves booking week-long canoe trips into the interior of Algonquin Park where, so far, the campsites remain beyond the reach of digital roam and there are no telephone jacks at the bottom of the jack pines. We were, I can admit now, *escaping* from the cottage.

Attrition is a curious thing. It can happen even to those with the best intentions without them fully realizing what's going on under their own hammock. I can remember a local cottagers' association many years ago where an older, white-bearded man put forward the notion that some of the smaller lakes near Algonquin Park should be restricted to canoes only. To me, it seemed a fine, if somewhat unworkable, notion. I had no idea at the time that I would evolve into the very creature he so clearly wished to avoid. But we had very young children then, and soon there were four, and far too soon they were teenagers, and somewhere along the way we had to build a separate shed down by the water just to hold the ropes and boards and tubes and – *good heavens!* – where did that ninety-horsepower boat with the wakeboard bar come from? We have two floating docks now, and they are not enough. I no longer show up for the annual cottagers' meetings. I am too ashamed.

Technology has become very much the double-edged sword of Cottage Country. The executive with his laptop and cell phone might believe he is whittling a few extra work days into his vacation, but in fact it is the office that is cutting deeply into escape. And as for those

wonderfully romantic memories of silly board games and marshmallows by the beach bonfire, how can "Sorry" possibly compare to a
Sony PlayStation or Bell ExpressVu and a choice of five hundred
different television channels? How can burnt marshmallows compare
to gourmet popcorn fresh from the microwave and a brand-new
rental movie from the little shop that, not so many summers ago, used
to keep bug spray and spark plugs on the shelves where Mel Gibson
and Halle Berry now rule? Cottagers used to watch for shooting stars
on a bright, warm summer evening. Now they count satellites, if they
are out at all.

It would be easier if we could just blame Benjamin Franklin,
Thomas Edison, and Alexander Graham Bell for what has happened
to Cottage Country over the past quarter century, but that would be
no better than blaming Cadbury for our cavities. The very rich, with
their gaudy cottages, big boats, and impossible-to-ignore presence,
are easy to fault, but they have not done this alone.

Even well-intentioned cottagers have become their own worst
enemies. Mass transportation first made Cottage Country more
accessible to more people. Prosperity, even limited, made a place at the
lake within reach, and better roads and vehicles extended that reach.
Retirement brought an air of permanency. The lake, much to our col-
lective shock, has too often become merely the latest layer of suburb
– the very thing from which the cottage was intended to offer both
escape and protection. We may have inadvertently been loving the
cottage to death.

There is something terribly worrisome about this rush to bring the
conveniences of home and the inconveniences of the office to the
bush. It seems to go against all that we have always felt about the very
nature of escape, even if we have not always been able to articulate
what we mean by getting away, periodically, from the overwhelming
bulk of our lives. In stretching the time spent at the lake so thinly, we
risk tearing the very fabric that makes up the summer delight. "I love
it," the American writer John Irving has a character say of a visit to
Georgian Bay in *A Prayer for Owen Meany*, "for a short time, it is

soothing. I can almost imagine that I have had a life very different from the life I have had."

Plug in that fax machine, however, or put in an extra phone jack for the modem, and the life at the lake is increasingly in danger of becoming very *similar* to the life left behind.

The office, with blackflies.

So much for what famed architect and author Witold Rybczynski called "an antidote to the city."

What we may in fact be doing is invading our own inner lives. The Canadian summer is supposed to be our secret time to ourselves, that two or three or four weeks when we believe we become our truest selves. And that truest self does not, I suggest, carry a beeper. At the cottage, the comforts are peace of mind, not how many channels you can get, and the game of choice should be crokinole rather than Nintendo. There is something so magical about a special place at the lake that it inspires the same feeling whether you are eighty or eight, that sense that this place is an extension of me, this place *is* me as I like myself best.

For those who might feel the same about the office, trauma teams are standing by.

A Statistics Canada study of social trends in the 1990s found, to the amazement of some, that Canada's rural and small town population has actually been growing in recent years, contrary to the usual interpretations. True, the population of larger urban centres was growing much faster, and true as well that provinces such as Saskatchewan and Newfoundland were in significant rural decline, but StatsCan researchers found significant growth in such areas as Quebec's Laurentians, Ontario's Muskoka, and British Columbia's Okanagan Valley. In all three cases, the two main reasons cited were increased retirement and the ever-spreading distance commuters were willing to travel, particularly if they had jobs that allowed them to come to the cities only irregularly.

It raises an intriguing question for future StatsCan studies: where do those who already work at their cottages go when they retire?

Such signs point irrevocably toward the increasing urbanization of Cottage Country, the encroachment of the very ethos that cottage life was always believed to counter. It was not so long ago – and there are still many who believe this – that the very lack of convenience of the cottage was considered a large part of its appeal. Coal oil lamps, wood fires, buckets of water from the lake, the outhouse – all were pointed out as welcome reminders of where we came from. It put us out of touch with the city, and in touch with our heritage. It is something of a betrayal to complain about download time today in the very same cabin where the greatest concern was once blackened chimney glass or whether or not there were enough three-inch nails in the shed.

This, surely, is what Thoreau was getting at when he said he took to the woods in order "to live deliberately, to front only the essential facts of life, and see if I could not learn what it had to teach, and not, when I came to die, discover that I had not lived."

The question is: if we truly feel more *alive* at the cottage, as we so readily claim, what is it here that makes the blood flow differently? The necessity of work? The joy of simple tasks? The lack of distraction that makes strangers of family in the city? The pull that brings us outdoors whereas in the city it is always easier to stay in?

The beauty of sacrifice has largely been lost. What many cottagers want today is all the conveniences of the city at the same time as they enjoy all the delights of the cottage. Perhaps they find time to read thick novels while they are downloading.

No one would dare argue that ideas about nature cannot change. Let us remind ourselves, just this once, that four hundred years ago the Italian philosopher Giordano Bruno was burned at the stake for daring to suggest that the outdoors was its own church, that all things were alive, and that, unbelievably, the earth itself had a soul.

There is still change in the air, and some of it viewed with such contempt as the Church once felt for Bruno's odd concepts. The permanent residents of Huntsville are still trying to get used to the fact that one of the stately old Lake of Bays lodges, Britannia Hotel, is now the Maharishi International Academy of the Science of Creative Intelligence, and that the once-charming little eighteen-hole golf course has been let go to seed while the Maharishi's adherents use the old fairways to practise yogic flying.

There is even conflict on the waterways, the canoeists and kayakers dreading the wake of the huge classic mahogany launches that are still spirited about the lakes by elderly men in white captain's caps and blue blazers, the occupants of the launches despising the boarders and pesky personal watercraft that chase them to use the high wakes as launching pads for tricks.

In the spring of 2000, Canadian Senator Mira Spivak, herself a cottager near Winnipeg, went so far as to introduce a private member's bill to Parliament that would, if it ever became legislation, give summer homeowners across the country the right to ban "horrendous" personal watercraft from their lakes and rivers.

"Dear Editor," a letter in the *Muskoka Sun* began on August 16, 2001, "fast boats have always been a tradition in Muskoka. Today's hot boats are no different than the early wood classics that roared across our lakes. . . . Many boaters have spent millions on cottages and hundreds of thousands on performance boats to enjoy the summer in Muskoka. A little noise during daylight hours never hurt anyone.

"The tree-hugging do-gooders that don't like loud boats should move to smaller lakes that ban power boats."

No wonder, then, that in 2001, on the traditional Opening Day weekend for Cottage Country – Victoria Day – a new issue of *Maclean's* magazine hit the stands with the cover line: "Paradise Lost: Dreaming of that Idyllic Getaway? Dream On."

In a "reality check" that seemed directly aimed at the Muskoka–Georgian Bay vacation land, writer John DeMont took on the popular myth of the Canadian lakes district. "You fantasize about days that begin with the loon's call from a curtain of mist and end in an Adirondack chair peering up into a star-filled sky," DeMont wrote. ". . . You picture a refuge that will be your children's and grandchildren's, a place somehow ever untouched, unsullied, no matter what the rest of your life may hold." But don't count on it, he cautioned. The Royal LePage real-estate company may have found that 10 per cent of Canadians own some form of summer retreat, and a huge percentage more hope one day to have one, but it is becoming increasingly impossible to find. Even the leaky scow and the single oar are now out of the reach of most Canadians.

According to *Maclean's*, the sudden influx of well-off and even early-retiring baby boomers, combined with dying parents leaving their nest eggs to children accustomed to spending in order to satisfy their every whim, has put an enormous strain on the already limited number of vacation properties available. Prices have been soaring everywhere: the Maritimes, the Laurentians and Eastern Townships of Quebec, the less desirable and more distant lakes of Ontario, Lake of the Woods in northwestern Ontario, Lake Winnipeg, Alberta's Sylvan Lake, Whistler and the Okanagan Valley of British Columbia. In Wasaga Beach on Georgian Bay, an old resort town already overcrowded and noisy, prices had gone up 50 per cent over the previous five years. Not only that, but prospective Canadian buyers have to compete with Americans looking north and Europeans, particularly Germans, increasingly looking across the ocean for vacation retreats. No wonder the rule of thumb in the vacation real-estate business has become four potential buyers for every available property.

"They're going to develop every square inch of it," bemoaned the head of the Muskoka Lakes Association a few summers back. "There's no question. That's what the future holds."

No wonder, too, that they come to gawk, to stare, to lust after what they cannot have. Millionaires' Row is now out of reach for mere millionaires. The wealthy and famous have spread so widely across lakes Muskoka, Rosseau, and Joseph that enterprising publications have taken to printing handy maps to the area to help curious visitors track down those fortunate enough to "escape" here for weeks at a time.

The famous, like the rich, are nothing new to Muskoka. Prime ministers used to holiday at the big resorts. The Eatons and Labatts and Seagrams and other wealthy families were early cottagers who stayed on. Actress Ursula Andress used to sunbathe nude on a small island rock when she was with actor Harry Hamlin, whose family owns a large cottage in Muskoka. The lakes are filled, as well, with the perfect seasonal residents, rich hockey players with entire summers free – including Steve Yzerman, Eric Lindros, Paul Coffey, Frank Mahovlich (now a senator) – and a constant summer rumour always has Wayne Gretzky looking for an isolated Muskoka island for his growing family.

Comedian Martin Short is a familiar figure around Lake Rosseau and has had Hollywood friends Mel Gibson, Tom Hanks, and Steve Martin up for stays. Actress Catherine O'Hara has a place near Bala. Author John Irving vacations on Georgian Bay, as does Blues Brother Dan Aykroyd. Rock drummer Alex Van Halen once had a sumptuous place, but then sold and moved on, perhaps because he found the retreat not quite as advertised.

Just across the water from Short's cottage on Lake Rosseau is the sprawling summer retreat that belonged to actors Kurt Russell and Goldie Hawn before they too sold up and moved, more discreetly, to a far more isolated cottage on the lake.

"People have been incredibly rude," Hawn told a New York City television interviewer after their first summer at the original estate.

"I cannot believe the rudeness of some of these people coming right up to our cottage, right up to the dock with binoculars and cameras.

"It's really been an invasion of our privacy – and I thought that wouldn't happen here."

What Goldie Hawn had just discovered was that she, like so many others, had brought with her what she was trying to escape.

Their summer retreat had become Hollywood. Complete with tours – by boat rather than bus – of the homes of the rich and famous.

Chapter Seven

CAMP LAKE

"This . . . is about getting to know a place so well that it becomes part of you. The boundary between self and place dissolves. Some kind of life force or shared blood supply flows evenly through you both without the slightest hesitation. You feel entirely and deeply comfortable saying, 'I am of this place; I am this place.'"

MONTE HUMMEL, *WINTERGREEN: REFLECTIONS FROM LOON LAKE*

The first time I saw this little overgrown spot on the south shore of Camp Lake, I was decidedly unimpressed. I thought it much too damp and steep and dark. I did not care for the northern exposure, which would mean no sunrise to get you going in the mornings, no long sunsets to stretch out the evening, and too much shade from the high hills behind squeezing what little of the day might be left. There seemed to me too much spruce cover, too many hemlock, far too much poplar and aspen tangle; there were no rocks to dive off, no sand to walk on; and the waterline began instantly where the tree cover either gave up or toppled over, giving the shoreline a ragged, uninviting fringe of dead, fallen, and broken trees, old stumps, jumbled rocks, and a soft, off-putting bottom of decaying leaves, sharp stones, and muck. I presumed, correctly, there were leeches.

The year was 1969, and I had come, by motorcycle, through twenty miles of skidding gravel and blackfly clouds to this newly surveyed lot because, back then, I would do anything to be with a certain young woman. Even if it meant fishtailing around corners, mashed bugs in the corners of my inflamed eyes, and raspberry-cane scratches as I tramped around on slippery moss behind a high-school chemistry teacher, her father, who saw a dock where I could see only deadheads, a cedar deck where I could see only scrub, and a cottage where I could see no possibilities whatsoever.

His $1,680 had been the only bid on this sloping pie-shaped lot. That should have told him something. But so determined was this quiet man who had been born and raised on Manitoulin Island to have his own sacred spot on the water that he probably would have bid against himself to win it. He had gone with another teacher to the Huntsville Memorial Arena, where the Ontario Ministry of Natural Resources was holding a rare auction of crown land. Some sixty lots would be opened up to cottagers on this small, isolated lake that bridges the northern tip of Muskoka and the beginning of the Algonquin Park highlands, and the two teachers were so determined not to be shut out by the hundreds of city dwellers who came to bid that they panicked and snatched up the first two properties to be put on the block that morning. There were much better lots – a lovely island, several points, some prized southern exposures – but they had calculated, correctly, that the city bidders would be waiting for the choice locations, and if they struck first, and fast, they might land lots together, at bargain prices, even if the light turned out to be bad and the slope all but impossible to build on.

There were no other bids on either of the first two lots. They had them, and they were already congratulating themselves on their investments, long before they could get a bulldozer in for a rough road, long before they could put up their simple prefabricated frame cottages, long before electricity, let alone television and laptop computers, would make it this far up Limberlost Road.

This was, for him, a lifelong dream come true. He had been looking for his own place of escape since the war had taken him out of Manitoulin's little Gore Bay. No longer would he have to store his tin cartopper in the back yard, muscling it up onto the old Dodge every time he wanted to go fishing. Here he could build a dock where the little boat could be tied and the six-horsepower Johnson fixed to the transom from late April to late November. Here he could fish on the weekends and, as soon as he could get out of teaching, fish whenever he wished. Here he would work with his hands and build the things that gave him more pleasure than teaching had ever provided.

To me, it was hardly worth bothering with. I was, but did not know it then, a cottage snob.

I had come from a strangely privileged background, one that had everything to do with circumstance and nothing whatsoever to do with money. I knew few others from my Baby Boom generation who had been toilet-trained on an outdoor privy, or who could remember having to be taught how to flush a toilet, turn on a tap, and flip a light switch, as I needed to be after we moved from the bush into town. My father was a lumberman who had lived all his working life in Ontario's Algonquin Park. My mother had been born at Brule Lake, in the heart of Algonquin, where her father had worked from 1907 until his forced retirement at seventy in 1954 and where he had served as chief ranger of the park for more than twenty of those forty-seven years. I was born at the Red Cross outpost in Whitney, on the eastern edge of the park, and went to school in Huntsville, the first town on the western edge of the park. For me, Algonquin could not only never be replaced, it must never be challenged.

The old ranger's reward for blazing the trail through the park that would one day become Highway 60 had been permission to build a permanent home on the site of his choice. He went to Lake of Two Rivers, approximately dead centre along the corridor, and selected a long, high, pine-covered point on a southern exposure, where the morning sun would slide down gently slanting rocks on the east side and the evening sun spread rich, thick light over the high rocks to the west.

He built a magnificent two-storey log home on the highest point of this long, rocky point; built it with his own hands, with a beautiful granite-and-quartz fireplace, and then three outer cabins and a cedar-log icehouse. When he was finished, he reached up under the eaves of what would come to be called the Big House and with a carpenter's pencil wrote the date, September 10, 1940, and his name, Thomas McCormick. An artist signing his masterpiece.

Nearly sixty years later, when cousin Don McCormick and I took my mother, Helen, back to the Lake of Two Rivers point for what we all knew would be the last trip of her long life, we found that pencil-signed section of one-by-four from under the eaves in a pile of rubble where the stone fireplace once stood. My mother took the small section of board home to Huntsville, wrapped it carefully in plastic, and labelled it "Grandpa's Foundation Stone." Shortly before she herself died, she gave it to me, and it sits on my desk as I type this.

It seemed that Tom and Bea McCormick had created this Eden for the dozens of grandchildren who swarmed over the point each summer, a few of us lucky enough to live there each year from the moment school let out in Huntsville at the end of June until early in September. My older brother, Jim, and I built a baseball diamond around the woodpiles, featuring the only first base on earth where, to be safe, you needed to run halfway up a slanted jack pine and touch the first branch. My sister, Ann, younger brother, Tom, and I built a miniature world on a sheltered bay by the point, with small roads and stone steps and tiny graveyards for minnows and tadpoles and newts and crayfish, where, if you had any decency about you, you spoke low and treaded softly.

It was a world removed, no electricity, no running water; a world where, on a hot day, you could twist your bare leg down deep in the icehouse sawdust and wiggle your toes against a thick ice block that had been cut from the lake the previous winter; a world of fresh trout, *Archie* comics, and deer named Sugar, Lady, Princess, Buck that ate from your hand.

Here was where we learned to paddle, where we built rafts and hoisted sheets for sails that let the wind take us down the lake but not back, where we learned to love the bush far more than we have ever learned to love cities.

We awoke to the slam of a screen door and fell asleep to the howl of wolves. We learned to swim on the morning side of the rocky point, where the rocks slanted gently down to form a natural granite "beach" of clear, clean water, bounded on one side by the walk to the enormous floating dock the old ranger had built, on the other by a boom of logs that kept the dock from floating away. We learned to dive off the high rocks where the evening sun struck the point, a level for each diver's ability. Unlike my own crashing attempts, Ann's magnificently arcing dives would slice into the water without a ruffle, my sister disappearing as neatly as a letter into an envelope.

And this – this pitiful, overgrown, ugly hill on the side of a lake that couldn't be bothered forming a proper shore – *this* was supposed to compete with such memories? There was not even a place to dive.

But time marched on. A bulldozer came in and rammed a rough road in to the lake that had no shore. Lloyd retired, and he and Rose began to construct their improbable dream. They laid footings and hauled lumber and, eventually, a small frame cottage went up in the shade of the hemlocks. He built his deck. He dug a hole on the only space that wasn't rock and put up an outhouse that also served as a storage shed for his chainsaw and a drying shed for the cedar kindling. He cut cedar logs and built a crib one winter that he filled with large stones he hauled over from the bay and far shore. And when the ice went out and the crib sank, he hammered a dock over it and built a wooden ladder off the far end so visitors could swim without having to put their feet down into the silty, branch- and dead-leaf-laden bottom. Furniture and appliances came from old relatives and from his insatiable urge to scavenge the back-road dumps for anything and everything: toasters that needed a new cord, clocks with hands that caught on each other, stove elements, kitchen chairs that needed only a little gluing and a new coat of paint. He would have no running water, but there would be electricity.

A hundred Teen Town dances later and the certain young woman and I, no longer teenagers, were soon married. Too soon, it seemed, we had four growing children. Much too soon, the retired teacher died and, naturally, we were expected to step in and help his wife become to the cottage what he had been: keeper, handyman, curator. The real question, of course, was whether or not this pitiful little attempt at a cottage could ever step in and become to me what the old ranger's Algonquin home had been. A selfish thought, but I did not know then that a cottage is a state of mind, not a fixed address.

And that's just what happened with this rustic little cottage on the sloping side of the lake with no shore. Slowly the place crept up on me. Gradually, as Monte Hummel, the head of the World Wildlife Fund Canada, wrote in his charming *Wintergreen*, "the boundary between self and place dissolves." It took years in my particular case, but that, I suppose, is understandable in that the comparison I was trying to make was so unfair. Regardless of the relative sweep of the two places – and first sight of the old ranger's log home on the rocky point was always followed by a sharp intake of breath – there was also the matter that the Lake of Two Rivers log cabin came wrapped, permanently, in glorious memory, in the magic of a child's endless summer.

Summer shrinks as we grow older, but the power of ritual expands. When rituals first come along, we often fail to recognize them for what they are, but soon they are as much a part of the lake experience as the first sighting of the baby loon on a parent's back. I remember telling our children, in yet one more effort to convince them that there was nothing here that could ever compare to Lake of Two Rivers, that the old ranger they never knew would offer a quarter to any kid who could swim the distance between the boardwalk and booms. There was, as well, a reward greater than money: if you could swim that distance, then you would be allowed to swim under the boom and out into the deeper water, and later, if you could prove you could swim from the dock to a distant point we called the Duck Rock, then it was worth two quarters and qualified you to begin diving off the high rocks to the west.

The kids loved this tale and adapted it to their own requirements. They demanded a dollar (inflation) when they could swim between the dock their grandfather had built and the small floating dock their mother built, then two dollars if they could swim from there to the diving platform of the next cabin down. This done, they decided it qualified them to try to swim across the bay. It was only when I realized that some of them might someday be measuring their own children in such a manner – telling them, God forbid, about an old eccentric they never knew – that I realized it is not the place but the experience we hand down.

Their grandparents' tiny cabin on the side of a hill – northern exposure, no shoreline – has twisted as deeply into their own beings as the old ranger's place had so long ago into mine. And if it is the experience that is important, not the place, then it struck me that perhaps it no longer mattered quite so much that an American had purchased the ranger's place away from us, torn it down, numbered the logs, carted them away, and burned what was left. The experience no one could touch, not with bulldozers, not with fire, and certainly not with money.

I had to learn to see this other place through the eyes of my own children. Long into summer nights, I have stood along this harsh shoreline I now worship with all of them, three girls and a boy, as each child passed through that precious phase when they stand, shaking and shivering, one bare foot scratching the bites on the calf of the other leg, their hands around a fishing rod while bats swoop out of the spruce trees and flit, seemingly beyond control, over the blackening water. Twenty years on, with them all now young adults, we still come here and stand, often in silence, remembering those precious evenings together when they simply could not let go of the day.

I understand that feeling, sense it myself year after year even though I know the Canadian summer to be fleeting, its joy transitory. Canadians eventually accept this fact of northern life, but we do so reluctantly. Summer, after all, is our secret time, the two or three or, with luck, four weeks when we believe we are our truest selves. This time away is very often also our sweetest thought, one held in parentheses by the Opening Up and the Closing Up, the season beginning with sparklers and ending in embers, when suddenly, without warning, the seasons reverse. The maple and birch leaves no longer shade but reveal; relief now is to be found inside rather than out, in fire rather than water. On an October morning so cold that the black lake steams, an outdoor toilet somewhat loses its July charm – but the place, never.

This is when we take summer down to the small shed and put it away with the half tank of mixed gasoline, strapless flippers, and tangled fishing reels. This is, sadly, when the air comes out of the cottage, when you pull the small plastic plugs with your teeth and stand stomping inner tubes and plastic boats while your own stale breath from early July hisses back at you. And yet with the next breath you take, you start looking forward to the summer coming. At this very same place where the "boundary between self and place" has long since dissolved.

It took me a long time to come around, but eventually I did. And now I know that for those children lucky enough to spend all or parts of their summers at the edge of a lake, any lake, in any circumstance, then that spot will take on permanent meaning for them. Forever.

Sometimes the effect is not noticed for years. Our youngest daughter, Jocelyn, spent her summers collecting toads and frogs and minnows, reading nature books and studying birds and eventually going to work at the bird sanctuary in Ottawa. Today she is at Trent University, studying biology and headed, she insists, for a life in the rain forests. She understands perfectly what Anne's creator, Lucy Maud Montgomery, was getting at in *The Alpine Path* when she claimed that the grove of trees near her school was "a stronger and better educative influence on my life than the lessons learned at the desk in the schoolhouse."

I learned my own lesson on this subject years ago at the end of one of those heavy, hot weeks when the days seem to follow each other with the lumbering rhythm of parading elephants. Our oldest daughter, Kerry, then perhaps eight, was sitting down by the water in what had, over the years, been reconfigured into her own private retreat.

There she had hauled in sand to make a beach that quickly washed away. She had strung a rope from a branch for swinging out over the water and letting go with a scream. She had built a small dock that wobbled. She had put in her own benches and, using spruce boughs, built her own beach umbrella for shade. The branches had turned brown as rust and the needles were falling off, but she still sat below it, staring out over the water.

"Don't ever sell this place," she said. "I want my children to come here."

At the time, there could be no question of selling, as we did not even own it. But that didn't matter to Kerry. The place owned her.

A few Christmases on, I was given another reminder. We were home in Ottawa, typical plugged-in suburbanites on a cold December evening, when, without warning, the hydro suddenly went off. One moment all was completely normal – television roaring, ghetto blasters pounding, Christmas lights blinking – and the next moment it was not normal at all. It was totally black, completely silent. No one said a word until a match could be located and struck, producing a nearly forgotten light – pale and yellow – that sent shadows leaping against the kitchen wall.

"*Neat!*" one of the kids called out.

A flashlight was found and, with the flashlight, two ancient coal oil lamps were brought from another room and lighted. The suburban kitchen filled with a liquid yellow colour it had never before known. The children stared at one another and their surroundings as if they were suddenly guests in a magic house.

"It's like being at the cottage," one of them said.

It was not just the light, but the silence – as if for once in this bedroom community two-storey home you might hear a squirrel scamper across the roof rather than the burst of a laugh track from the television room. The two youngest children ran with the flashlight for their comforters, brought them downstairs, wrapped themselves up with exaggerated squirms of delight and asked for a fire.

While the kindling stuttered and snapped in the fireplace, they filled the space usually taken by television and compact disks by talking about their most treasured moments of the year just past.

"Remember the big snapping turtle?" someone said.

"Remember the deer tracks by the sand pit?" someone answered.

I stood by the window, remembering another house in the bush when these same coal oil lamps would cast just enough light for an old ranger to work on his crossword puzzles and an old woman to prepare her Christmas baking. Our mother would be testing the oven of the wood stove with the back of her hand. Our father would be due soon from the mill. Jim and Tom would be reading comic books; Ann would have a jigsaw puzzle out that had been put together and taken apart so often certain pieces looked like splayed books.

Once, as adults, Ann and I had gone back in search of that minia-ture world we had once built back of the icehouse. More than thirty years had passed since we had played there. The icehouse had col-lapsed and only dried sawdust remained in the cracks of the rocks, and the area was now so stunningly overgrown that we could find but one spot, like a miniature Mayan ruin, where it seemed as if stone steps might once have been laid out. The place could not live up to the memory, but the memory had not been harmed in the least by this realization. If anything, it was all the more valuable, because it was something we would share forever.

Or at least so I thought. Forever, unfortunately, sometimes runs out far too soon. I had no idea that in a very few years I would be back at that same spot, the point even more tangled and overgrown, in search of several of those stones to place in Ann's casket.

The day before cancer took her we had been talking about all that had gone before – both of us acutely aware of how little had gone before – and I happened to ask her what her favourite time had been. She had not wasted a moment. She had so few to spare.

"Lake of Two Rivers," she said, "of course."

Of course.

Those children in their comforters by the fire were talking, I realized at that moment, of the most beautiful place I now knew on earth. The place that held my children's best memories, many still to be formed.

"Remember the big toad?" a small voice wondered.

But before anyone could, the power surged back on. Lights, television, tapes, buzzers, clocks.

"*Boooooo!*" the children shouted.

It was a false alarm. The power failed again; the coal oil lamps regained their place; the children cheered. And while they returned to their Camp Lake memories, Ellen and I quietly left the room to the crackling fire and their low, excited voices.

And we walked about the suburban house turning off every electrical switch we could find.

For twenty summers now, I have been keeping a journal at the cabin. It has become such a daily ritual that God be with the family member or visitor who does not sit down and record something significant, or completely insignificant, about the day just past. A blank page has become, in this ritual-bound world at the edge of the lake, a crime about as serious as failing to take a replacement roll of toilet paper up the hill.

I began this journal, somewhat basically, on Saturday, July 23, 1983. The previous fifteen years of the Camp Lake cabin's existence had been recorded on a haphazard series of children's drawings, tree fungus art, and a stack of old Milk Marketing Board calendars, noting how many fish had been caught, either trolling or through the ice, and how much the official recording secretary claimed they had weighed.

Tom McCormick had always kept a journal. He would take a sharpened pencil, open a small tally book, and record the weather – wind, temperature, sun, rain, or snow – and where he had gone that day in his duties as chief ranger of Algonquin Park. Nothing else: no personal observations, no anecdotes, just the bare facts of a day well put in. When he died in 1962, his widow, Bea, placed all the daily journals in a box and had my father take them down to the Rock Lake mill, where he cranked open the big metal door on the burner and heaved them from his shoulder into the howling inferno of bark, wood chip, and sawdust. I do not know why she wished them thrown away – I doubt she gave it a moment's thought – but I would give anything to have them back, even if they told me nothing more than where he had been on the first Tuesday afternoon in April 1931, what the weather was, and what jobs had been completed. The only thing I know for sure is that he would have been on the job. Rangers were always on the job. No, not quite. They did not think of it as their job, but their life.

I must have been feeling the old ranger's influence as I wrote my first entry in the Camp Lake journal, for it reads as spare and straightforward as if he himself had pencilled it in: "Arrived around supper time. Weather fine."

The evolution began the very next day. "Clouded over, slight drizzle," but also a note that cousin Tom Pigeon, himself once a park ranger, was out to help bring down a difficult hemlock, a reference to youngest daughter Jocelyn's very first fish (a perch), and mention that the grandmothers had come out from town for supper.

It is fascinating to sit here and see how the journal has evolved over the past two decades. Gradually, the entries grew longer and longer. The weather became incidental, and the real meat of the book (now two) soon became the stories and tales of what happened each day spent at the lake. Less about the lack of sun and much more about the abundance of turtles, the joy of a long rope hanging from a tree branch, the success (or failure) of a certain trick over the wake, the old and new friends dropping by, the progress of the lake's baby loons, the tipped canoes, successful dives from the high rocks, and who showed up from around the lake for the evening campfire.

There is something to be said for photographs, obviously, but there is also something not entirely accurate about the seasons they record. In summer photographs, everyone seems always to be bunched in together as if they've just been lassoed, and the subjects are always smiling and the sun is always shining, and the picture is usually taken, unfortunately, after an event of such enormous impact that someone has finally thought to run for the camera.

I'm not at all convinced a modern camera captures a moment better than an old-fashioned pencil.

A journal is different. It tells us what it was like the day the rain seemed to be ringing off the lake. It captures the sense of defeat the losers must surely feel (for how would *I* know?) at the end of a game of Monopoly or Risk that goes on well past midnight. And it reminds us of times that are significant only in the small history of a family: birthdays, first swim, first boyfriend/girlfriend, even last fish.

Ours is a book by many authors, with children and visitors invited to write whatever they feel about anything that happened that particular day at the lake. Some of the children's entries come complete with illustrations, and they are prized as much as if they were sketched by the Group of Seven. Others are by those who are no longer here but whose presence is felt, and will always be felt, in every corner of this little property on the side of the lake. "Came out alone," Ellen's mother, Rose, has written on July 7, 1988, eight years after she lost her husband. "A good place to be with memories on this our anniversary. The weather is hot, the lake warm. I remember one such night some years back we both went in swimming at midnight." I never once saw them hold hands. After reading this innocent little passage, I now think of their relationship as a lifelong romance.

The journal is the record of our times, and the one part of life at the lake that opens up and closes up dozens of times a year. No tools required.

I cannot pretend that all is sunshine in these small notes. There is great joy in going back through these pages, but also great pain at times. The year 1999 burns the eyes to scan. Both grandmothers passed away and, as high school let out for what promised to be a carefree summer, five young lives were lost in a tragic automobile accident. Three of those boys – Stan Thomson, Lyle Siew, and David Rider – had spent considerable time with us at the lake, and all have left their mark in the journal. Dave Rider had, with our son, Gordon, become the first to bicycle completely around the lake using the old logging trails, an event he had marked near the dam by scratching "Hell Ride '98" into the wood with his penknife. It is still there, and whenever I go down to the dam I run my hand along it. The following February, after a winter visit in which we ran and slid over the entire lake, Dave has written, "Keep the good times rollin'" into the log book. No way should such times, ever, stop rolling when you are only sixteen years old.

But this bright winter morning, I also read through the happier entries and am struck by the richness and variety of the Camp Lake tales.

June 29, 1984 – Still cool, overcast. Set up boat and took kids for ride. Went to dam and found signs of a wild fight between bears and suckers. Dead, swatted, torn, half-eaten suckers all over the rocks. Found one large sucker still alive but with dorsal fin torn off, blinded in one eye and with small "nail" holes in one side, obviously from the cuff of a bear's claws. It died shortly after we found it.

February 3, 1987 – Tom Pigeon came out to shovel off the roof – could step right off roof onto snow when finished.

July 28, 1987 – Kerry and Christine spotted smoke on Blueberry Island. Someone had failed to put out their campfire. Fortunately, the kids found it in time and drowned the fire before the whole island went up. Now the girls are heroes around the lake.

August 27, 1989 – Bumps [our dog, then fifteen] fell in while going down to the dock in the dark for a drink and, being mostly blind, headed out into deep water. Luckily, Ellen heard the splashing around and went down with a flashlight. Roy chased her in the canoe, finally hauling her up and in and back to safety, her old heart pounding like a bird's.

July 22, 1990 – About 20 suckers are trapped in the dam. Gordie plans to "rescue" them by catching and releasing them back in Camp Lake. By dark he had four rescues to his credit, with more planned for tomorrow.

August 21, 1990 – Duncan [who would turn eighty-three the following week] out for his annual fish – he caught one (2 lb) on *first* pass of the island. On second pass, nailed another – "Bigger!" – which took a long time to pull in and shook off 20' from the boat. Went well. [It would be his final fish.]

August 23, 1991 – Christine shinnied forty feet up the big yellow birch hanging over the water and tied a rope to a high branch. It works brilliantly! You swing well out over the water and must be twenty feet in the air when you let go – you can see the bottom as you're falling!

August 8, 1997 – Jocelyn, who is terrified of snapping turtles, attacked one herself today. She saw the big turtle rise up and snatch one of the baby loons. She raced through the water, grabbed the turtle by the shell and shook it until it released the loon underwater. We think the baby escaped but no sign of it yet. Everyone on the lake is talking about Jocelyn's act of bravery.

August 26, 1997 – Summer is over. We are cleaning up to head back to Ottawa after most of two months here. [Gord, then fourteen, writes the final passage.] "Thank you, Camp Lake, for the best summer of my life."

There is surprisingly little written in the journals on projects. There was no journal kept when Lloyd Griffith felt he had to make each day count for something measurable – some new stain on the deck, felling the dead beech back of the parking area, cleaning the chainsaw, making a list of things to do tomorrow – and only scant mention made of the two docks, the new deck, and the shed Ellen has built since we took over the place. This, of course, is because I tend to keep most of the journals, and a new coat of paint for the cottage takes only a sentence to note while the search for Ermine Lake might run several pages, complete with illustrations.

There is no use pretending. I am not a projects person. If I kept a list at the lake of *must do*'s, it would read something like this:

- Breakfast on the deck.
- Check hummingbird feeder.
- Take dog for brief walk.
- Go for paddle before wind comes up.
- Have second cup of coffee.
- Boat over to secret rock to see if bass are lounging about in the sun.
- Drive slowly by various docks to see who's up and who might offer a third cup of coffee.
- Fish, maybe.
- Go for swim. If kids up, jump off rope. If kids not up, jump off rope anyway. Tell dog to quit barking.

- Lunch on deck.
- Start new mystery novel.
- Nap.
- Go for long afternoon walk into bush with dog.
- Swim. Tell dog to quit herding me back to shore and quit trying to bark when she's in the water.
- Journey about lake looking for people to bug.
- Do something useful to ease minor guilt pangs: e.g., cut some kindling, double-check hummingbird feeder.
- Think about having cold beer before dinner.
- Eat on deck.
- Paddle, fish, or visit about the lake.
- Evening swim, tell dog her barking carries.
- Build campfire.
- Go to bed.

The place is hardly without a Project Manager. Ellen is one of those who must have something concrete (sometimes literally) to do at the lake or there is no point in being there. I would argue that the *point* is to do nothing. Fortunately, it works for us. She builds the steps, replaces the deck, puts up the shed, hammers together the docks, puts in the new floor, and, if we ever get around to it, will likely install the bathroom so that we can get rid of the outhouse – which, of course, is quickly becoming a problem because I never seem to get around to digging it out.

I did once install a small electric heater one winter weekend. It came in a box and had to be removed and plugged in. So I am not entirely useless.

My own father lost his father when he was only four years old and once explained to me that he had no tools, and no knowledge of how to use them, because he had no one to pass the knowledge down to him, and thus could pass nothing down to me. My own son adores tools; he borrows his mother's.

A worthwhile project, to my mind, would be something like trying to figure out what the bottom of the lake looks like. This comes, I think, from one of my two recurring dreams – the other being that I have failed grade 12 yet again and must repeat it for a third time. This particular one concerns Lake of Two Rivers. I am sleeping in one of the small cabins, and when I wake up in the morning all the water has somehow drained out of the lake.

Exactly how this happens I do not know. It is as if the Madawaska River, which enters at the west end of the lake, has been dammed and a great rubber plug has popped free somewhere in the centre of the lake, leaving the bottom wet and muddy where it is not solid rock, but firm enough that I can race across the shoals and see everything that I have ever imagined down there.

This must come from something that happened to my brother Jim at Lake of Two Rivers in the 1950s. He found money – two ten-dollar bills, three one-dollar bills, twenty-three dollars in total – *floating* in the bay one still July morning. It was an enormous sum then, and we could not fathom where the money might have come from. The first speculation was a boating accident, but no canoes had been seen overturned, it had not been windy, and no one was reported missing. Some thought a camper's pack, but only the money was ever found. Perhaps the explanation was more simple – money in a camper's bathing suit that had come free while swimming? bills stuffed into a pocket that had been sent flying when the owner grabbed for a handkerchief? – but what to do with the money was hardly so simple. With the old ranger overseeing the operation, we reported the find to the ranger's office at the Lake of Two Rivers camp grounds, reported it to park headquarters, and, after a day without anyone claiming the money, took the money down to the Ontario Provincial Police station at Whitney, where Jim was questioned and the bills placed in a plastic bag, awaiting their claimant. When ninety days had passed without anyone stepping forward, the twenty-three dollars were given to the finder, and Jim bought his first new pair of skates with the windfall.

In my dream, I worried more that the money had drifted free of a drowned fisherman and I would come across the body as I raced around the lake bottom. But there were no bodies, only treasures: new, sparkling Williams Wablers to scoop off the rocks and sunken logs, rods and reels that had fallen overboard, even perfectly preserved outboard motors that had vibrated free and dropped down into the deep lake.

I could see where the shoals ran, and knew, then, exactly where the trout would feed. I could stand looking down into the deeper depressions in the lake, one hundred and twenty-five feet deep in spots, and see where the lunkers hid out, the huge lake trout that sometimes struck our steel line as though we'd been rear-ended by a truck and then broke free, leaving nothing but our wildest imaginings as to what had hit the line.

This obsession with what lies below the surface of a lake has been lifelong. I used to rise early at Lake of Two Rivers and go out and lie on the high rocks, staring down on a calm day when I could watch big bass lolling about as the sun danced along the rocks just below the surface. I have lain so long on docks, staring down through a swim mask, that when I have finally stood up my chest has taken on the exact imprint of the boards. I will paddle for hours on a calm morning around the entire perimeter of Camp Lake, endlessly staring down through the clear water in search of fish or minnows or snapping turtles. There is a sunken speedboat that lies in a dozen feet of water in the near bay; it has been there for decades, slowly rotting, and each summer it strikes me as a delicious mystery I would someday love to read.

If this has made me, literally, a rather shallow person, so be it. I stare down only where it is possible to see the bottom, which restricts me to a certain depth as well as to calm, sunny days. I will look at anything, even stumps. And I count it a highlight of my life that I was in a canoe, with two of the kids, when a loon dove directly under us and let loose what we have always presumed bears do in the woods.

Just for the record, it is like white shrapnel exploding in the water.

My interest in the secrets of the lake bottom is the reason I recently became the only person ever to move about the lake with a fish finder but no fishing pole. I picked up the fish finder during the National Hockey League playoffs, which I was covering for the *National Post*. I remember standing in a massive Dallas sporting goods store watching a demonstration of the gadget – the bottom rolling along, accurate to the inch, with pings and boings and beeps for the various-sized fish, from schools of minnows to what appeared to be a small whale – and thinking that for $79.99 U.S. I could finally find out the hidden secrets of my lake.

This fish finder would make up for my bad hands. Ellen's father, Lloyd, and my father, Duncan, both had "soft hands" for fishing, and so, too, does Gordon, my son. How, or why, these soft hands chose to skip a generation, I do not know, but I do not like it. My hands tell me only when the lure is hopelessly embedded in a log or caught in the crack of a large rock. I cannot tell the difference between silt and weed. My father could tell exactly when he had lost his minnow; I sometimes have trouble knowing when I have caught a fish. With nothing more than a trolling rod, these "soft-handers" can *feel out* a lake, delicately bouncing a lure off the bottom until a perfect map forms in their memory. They are, I think, freaks of nature.

I do not have that ability. I do, however, have a plastic credit card that provided me with the electronic equivalent.

The day I set out to map the bottom, John and Denis decided to come along for the ride – presumably to find out where the lunkers, if there were any, happened to be hiding.

I loaded up the finder with a fresh battery. I attached the suction cup to the bottom of the boat, aimed the sounder directly down toward the mysterious bottom, clicked the "on" button, and we set out, like David Thompson nearly two centuries earlier, to map out the last great unexplored mystery of the Canadian wilderness.

The little machine beeped a few times and something dark began rolling across the screen, complete with readout numbers. I was, finally, seeing my bottom.

"*It's 120 feet deep here!*" I called out. I could barely believe it. I would have guessed sixty feet, at best.

"*Twenty feet now!*" John called out.

The three of us leaned over the sides, expecting to see a small volcano rising where previously we had thought there might be a shoal.

"*LOOK AT THE FISH!*" Denis yelled at the screen.

We stared, stunned: the graph was filling with fish after fish after fish, the various pings and boings and beeps growing louder and louder.

Finally, a beep like an alarm signal. "*GOOD CHRIST!*" I cried, pointing. "*There's a WHALE down there!*"

Whatever it was lurking beneath in the deep, it took up the whole screen. Smaller fish seemed to scatter. The beeper was now sounding as if one of us had just walked through an airport checkpoint wearing the nail apron that the lake handyman, Lanny, sometimes wears when reshingling a roof.

Denis, who is also handy, shook his head. "Impossible."

He reached out and slowly ran a callused finger down the side of the fish finder until he found a small switch, which he then pushed.

Suddenly the screen changed: seventy feet deep, no fish.

I looked at it, thinking he had broken my great prize from the state of Texas.

"*What happened?*"

Denis looked up, smiling in pity.

"You forgot to switch it over from 'demonstration' mode."

So I am not a hammer and nails person. So what? I do not wear a tape measure as if it were attached at birth. I look at empty space and see empty space, not bunkies or deck extensions or sheds. But that does not mean I am without my ambitious summer projects. Mine happen to be adventures, even if some are so small they amount to little more than spending a day biking around the lake, or heading off to canoe on a river I have never before been on, or hiking in to an isolated body of water I have seen only on a map.

I also like, once a summer, to escape from escape.

I begin planning in early spring, when the snow clears and the first crocuses appear on our front lawn. I find myself in the garage, lovingly running a hand along the red canvas canoe that hangs from the ceiling. I take out my paddle and go against the air currents. I check rope and gear and tent pegs and packsacks and tarpaulins. I pore over maps. Not maps of I-95 to Florida, as so many of my neighbours will do this time of year, but in *Canoe Routes of Algonquin Provincial Park*, using an adding machine to tally up portages and a calendar to work out what is possible for the various members of a busy family of six. I then take out my battered credit card, dial 1-888-ONT-PARK, and book what has increasingly become a major part of each coming summer.

This strange ritual began, as most do, by accident. It grew out of something Gordon said at the end of yet another year in which we had contrived to spend every conceivable second we could at the lake.

"Next summer," he said, "I want to do some different things at the cabin. I don't like it when I look back and it all seems the same." He was speaking, of course, from the viewpoint of the Life Cycle of the Lake Teenager: sleep in, get up, eat, swim, hang out, eat, sleep.

Something was needed to break the pattern. Day trips were fine, but the real breakthrough came when, one summer a few years back, we all headed off into Algonquin Park to spend the better part of a week exploring where the kids' grandparents and great-grandparents had once lived their lives.

The initial planning was exhausting. I assigned myself the task of staring at the map and daydreaming, while Ellen took on arranging what equipment we had – most of it dating from when we had first married – purchasing the new equipment we would need, planning and buying the food, ironing out compatible dates with all the family members, and finding Ziploc bags big enough to hold rolls of toilet paper. Several weeks later, we launched the three canoes and headed off toward the first portage in what, over the next few days, would become our full-time, dawn-to-dusk life.

We loved it, of course. There is something about what John Muir called "this sudden plash into pure wildness" that creates a fresh awareness of what we presume, wrongly, we already fully appreciate. Here, there were no board games, no soft beds, no wine on the dock, no electrical outlets for CD players or, God forbid, portable video cassette recorders. Instead we enjoyed mornings where the only sound was the red-winged blackbirds along the river routes, meals together, endless animal sightings, glorious sunsets, long evenings to put in together around the campfire, and sleep that no bed anywhere can equal.

We saw what we had expected to see: moose and osprey, once a wolf, and the charming lakes the grandmother of these children had paddled and skied until she was well into her teens. But there was also the unexpected, and this was felt rather than seen. We felt the joy of long paddles, something too often forgotten when the boat requires only a turn of a key. We found the delight of our own conversation, when too often the phone, the radio, the CD player, or that cursed old one-channel television takes talk away.

We gained a renewed respect for the simplicity of the outdoor life, the agreed highlight coming at the end of a difficult mile-long portage when Ellen, the planner, reached deep into her pack and produced six large oranges – the finest gourmet meal ever served at the edge of a northern lake.

When we came out, even after such a short time, we felt the way travellers do when they return after months away from home, everything taking on a new light and new meaning. For us, it was a welcome, and now annual, reminder of the original purpose of a summer retreat.

To get close to nature.

Sunday, June 10, 2001 – Came in alone. There must be a dozen different shades of green along Limberlost Road and saw eight snapping turtles laying eggs in the soft gravel along the sides of the road. Two huge ones were hunkered down side by side at the turnoff into Toad Lake, their bored, patient looks almost as if they were in a hairdressing salon waiting for new perms to dry before lumbering back into the water.

I like to swim early, before the bugs wake up, and sometimes wonder if I'll survive the shock of that first dawn dive off the end of the dock. The water seems somehow harder that time of day, the splash louder, and the towel rougher, yet there is a certain smug delight that comes to those who get up and get going early that makes it all seem worthwhile when your skin is tingling all over, your heart happily pounding, and, if you stand on the end of the dock and look down the lake, you can watch the sun gild the far hills.

Surely there is some connection between the decline of the Church and the rise of nature worship. I even know people who will say they find all the old church comforts in a Sunday at the lake, or hiking through the woods, and these comforts come without having to get into clothes you shouldn't wear this time of year unless you're lying in a coffin.

People might no longer believe much in the old concepts of heaven – clouds you can walk on, stringed instruments you can finally play – but they do believe, more and more, in finding pieces of heaven here on earth. Mine happens to be – though I could never have predicted this when I first motorcycled out here more than thirty years ago – this deep little northern lake where the waters drain from Algonquin Park, but there are as many such special places as there are people to treasure them.

Everyone finds his or her own level in the outdoors. It might be dangerous mountain climbing; it might be no more dangerous than lifting your second leg into the hammock and cracking open a new mystery novel.

Unlike that other heaven, we don't tend to judge here.

My old journalism hero Bruce Hutchison found the bush and lake the perfect antidote for the excesses of the political and journalistic worlds in which he spent the salaried side of his life. "To me," Hutchison wrote in his memoir *A Life in the Country*, "boats and cabins were among the few stable things left in a mad, reeling world to indicate the quiet, abiding rhythm that endures beneath the outward disorder of our times. Other men find this comfort in churches, money, power, or drink. Let them find it where they can. I found it now and then, not always, when I had shucked off the garments of society, the masks and flatulent pretensions.

"Reality seemed to await me at the trail's end, the water's edge."

I don't intend to engage in theological argument. The connection between nature and religion has long been made in North America, as might be expected of a continent of which large parts were settled through religious fervour and flight. The Jesuits found it in Canada, the Pilgrims in the United States, and the story is told in a hundred different forms in a thousand different locations.

To no surprise, this has often been pushed to excess. Even before the pious Thoreau came along, Susan Fenimore Cooper, whose father, James, wrote *The Last of the Mohicans* and other American classics, was hugely popular with her writings about the outdoor church. "The humble moss beneath our feet," she wrote in *Rural Hours*, published in 1850, "the sweet flowers, the varied shrubs, the great trees, and the sky gleaming above in sacred blue, are each the handiwork of God. They were all called into being by the will of the Creator, as we now behold them, full of wisdom and goodness. Every object here has a deeper merit than our wonder can fathom; each has a beauty beyond our full perception; the dullest insect crawling about these roots lives by the powers of the Almighty; and the discolored shreds of last year's leaves wither away upon the lowly herbs in a blessing of fertility."

Canada's Catharine Parr Traill, the sister of Susanna Moodie, was a contemporary of Cooper, though Traill did not get around to laying out her own philosophy until 1894, when she was ninety-two years old and had just finished *Pearls and Pebbles: Or, Notes of an Old Naturalist*. She found God, she believed, in the lowly twig-borer, one of the least-noticed insects of the Ontario bush. "How marvelous and wonderful is their instinct!" Traill wrote. "Note the curious means employed to accomplish an end which could not be foreknown by experience, by teaching or by reasoning, in the creature working for the future preservation of her unseen offspring. The calculating of the exact date when it should come forth, and the corresponding time when the girdled branch should part from the tree, thus providing a nursery for her infant and sufficient nutriment to sustain it, until in its turn it arrives at the perfect state of the mother beetle, to enjoy like her a brief term of life, prepare a cradle for its offspring, and die.

"Surely this leaves a lesson for man to ponder over and confess that he knows but little. The wisdom of man must be but foolishness in the sight of God, since he cannot fathom even the ways of one of the most insignificant of the works of the Creator. How then can man by his puny wisdom find out God?"

Years after Cooper published her *Rural Hours*, Emily Dickinson said it all much better, in only eight words. "Take care, for God is here," she wrote in one simple poem about the breaking of the day. "That's all."

The notion that you could find the spiritual in a setting in which there was no church and no preacher came from Emerson, only to be refined by Thoreau. Ralph Waldo Emerson was an enormous influence on Thoreau and in fact owned the land on Walden Pond where Thoreau squatted and began his famous journals. Many believe that Emerson talked the impressionable younger man into the unusual exercise that resulted in *Walden Pond*, as Emerson had himself written a book here, *Nature*, in which he embraced transcendentalism and argued that even the simplest natural object could hold universal truths. "Nature," he believed, "is the symbol of spirit."

The two, Emerson and Thoreau, brought about an entirely new perspective on the outdoors. Until their time, those who came to settle in North America, in sharp contrast to those who were already here, had no particular love for what nature represented: danger, cold, wild animals, impediments to land-clearing, bother. The Puritans believed that in God's kingdom the wild should be tamed. After all, did God not command in Genesis that man "be fruitful and multiply, and fill the earth and subdue it"?

How different from what Thoreau was soon trying to tell Americans. "To ensure health," he recorded in his journal on January 23, 1858, "a man's relation to Nature must come very near to a personal one; he must be conscious of a friendliness in her; when human friends fail or die, she must stand in the gap to him. I cannot conceive of any life which deserves the name, unless there is a certain tender reaction to Nature."

Out of such thinking came the likes of Bob Marshall, founder of the Wilderness Society, who would soon be arguing that rather than be beaten back, nature should be *entered*, as if the visitor were a lover or, equally true, had been invited to become, even briefly, a part of the wider landscape.

"One looks from outside at works of art and architecture," Marshall believed, "listens from outside to music or poetry. But when one looks and listens to the wilderness he is encompassed by his existence of beauty, lives in midst of his esthetic universe."

He went even further. Wilderness, Marshall contended, "exhibits a dynamic beauty. A Beethoven symphony or a Shakespearean drama, a landscape by Corot or a Gothic cathedral, once they are finished become virtually static. But the wilderness is in a constant state of flux. A seed germinates, and a stunted seedling battles for decades against the dense shade of the virgin forest. Then some ancient tree blows down and the long-suppressed plant suddenly enters into the full vigor of delayed youth. . . .

"Another singular aspect of the wilderness is that it gratifies every one of the senses. There is unanimity in venerating the sights and sounds of the forest. But what are generally esteemed to be the minor senses should not be slighted. No one who has ever strolled in spring-time through seas of blooming violets, or lain at night on boughs of fresh balsam, or walked across dank holms in early morning can omit odor from the joys of the primordial environment. No one who has felt the stiff wind of mountaintops or the softness of untrodden sphagnum will forget the exhilaration experienced through touch. 'Nothing ever tastes as good as when it's cooked in the woods,' is a tribute to another sense. Even equilibrium causes a blithe exultation during many a river crossing on tenuous foot log and many a perilous conquest of precipice. Finally, it is well to reflect that the wilderness furnishes perhaps the best opportunity for pure esthetic enjoyment."

I can read all this, and enjoy it, but sometimes I have to admit it makes me giggle. Sometimes we make too much of it all when it simply is what it is. Bob Marshall, like a lot of us, was terrified of the dark woods when he was a child, and he used to force himself to walk alone through them, first with a lantern and then with nothing but his own senses for protection and guidance, and if one day later on he made a bit too much of them, so be it. He's welcome.

Personally, I like to keep it a little more simple than that. I remember Bill Mason, the legendary Canadian paddler, once regretting that so many had come to see the wilderness as some free amusement park. "What wilderness should be doing," he thought instead, "is speaking to our souls and teaching us about being quiet . . . and respecting the world we live in."

My own sentiments lie far closer to Calvin Rutstrum, the great iconoclast of the American nature movement, who found, in Minnesota and northern Ontario, a bush experience remarkably like my own father's. Both Calvin Rutstrum and Duncan MacGregor had little formal education, both were, nevertheless, the best-read men any of their friends or family knew, both lived into their late eighties, and both had a charming, if sometimes exasperating, contempt for material things. My father used to dream of winning the Irish sweepstakes so he could give his money away. When he died, he had but one possession, his old trolling rod, a change of clothes, and almost exactly enough money in the bank to cover his funeral. The only time in his life he was ever tidy was when he died.

"People have more interest in the dollar than anything else," Rutstrum once said. "They fight for it until they become the richest man in the graveyard, and they die. No one remembers them. They're a lost entity."

Rutstrum wasn't big on the afterlife. "I'm convinced," he said, "beyond any question or doubt that when this life is gone you are a forgotten entity. I don't think there is any afterlife. The same biological process that occurs when a cockroach dies is when you die. Exactly. . . . Man has no concern for the hundreds of billions of years that occurred before he got here; that doesn't bother him at all. He wants to be considered as living forever. The only promise you got of living forever is that you'll be taken up into the ether to a platform somewhere and you're going to be allowed to strum on a harp all day long.

"I don't even like music that well."

The only better thought I ever encountered came, as is fitting, from an old man who had spent his life in Algonquin Park. Ralph Bice was like an extra grandfather to our family, a wise and comical old trapper and guide who claimed he had paddled or camped along more than eight hundred of Algonquin's one thousand lakes. His father had been a park ranger at the time my own grandfather was a ranger, and both had known Tom Thomson well. The Bices lived in Kearney, on the western edge of the park, and whenever my mother or her siblings had to go out of the park to get medical attention or write school exams, they always stayed with the Bices. It was their second home.

Not long before both my mother and Ralph passed on, I took her up to Kearney for one last visit with the old man, then ninety-six years of age.

"I'm not looking good," he said to me when my mother and his daughter went off to make tea.

"You're looking fine," I argued.

He shook his head. "No," he said. "I know I'm going down. I can feel it. I'm getting weaker and weaker, you know. The end is coming."

I had no idea what to day. I sat, fidgeted, and smiled – until he winked and burst into laughter.

"Doctors figure I've only got ten to fifteen good years left in me."

In fact, he had only one, and was dead at ninety-six in the summer of 1997. He had led a wonderful life even without that extra ten to fifteen years. Before he died, he had attained widespread recognition for his wilderness lore, and was even awarded the Order of Canada the same year it went to Pierre Trudeau.

For whatever reason, certainly not alphabet, these two recipients had been seated together at Rideau Hall for the investiture ceremony, and Ralph, not realizing Trudeau had little time for small talk, had immediately started chatting. Not long into the one-sided conversation, Ralph pronounced Trudeau "the luckiest man in the room."

"And why is that?" Trudeau had asked.

"Because there's only one old trapper here," Ralph said, laughing, "and you got to sit next to him."

Like Duncan MacGregor, Ralph Bice, when he died, did not leave behind much more than memories, which was more than enough for his family.

Memories, and a few choice sayings.

"Nature," he used to say, "is God."

He was, unlike Calvin Rutstrum and Dunc MacGregor, a deeply religious man and a regular churchgoer. Someone asked him once what he would do with himself when he got to Heaven.

"Probably ask for a map," he laughed, "so I can find my way around."

But then he had paused, thinking about it a little more, and he shook his head.

"Anyone who has been to Algonquin Park," he said, "will be quite disappointed when they get to Heaven."

EPILOGUE

I am at Camp Lake this afternoon, a brief escape in the early summer. A solid week of blue sky has turned to purple as the predicted storm moves through. The thunder has at times been far off, at other times so close that the cabin itself shakes as if in fear. The dog shows none of her usual inclination to race outside in pursuit of anything that sounds or moves; instead, she lies at the foot of the bed and may yet wriggle in under it. There are periodic flashes in the clouds, but so far the lightning has kept its distance. Rain has fallen in cold sheets and like a warm and gentle garden spray. I have just come up from a swim, a fading rain now lightly chiming off the suddenly still lake, and the sky, for the first time in a long, teasing day, hinting at recovery.

The shifts have been fascinating to watch, but they cannot compare to what went on here over the past few weeks. If I wish to see a demonstration of what nature roused can do, all I have to do is step out the cabin door and push through the wet, sagging branches that have narrowed the path that leads to the next cabin over.

It has been squashed.

Two weeks ago, a hard wind reared up out the east, blew down our bay, and knocked one large hemlock onto the little sleeping bunkie beside the neighbouring cabin, destroying the small structure beyond repair, and another younger hemlock onto the cabin itself, ripping off a large portion of the roof. The damage wasn't nearly as bad as it might have been, and fortunately there was insurance to cover it, so our neighbour immediately began to restore things to the state they had been in before the wind hit.

The roofers had just finished the new shingling when, in a coincidence that defies comprehension, a second high wind roared through, this time out of the west, and snapped off an even larger hemlock – the forest's least trustworthy tree – which toppled straight onto the brand-new roof and squashed the cabin as surely as if the heel of a work boot had slammed down onto an empty pop tin.

Those who were working on the repairs at the time were lucky to escape with their lives. Our neighbour, who spent much of the night in hospital being monitored for shock, described the arriving wind as sounding like "a freight train coming through a tunnel" – a curious description to hear in a place where people go for the peace and only on certain nights, when the wind is out of the south, can you even hear the logging trucks moving down distant Highway 60.

They heard the wind coming, they heard trees falling all around them, perhaps a dozen within easy sight of the property, and they ran for a nearby clearing. A wise choice: had they stayed around the cabin, someone might well have been killed. Our neighbour ran carrying the eight-foot-long board he had been sawing when the wind hit. A branch that broke off the falling hemlock struck the large board as he held it up for protection, snapping it in two as though it were a dried twig.

There is a black side to nature, and we are foolish to pretend it does not exist. Disaster can strike at a moment's notice, and occasionally it does. As Thoreau said so many years ago, "Nature, as we know her, is no saint."

We welcome a breeze yet fear the wind; the sky can be both magical and deadly; the lake can seem so inviting one day and take a life the next.

We can see this every day, not just after a fierce wind has bullied through. When my daughter Christine and I drove up here from Ottawa earlier this week ahead of the rest of the family, we turned onto the gravel road and had to brake quickly for a sleek-coated red fox, slowly crossing in front of us with a rabbit still twisting frantically in its jaws. That, too, is nature.

And yet nature can also appear divine, if not exactly saintly. On the very path that the workers used to flee the falling tree, the same path where broken tree limbs have punched into the soft earth and torn up the ground, stand two glistening pink lady slippers, the gorgeous wild orchid of the Algonquin highlands, defying both the fury of nature and the trampling of man. Their delicate beauty seems all the more breathtaking given the violence they have somehow escaped.

Several times since we arrived I have gone down the path to stand and stare at the destruction brought about by the giant hemlock that decided, after nearly two centuries – we counted 172 rings – of standing free and strong, to snap off at the roots like a tulip clipped by scissors. I try to imagine the roar of the "freight train" as the wind arrived and the terrifying sounds of trees going down and the sickening crunch as this largest one flattened the cabin.

It is quiet at the lake in the days before school lets out for the summer. The fogs are heavy, the high water has logs floating freely about the bay, and fortunately there are no scurrying boats to worry about warning. It is so peaceful here, now, it is hard to believe this ugly scene was able to pry its way into such an exquisite landscape. The sight is a stunning reminder of how insignificant we are and how immediately significant the world about us can be.

"No one ever owns a cabin or an acre of forest, whatever the title deeds in the land registry may say," Bruce Hutchison wrote of his small retreat on Shawnigan Lake. "We were transient tenants to be quickly forgotten. . . . But the forest lived on, perpetually renewing itself."

Time is a rather different concept here in the bush, where the only clock is the shifting seasons. That fallen hemlock was a seedling when Laird McNab was setting up his feudal system on the other side of the park. It was just part of the undergrowth when the *Anne* came sailing into the mouth of the St. Lawrence River carrying Susanna Moodie, the same year Edward Michell Pierce was born in Somerset, England. It was a small tree when David Thompson came through this area grumbling about the swamps and the "rude rocks," when rebellion rocked the two Canadas and led, in so many ways, to the opening up of this country for new settlements like little failed Mizpah just down the road, where little Thomas Alvin Hart's blackened stone asks that we not forget him in death. It was a tree of some substance when

Algonquin Park was established within sight of where it so unexpectedly fell late this spring.

I have never quite known how to measure my time at Camp Lake. The battery-powered clock on the wall of the cabin seems unnecessary. Morning breaks and night falls; weekends come and weekends go; school lets out, school goes back in; work stops, work starts up again; the bugs begin biting, the fish stop biting; the seasons tease, finally settle, and then start their teasing all over.

I do, however, know the value of time at the lake and in the bush. In the cities, where my work takes place, I have too often felt like one of Willa Cather's characters, a woman who believed she had somehow been born behind time and could never quite catch up – except when she was able to get to a cabin so isolated that time lost all meaning and measure for her.

This is a common theme among escape artists. In the middle of the Great Depression, T.S. Eliot wrote of our need to locate "the still point of the turning world." And this past year, when escape has taken on heightened meaning for so many, Van Morrison released a song about a secret place he knows in the mountains "Where the world / Keeps standing still."

I know I can no more stop time than I could have stopped that enormous hemlock from crashing down on the cabin, no more than I can hope the pink lady slippers hold their delicate bloom through the summer, no more, for that matter, than I could prevent them from blooming again a year from now on the south shore of this cold, clear northern lake.

What I do know is why I come here, why so many of us have such deep need of a special place in our lives, a small retreat where, when required, and even when not at all necessary, we can escape temporarily from the even-more unpredictable winds that blow elsewhere.

For here, and perhaps only here, time is my own.

To do with, or to do nothing with, as I wish.

ACKNOWLEDGEMENTS

My thanks to those escape artists who were along for the research, if not the writing: Don, Marcia, Brandon, and Vaughn Harris of Raymore, Saskatchewan; Alannah Campbell and John, Shauna, Logan, and Hope Kearns of Toronto; Denis Menard and Merryl-Jeanne Mason of Ottawa; Ralph and David Cox of North Bay; Barbara Gibson of Pittsburgh and Camp Lake; Ellen, Kerry, Christine, Jocelyn, and Gordon MacGregor, and, of course, Bandit.

Expertise on the sexual habits of the snapping turtle was provided by nature wizard Justin Francis of Low, Quebec, and the good-humoured Bob Johnson of the Toronto Zoo.

The author is also considerably indebted to two remarkable editors: Edie Van Alstine, a dear friend from forever who not only knows what works but has the background to know what's right; and Alex Schultz, who also edits the Screech Owls mystery series, who has the courage and sense to throw a chapter back in the face of an author and tell him to start over.